Global Media Governance

CRITICAL MEDIA STUDIES
INSTITUTIONS, POLITICS, AND CULTURE

Series Editor
Andrew Calabrese, University of Colorado

Advisory Board

Patricia Aufderheide, American University

Jean-Claude Burgelman, Free University of Brussels

Simone Chambers, University of Colorado

Nicholas Garnham, University of Westminster

Hanno Hardt, University of Iowa

Gay Hawkins, The University of New South Wales

Maria Heller, Eötvös Loránd University

Robert Horwitz, University of California at San Diego

Douglas Kellner, University of California at Los Angeles

Gary Marx, Massachusetts Institute of Technology

Toby Miller, New York University

Vincent Mosco, Carleton University

Janice Peck, University of Colorado

Manjunath Pendakur, University of Western Ontario

Arvind Rajagopal, New York University

Kevin Robins, Goldsmiths College

Saskia Sassen, University of Chicago

Colin Sparks, University of Westminster

Slavko Splichal, University of Ljubljana

Thomas Streeter, University of Vermont

Liesbet van Zoonen, University of Amsterdam

Janet Wasko, University of Oregon

Recent Titles in the Series

Deliberation, Democracy, and the Media,
    edited by Simone Chambers and Anne Costain
Deregulating Telecommunications: U.S. and Canadian Telecommunications, 1840–1997,
    Kevin G. Wilson
Floating Lives: The Media and Asian Diasporas,
    edited by Stuart Cunningham and John Sinclair
Continental Order? Integrating North America for Cybercapitalism,
    edited by Vincent Mosco and Dan Schiller
Social Theories of the Press: Constituents of Communication Research, 1840s to 1920s, second edition,
    Hanno Hardt
The Global and the National: Media and Communications in Post-Communist Russia,
    Terhi Rantanen
Privacy and the Information Age,
    Serge Gutwrith
Global Media Governance: A Beginner's Guide,
    Seán Ó Siochrú and Bruce Girard

Forthcoming in the Series

From Newspaper Guild to Multimedia Union: A Study in Labor Convergence,
    Catherine McKercher
The Eclipse of Freedom: From the Principle of Publicity to the Freedom of the Press,
    Slavko Splichal
Elusive Autonomy: Brazilian Communications Policy in an Age of Globalization and Technical Change,
    Sergio Euclides de Souza
Internet Governance in Transition,
    Daniel J. Paré
Herbert Schiller,
    Richard Maxwell
Digital Disability: The Social Construction of Disability in New Media,
    Gerard Goggin and Christopher Newell

Global Media Governance

A Beginner's Guide

Seán Ó Siochrú and Bruce Girard
with Amy Mahan

ROWMAN & LITTLEFIELD PUBLISHERS, INC.
Lanham • Boulder • New York • Oxford

ROWMAN & LITTLEFIELD PUBLISHERS, INC.

Published in the United States of America
by Rowman & Littlefield Publishers, Inc.
4720 Boston Way, Lanham, Maryland 20706
www.rowmanlittlefield.com

12 Hid's Copse Road
Cumnor Hill, Oxford OX2 9JJ, England

British Library Cataloguing in Publication Information Available

Library of Congress Cataloging-in-Publication Data

Ó Siochrú Seán, 1955–
    Global media governance : a beginner's guide / Seán Ó Siochrú and Bruce
Girard with Amy Mahan.
        p. cm.—(Critical media studies)
    Includes bibliographical references and index.
    ISBN 0-7425-1565-6 (alk. paper)—ISBN 0-7425-1566-4 (pbk. : alk. paper)
    1. Communications—International cooperation. 2. Mass media—Political aspects. I.
Girard, Bruce, 1955– II. Mahan, Amy. III. Title. IV. Series.

P96.I5 O17 2002
302.2—dc21
                                                                    2001057855

Printed in the United States of America

⊗™ The paper used in this publication meets the minimum requirements of
American National Standard for Information Sciences—Permanence of Paper
for Printed Library Materials, ANSI/NISO Z.39.48–1992.

Contents

Preface

A few years ago, we sought in vain a publication that would succinctly present the main issues confronting media and communications governance at the global level. We were not the only ones searching, and so this book was written.

Media and communications have always been singled out for special attention by governments, nationally and internationally. Recognizing the power to disseminate information and influence people, political leaders have used media to muzzle opposition and to present themselves in the best possible light. But media potential goes far beyond propping up, or even toppling, individual regimes.

The sphere in which the public debates, understands and forms opinion, and takes decisions on the future of society is marked out by the characteristics of its media and communications. It is through media and communications that mutual understandings and differences become apparent and are thrashed out, an especially important function in societies with democratic political structures. The extent to which the media introduce diverse possibilities, educate on alternatives, and mediate between people and ideas and their freedom from partisan interests are good barometers of the health and depth of political democracy in a society.

Media and communications also play a critical role in establishing and sustaining our sense of identity, both individually and collectively. Particularly in industrialized societies, among the middle classes in less industrialized society and in urban areas everywhere, the media occupy the vacuum left by the dissolution of extended families and close-knit communities and the retreat into the nuclear family and stratified work environments.

It is thus no surprise that governments and those governed have a deep and enduring interest in the freedom and constraints that affect their media and communications institutions.

Media and communications also constitute a major and ever growing sector of economic activity, highlighting a second major dynamic. Media and communications enterprises are increasingly commercialized, moving to a market-driven and profit-oriented environment. In many countries, ownership and control of newspapers, magazines, radio, television, film, and telecommunications is concentrating into fewer and fewer private companies and is on a trajectory impelled by trade and commercial exploitation. The proliferation of media outlets is paradoxically accompanied by fewer forms of ownership and less diversity of content.

This tendency toward profit creation and commodification, not surprisingly, often comes into conflict with social, cultural, and political dimensions of media and communications. Such conflict generates the necessary complexity of their governance, and so constitutes a constant theme of this book.

Much has been written on the struggles of media and communications at the national level. Although we briefly review these issues, our focus is on the global level. Our central concern is to explore the issues and actors, and the trends and possibilities, in the governance at the global level of media and communications.

Although media and communications have always had an international dimension, national boundaries have hitherto circumscribed most of their influence. Newspapers, television, and radio had traditionally been nationally owned, with coverage focused on national issues and perspectives. For many, they have been a key instrument in "nation building." Telecommunications has also been held for most of its history as subject to national sovereign control, whether publicly or privately owned.

The international dimension, however, has now come to the fore. Technological advances and the commercialization of media have long overrun national boundaries. Vast swathes of the world's media are now controlled by multinational corporations whose national allegiance, if any, is subsumed under corporate exigencies. Satellite television and the Internet know no boundaries; even local radio stations are deemed worthy of control and are swallowed up by major media conglomerates. Likewise, most countries have shed all claims to their telecommunications sector as a matter for strategic sovereignty. One by one national telecommunications networks, especially in less industrialized countries, are moving to multinational ownership, their growth and spread motivated by narrow commercial goals.

Media governance at a national level, hitherto driven by a diversity of competing economic, social, political, and cultural goals—not all of them worthy—is giving way to international structures of governance emphasizing trade and commercial considerations above all else. Through organizations such as the World Trade Organization (WTO), governments are relinquishing the power to regulate and govern the media. More and more, global structures and dynamics dictate what happens at the national level. These dictates impose a purely commercial logic on the sector, threatening the social, political, and cultural roles of media and communications.

For all these reasons, the analysis of media and communications, the role they play in society, and the forces that impel them forward must move beyond the national level.

The process of the globalization of media also makes them less accessible. Not only national governments, but also civil society organizations are left with far fewer avenues by which they can engage the media. While their influence grows, the capacity of people to influence media and communications structures and content diminishes. They become separated off from the people, fracturing the public sphere, and closing down voices of diversity.

But there are signs of emerging countertrends. Most significant is the rise of what has been called global civil society in the form of networks of nongovernmental organizations that are increasingly vocal in their demands for a presence at global governance tables. These include protestors not only outside the meetings of the WTO or of the Group of Eight industrialized countries, but also some with a substantial presence *inside*, thanks to a series of reforms adopted by many bodies in the UN system. There are also signs that less industrialized countries are becoming more effective in their participation in these forums, working out common agendas for cultural and economic alternatives for media and communications.

At this time, when civil society is just finding a global voice and establishing a legitimate claim to be heard, to neglect the central role of media and communications would be a major, perhaps irrevocable, mistake. Much more than an instrument to reach a wider public, media and communications are perhaps the single most important factor molding what is acceptable and unacceptable in terms of social, economic, and political action. Yet not just governments, but also civil society and its organizations, as well as the intergovernmental system as a whole, appear all but oblivious to the inherent dangers and the enormous influence that media and communications have on the process of globalization as a whole.

At its starkest, the issue is about the struggle for control, at a global level, of media and communications. On the one side are people, social, political, and cultural rights, and those organizations that stand by people. On the other is economic power, currently dominated by narrow commercially driven forces primarily controlled in the interests of the more powerful nations. The interaction between these is, however, not reducible to simple formulae. In this small volume, we emphasize the major significance of matters at stake here, and we also underline their complexity. This book aims to further our understanding of the main issues and forces at play in global media and communications governance and, hopefully, to make a contribution to the debate about options for change at the global level.

Introduction

This book is about *media governance* at a global level and the key influencing forces and elements. Governance encompasses regulation, and questions addressed here include: Why do we regulate the various media at all? What currently are the major forms of global regulation, and how do they work? Who participates in, and who benefits from, media regulatory and governance structures? And what are the trends?

People interested in the media and their progressively rising influence over so many dimensions of society will sooner or later find themselves confronted with these questions. This book is intended as an aid to such an interested reader. It does not pretend to answer all the questions, but it does at least raise most of the key ones and points in directions where more complete answers can be found.

GLOBALIZATION

Our perception and understanding of "globalization" at the beginning of this new millennium depends on who we are and where we are looking from. For much of the world, the tip of the globalization iceberg has not yet appeared on the horizon—either explicitly wreaking havoc or bestowing benefits. Yet just because most of the world's population has never made a phone call, accessed information via the Internet, or flown in an airplane does not mean that it has not been touched by globalization. It may well be that globalization subtly entrenches marginalization without being directly perceived, its role in local price fluctuations concealed and its impact on employment, on services, and other areas obscured behind layers of mediating factors. Or perhaps not.

Globalization, depending on your information and worldview, could be the great equalizer, a bleak exacerbator of inequalities, or just the latest hype soon to be replaced. The term as used embodies various combinations of all three. Recent work groups theories of globalization into three broad theses: (1) *Hyperglobalist*, which describes a world increasingly dominated by a single global market, and characterized by the irrelevance of the nation-state and the emergence of a single world order, government, and global mass media. (2) The *skeptics* claim that the current globalization controversy is much ado about nothing. Globalization is understood as distinct from internationalization in that it invariably evolves from the breaches of control of nation-states. The skeptical thesis implies that *internationalization* is in fact the current trend since economic policies and regulation emanate from nation-states and their respective regional trading blocs, rather than through top-down global coordination of a single world economy. Finally, (3) *transformationalists* argue the case that, for good or evil, a fundamentally more interconnected world is now emerging, in which "globalisation is a central driving force behind the rapid social, political and economic changes that are reshaping modern societies and world order."[1] The local and distant, the periphery and center, do not exist in isolation of one another, as the reality of one is inextricably intertwined with, for example, the poverty, the environment, and indeed the media of the other.

This book does not venture into the theoretical terrain of globalization theories. But it does situate itself loosely within the *transformationalist thesis*. Historically distinct technologies are now interchangeable means of delivering media products on a global scale; historically separate cultures now have Disney and CNN in common, but also have opportunities to produce indigenous cultural products locally and disseminate them globally; and organizations previously uninvolved with media regulation are now finding cause and interest to become so. Viewed from within this thesis, the media could play a critical role in the eventual impact of globalization on people everywhere and on how different interest groups fare. Thus, the regulation and governance of media is an important issue, since this in turn will circumscribe the thrust and nature of media influence on globalization as a whole.

MEDIA GOVERNANCE

The main current issues for media governance can be simplified into a set of questions, for which answers must be forthcoming. Some relate to economic issues, others to human rights and social issues. Some issues are stable, with no serious debate or contention, but they may not remain so indefinitely. Others are central to the agenda. Others still are emerging for the first time.

At the national level, limits are placed on the concentration of ownership within and between media in order both to prevent excessive industry control and to ensure a plurality and diversity of media sources for social, cultural, and political development. At the global level, should media concentration be the subject of specific measures to regulate media corporations (combining transnational and national holdings) that have significant control of a market? Are more complex regulatory needs emerging, such as regulation to ensure fair access to "gateways" and "filters" between different layers of media, where excessive control exists internationally? Is there a need for regulation to support a global public service media to counterbalance the private-sector control of transnational media, as midwife to a global public sphere and to ensure greater diversity in the media?

Questions also arise in relation to telecommunications and content access. Is there an economic and/or equity case for a redistribution of a fraction of the international telecommunications revenues to develop the networks, services, and content in less industrialized countries and regions?

Copyright bestows ownership of intellectual work for a period, and the media are a primary means to disseminate such work and derive an economic income from it. Yet the rights of different parties, the creators, owners, and users of information must be balanced. Should the creators of ideas retain moral rights to creations, including control of editorial changes and the right to retain authorship? How can the rights of owners of intellectual property be balanced against the rights of communities to protect and sustain their cultural heritage? To what extent is it justified to make exceptions for the use of intellectual output for educational, cultural, research, or other socially beneficial activities?

The media uses global public resources that are in limited supply, such as radio frequency and orbital slots. As public resources, governments are under an obligation to use them optimally in the interests of the public. Should certain frequencies be reserved for use to develop a global public sphere, such as for public service media? Should part of the profits derived from the use of such public property by private interests be diverted for public use?

There is also little doubt that the means to tackle these questions, in terms of regulation and the appropriate and effective form of governance, are going through a period of rapid and fundamental change.

Media regulation has historically been applied quite separately to the different modes of media transmission: radio and television were covered by broadcasting policies; telecommunications had its own regulatory instruments; and newspapers and print were protected by free speech doctrines and libel laws. The state has always played a significant role in creating and overseeing media regulation, and likewise, there is an understandable reluctance to excessively delegate these functions to the market. The ideological foundations of a nation-state—including ideals such as access to information, freedom of speech, the nation-state's own promotion of national identity, and so forth—are strongly connected with independent media. In this regard, it is natural that the state has maintained an interest in promoting and ensuring the functioning of media. Convergence of media has led to new questions for and new demands on the role of the state. Yet convergence also heightens and highlights the need for the continued role of the nation-state in media governance.

A key question here is whether the institutional structures and regulations emerging will operate genuinely, impartially, transparently, and democratically to the benefits of all, or whether they will succumb to powerful sectoral interests, becoming yet another means to support the interests of the powerful over those of the majority.

OVERVIEW OF THE BOOK

This book is divided into three parts. Part 1 explores the overarching issues of governance and globalization in the context of media industry and media convergence. Its three chapters set the scene for the rest of the book in three areas: media regulation and the forms it takes at the national level; governance in general and how it has emerged at an international level; and the main trends and dynamics driving the media themselves.

Part II provides an overview, in five successive chapters, of key institutions of media global governance. It is primarily descriptive rather than judgmental, and reviews their history, describes their functions and structures, and analyzes their central dynamics as they relate to media

Part III synthesises, summarizes, and looks to the future. In three chapters, it provides an overview from several perspectives of current global regulatory mechanisms that impact on the media; it looks at the governance of these instruments, focusing especially on their adequacy in terms of democratic principles; and it describes two realistic but contrasting scenarios for the future.

NOTE

1. D. Held et al., *Global Transformations: Politics, Economics and Culture* (Cambridge: Polity, 1999), 7.

I

1

✛

Introduction to National Media Regulation

WHY MEDIA REGULATION?

The question is occasionally asked about the media: Do we need regulation at all? Why not let the market decide what television, radio, newspapers, and the rest can offer, just as it does for other goods, with governments intervening solely to ensure a level playing field? Why are media products so special that we cannot let enterprises get on with what they claim to do best—producing what people want, measured by what they will pay for?

Media products *are* different, not least because they are more than just consumer goods—in important respects they also "produce" us. Mass media and electronic media in today's highly differentiated and compartmentalized world are becoming the primary means through which people interact with each other, beyond their immediate everyday contacts. Our sense of belonging, of being part of a wider community, a society, a culture, a nation, a single human race is more and more "mediated through media." Beyond even an individual's relationship to society, the very mode in which society as a whole realizes its aspirations and fulfils its claims to offer freedom and democracy to its members, to support rational and fair legal, political, and social institutions—its legitimacy in claiming to act in the best interests of people in general—all of these ideas and realities are represented to us and brought to us primarily by the media. They provide us with the raw material, often even the tools, to comprehend what our society is beyond our immediate experience, and ultimately to participate in that society and perhaps even to change it.

The idea of "media products" seems somehow too narrow to encompass the role this plays in our lives. In listening to, watching, and reading media we do not just consume, we interact. We interact with other people and through them with society in general. We interact with ourselves, sometimes unconsciously, with our sense of sharing a common culture and of being a part of something beyond ourselves.

But how can we regulate or legislate for these things? How can society draw up and impose agreed to criteria and rules especially on the *content* of media—what is delivered by and to people—without at the same time imposing a single view, filtering out some ideas, and allowing in others, in short inflicting a form of censorship? And if media regulation is carried out by government, surely the risk is ever present of manipulation by political self-interest?

Yet it is also important to understand that the *absence* of regulation, for instance in the sense claimed of a "free market," is also a filtering and selecting process—regulation by another name. The criteria and rules may not be set down in legislation and enforced through agencies or the courts, but they will always be there. In a purely commercial environment, these would come down to what secures the greatest return for investors.

The very fact that every individual does not, and if only for practical reasons cannot, have an equal level of access to the media, as producers and users, means that content and access to it are inevitably controlled by entry barriers, perhaps by several competing sets of barriers. The idea of totally "free" media is in this sense an absurdity, since all media are motivated and constrained by a great number of factors. Regulation in the end is about the use and abuse of power. The real question is how regulation, by that name or any other, is shaped and implemented in a society, who controls it, how informed people are about it, and how they can participate in determining its priorities.

RATIONALE FOR MEDIA REGULATION

Virtually every society has thus developed special ways of treating media. Justifications put forward for regulation and the particular forms adopted can usefully be categorized under two broad headings, each offering a distinct rationale for regulating the media, deployed in very different configurations by different societies. They are:

- Regulating the media as a sector of the economy, or *industry regulation.*
- Regulating to sustain and strengthen the social, cultural, and political role of media and communications or *societal regulation.* This in-

cludes *prohibitive content regulation*, that is, regulating the acceptable "outer limits" of specific content based on social norms.

Industry Regulation

Although the media sector has its unique characteristics, it is nevertheless still a sector of economic activity and is thus a subject for industry regulation. Increasingly, and this is a global phenomenon, it is becoming a market-driven sector and thus the emphasis is on regulating for competition in the economy.

A market must be regulated not just in exceptional circumstances of a breakdown in mechanisms. Regulation is prerequisite to the operation of any market. Indeed, a market-driven media sector usually requires a lot more regulation than a monopoly sector. Thus, conventional economic regulation is applied to the media, justified as necessary to ensure fair competition, and to combat oligopoly and unfair trading practices. The regulation of intellectual property rights (IPRs), in the form of copyright, is a particularly important prerequisite for media markets and has become a major battleground on the international scene.

Although no different to other sectors in some respects, regulating media competition does produce complexities that may require special attention. Concentration of media ownership that can lead to excessive market control and hence to higher prices and barriers to entry is regulated in most countries. But with media convergence, existing simple formulae for detecting and measuring market dominance become increasingly difficult to apply. This is because of the layering of individual media, especially electronic media, and the convergence and interchangeability of content between media.

Distinct layers are emerging in some media sectors, such as the Internet and television. These may comprise, for instance, content production, content compilation and management, signal/broadcast management, infrastructure provision, and user equipment production and distribution to final consumers. Control of gateways between these layers can lead to huge market influence, but with insignificant levels of actual ownership. Examples include access to search engines on the Internet, the bundling of popular programing in with television station takeovers and mergers, conditional access to subscription services, and the barriers placed to unbundling local services in telecommunications. At the same time, convergence of different media in several forms, for instance Web television or radio, cable television, and telecommunications, make it more difficult for regulators to determine the extent of control exerted by ownership of one medium over another and to assess the "media control exchange rate."

The political and cultural importance of media introduces a level of complexity to economic regulation of the industry that is not characteristic of other sectors. For example, in some countries constitutional guarantees of press freedom have been invoked by the media to defend their monopoly positions from regulators intent on encouraging competition as an industrial policy. These complexities have required the development of very specific regulatory instruments and agencies.

The allocation of radio spectrum for the media industry, as a scarce public resource, also presents problems. Issues arise in allocating to competitors within a single medium, for instance the licensing of FM broadcasters within the FM allocation, and between different media, each (along with special interests, such as the military) striving to claim a larger slice of bandwidth. Several approaches can be taken to the problem, with significantly different outcomes.

There are other aspects to industry regulation. Drawing at least partly on economic grounds, telecommunications regulation is often used to extend the network beyond the point that is commercially feasible for an individual network provider and also to reduce tariffs for some customers. The economic rationale associated with network and interactive services is based on the idea that the utility of the network as a whole grows with the addition of each new member. Thus, for example, new users might appear uneconomic in their own right, but are viable when the additional revenue gained from existing users communicating with new users is added. A second economic justification can apply where only part of the full economic benefit of infrastructure development can be secured by the infrastructure provider, justifying further (usually government) expenditure to capture the economic externalities to the benefit of general economic growth.

The upshot of complexity is that industry regulation in the media sector is often undertaken by specialized instruments, distinct from competition regulation more generally.

Societal Regulation

The media sector stands out more clearly from others when we turn to forms of regulation that go beyond competition and industry, since these are peculiar to it, at least in combination. This leads to the second area of media regulation: regulation for enrichment of the social, political, and cultural spheres, or more succinctly, societal regulation. This raises the most profound dimensions of media and communication in society. The rationale for such regulation points to the role media play in the cultural, social, and political evolution of society: in a cultural context by renewing cultural integrity and sustaining diversity; in a social context by enhancing public understanding and education; and in a political context by constituting the sphere for open public debate that is essential to a healthy democracy and as means to express fundamental human rights including freedom of speech. These three domains of society, politics, and culture are closely intertwined, with the media playing overlapping roles:

- Media have grown in importance in terms of how people learn about their own communities, develop social affinities, and form group identities
- Media play an ever more critical role in expressing, celebrating, sustaining, and evolving diverse cultures and groups within society, especially minority groups, and in enabling people to develop mutual understanding and respect
- Media are at the core of enabling democratic debate and understanding, and of facilitating and encouraging open, transparent, and impartial public debate on issues relating to society, politics, and government.

Societal regulation mostly takes the form of measures to ensure diversity and plurality of the media.

Regulating for media diversity aims to ensure that news reporting, current affairs, and political/economic media coverage generally reflect a diversity of views, including dissenting views, and that the media remain in some sense impartial and refrain from siding with a specific sectional interest. At the same time, content, whether news, entertainment, education or otherwise, may also be regulated to ensure that it caters to a diversity of viewer interests and not only, for example, to those most attractive to advertisers.

Plurality, on the other hand, refers to encouraging a multiplicity of different types of media, offering people different avenues for media participation, and reaching different audiences with a variety of range and depth of content. Some countries take this form of regulation so seriously as to enshrine it in their constitutions—Germany and Italy for instance—pointing to deep philosophical roots, not simply as a facilitator of public understanding and democracy, but bound up intimately and inextricably with the very notion of a democratic society.

The concept of the public sphere (see textbox) offers insight into the justification of regulating for media diversity and plurality, as well as what is meant by terms such as "freedom of the press." Diversity in media content is not simply, or even especially, about reflecting an actual diversity of ideas among people. It is about ensuring that within the overall communications domain there exist voices that are disinterested, in the sense of being motivated not by sectional interest, but by the need to achieve transparent and open communication and debate on matters of common concern. The issue is not one of "objectivity" or "balance," although such ideas are important in certain contexts. It is about the *intent* of communication and ensuring the conditions in which distortions of various kinds are minimized. And although this applies a fortiori in news media, such forms of communication are also relevant to entertainment, educational, and other media content in so far as they imply and impinge on such political and democratic ideas and issues.

Media and the "Public Sphere"

The philosophical antecedents of societal regulation are deeply ingrained in the Western psyche and go back to one of the major strands of the liberal democratic tradition.* Representative democracy is premised on the notion that individuals are morally sovereign because they are endowed with reason. Put simply, each person is entitled to make individual moral judgments since each is capable of rationally assessing the effects of his or her actions on others, and therefore, within generally shared social norms, to judge the difference between right and wrong in a social context. This gives people an a priori capacity to make and accept laws that govern their actions (in this tradition, this is also the basis of human dignity).

In representative democracy, a small number are chosen by everyone to take decisions on their behalf. The selection procedure—elections—must of course be transparent and fair. But the real test of liberal democracy is whether the public has ongoing access to information on the rationale and circumstances of decisions taken by those vested with such power and the capacity to understand and articulate views and beliefs on them. In principle, liberal democracy is thus *not* an abrogation of power by the people to their leaders for a given period of time. It demands constant renewal, through the general affirmation that decisions are being taken rationally on behalf of the general good, and stands only as long as the leaders can rationally defend their actions. The more thorough the understanding of the populace concerning these decisions, the deeper and more robust the democracy, and indeed the more cohesive the society.

The "public sphere" is the arena in which such deliberations are debated. It is not a single forum, but a multiplicity of contexts and mechanisms where people debate and interact to gain an understanding of matters of general societal concern and to participate in the democratic process through formulating views and conveying them to political leaders. The public sphere can encompass newspapers, television, "soap-box" gatherings, public demonstrations, discussions, and a myriad other forms; it may be pursued directly by people or vicariously through surrogates such as journalists, commentators, or writers—the form or even the intermediary is not what is important. Rather, the essence of the public sphere is that it is where people openly and transparently debate on the basis that they can be *convinced by reason*, by the rationality of argumentation, and not by appeals to amusements or desires, or through suppression or distortion of information. Thus, the argument is that deepening democracy, and seeking the democratic ideal, is possible only where there is continuous support for and extension of the public sphere and of the central role of the media within it.

What distinguishes the public sphere from other forms of communication is thus its intent and the characteristics it must have to realize this. The objective of enabling general public participation and renewing the legitimacy of political structures can be distorted significantly by the intrusion of sectional interests, including, among others, those of politicians in maintaining power and of economic interests in maximizing accumulation. The interests of media themselves, in so far as they are economic actors, is also clearly an important factor. The characteristics of the public sphere, striving to achieve an "ideal communication sphere," include transparency, full knowledge, sincerity, and nondistortion of communication. But effective participation also points to other prerequisites, such as formal and informal educational structures and the general capacity for informed reasoning.

* This sequence of philosophical understanding from Immanuel Kant through Karl Marx and Max Weber to Jürgen Habermas is succinctly summarized in Shalini Venturelli, *Liberalising the European Media: Politics, Regulation and the Public Sphere* (Oxford: Clarendon, 1998).

Similarly, regulating for plurality is not just about supporting a diversity of media forms, but also about encouraging them to bring more people into the public sphere and to engage at different levels in debate and discussion. A growing aspect of regulation for plurality aims to support more direct means for people to become involved in media not simply as consumers, but as producers and broadcasters. For instance, cable carriers or television broadcasters can be obliged, by means of "must-carry" regulations, to distribute community media programing, under the control of civil society organizations. Open access television, a version of this, carries output produced by individuals and groups in society on a nondiscriminatory basis. In many countries, community television and radio channels are supported by a levy on a city cable license holder or through forms of public funding.

One form such regulation may take sometimes leads to confusion as it can appear very similar to industry regulation. Curbing concentration of media ownership is justified on the grounds of undue control of content by private economic interests, quite distinct from economic arguments concerning profiteering and allocation of resources. Another particularly important form, public service media, earns its relative protection from competition regulation from the need to present independent, impartial content, although not without introducing a set of tensions around undue political interference and even class-inspired cultural control.

DUAL ROLES OF SOCIETAL REGULATION

Societal regulation can take yet other forms.

IPRs lay down the terms on which information enters the public domain and is freed of copyright restrictions, of vital relevance to the public sphere. However, unlike regulating for media concentration of ownership, IPRs must struggle with an inner tension—extending the rights of private intellectual property owners is always at the expense of the release of information into the public domain. Thus, IPRs must strike a balance between ensuring a reasonable return to creators and owners of ideas and improving public access to information and ideas by extending what enters the public domain.

Regulation for universal access also serves a dual role, extending economic and social opportunities offered by telecommunications and other networked electronic services to rural areas and to disadvantaged social groups, justified both on grounds of equity and to generally provide access to the public realm. Such justification will vary by the norms and competing resource demands: The basic norm of a digital line in every home and access to the Internet in schools and libraries might be justified in wealthy societies, whereas a phone within an hour's walking might be acceptable in another environment. The allocation of radio frequency can also be relevant here since it can be used to prevent or to facilitate access to radio and other services in defined geographic areas.

In the context of culture and identity, a similar issue has arisen around television rights to broadcast particularly popular and nationally significant sports events. In several countries of Europe, for instance, attempts by "pay-per-view" operators to use exclusive access to major sporting events to leverage subscriptions have been partially thwarted by regulation to ensure such "listed events" are available over free-to-air services. Regulation of public service broadcasting, in general, also includes access stipulations that can include geographical extension of transmission services as well as obligations on others to carry the signals.

Another side to societal regulation is whether, and the circumstances in which, the state has the right to intervene in and access private transmission and communication in the general public interest. The balance of privacy and the public good is relevant to all media but is topical in the area of Internet encryption and whether the state should in principle be allowed to intercept and interpret encoded messages.

Finally, prohibitive content regulation is concerned with ensuring that media content is kept within accepted normative or ethical boundaries of society and that anything falling outside this is prohibited. It draws a perimeter around what is acceptable for people to receive from the media, based on appeals to generally held normative boundaries. Regulation attempts to police that perimeter in various ways. Restrictions on sexual and violent material are common, often taking the form of specific censorship instruments for films and books. Defamation of character and breaches of confidentiality are also covered here, to which recourse is usually through the courts. In some countries, communication construed to subvert the state, acts of treason, and offenses against state symbols may also end up in a court of law.

The Internet has given a new lease on life to debates on this form of regulation. Early cases in Germany, for instance, aimed at forcing Internet service suppliers to take responsibility for content, in the United States and Canada to revise public decency laws, and in the United Kingdom to restrict satellite pornography suggest that these issues remain important.

Of course, such normative boundaries are not fixed in the same place in all societies. While an abhorrence of child pornography is virtually universal, general societal tolerance for public displays of sex and sexuality vary enormously between societies, as do definitions of what is sacred and what is sacrilegious, both legally and in terms of social acceptability. These differences point to where the rationale for different forms of regulation blur, merging into or conflicting with each other. Thus, content regulation can come into conflict with other aims of regulation, for instance in deciding where to draw the line between ensuring freedom of expression and preventing incitement to hatred or violence (see table 1.1).

INSTRUMENTS OF NATIONAL REGULATION

At the national level, a variety of instruments have been designed or adapted to meet regulatory needs as they arise. Although occasional attempts are made to rationalize these into a single coherent institutional context driven in recent years by convergence and commercialization of media, they are likely to remain distributed through various institutions of government, economy, and society.

A variety of actors and institutions, not just governments, are involved in regulation.

Largely because it impinges on constitutional or common law rights, media regulation is often played out, in practice, in the courts. This is especially true in the United States with landmark cases over recent decades leading to legislation that largely determines the contours of telecommunications, broadcast, and cable regulation, as well as the ongoing evolution of IPRs and freedom of speech. Broadly, the courts have three functions here:

- They create and police a framework of basic rights, within which the media and public authorities must operate.

Table 1.1   Rationale for National Regulation

Rationale for Regulation	Regulatory Measures

Industry Regulation:
  To regulate the media as
  a sector of the economy
	• Limiting concentration of ownership within and
	  between media to prevent sectoral control
	  and support competition
	• Establishing fair conditions of access to infrastructure,
	  broadcasters, and gateways to "layers" of the media
	  industry in order to limit control by a few players
	• Extending universal access to telecommunications
	  services to generate network economies and capture
	  externalities
	• Securing intellectual property rights to provide a fair
	  economic return to the creators and owners of ideas
	• Allocation of radio spectrum as a scarce public
	  resource of major economic value

Societal Regulation:
  To sustain and strengthen the
  social, cultural, and political
  role of media in society to
  enrich and enlarge the
  public sphere and to restrict
  media content contrary to
  social or other norms
	• Limiting concentration of ownership in order to
	  ensure diversity of content and plurality of media
	• Protecting public service media from industry
	  regulation to enhance diversity and provide a sphere
	  for political debate
	• Providing universal access to cultural events to
	  sustain common identity
	• Providing must-carry obligations to broadcasting to
	  ensure community access and program diversity
	• Allocating radio spectrum to ensure fair access
	• Extending access to telecommunications to excluded
	  groups as economically and socially essential
	  services
	• Intellectual property rights that expand the volume of
	  information in the public domain
	• Legal prohibition of content and of production by
	  direct censoring of content before
	  transmission/distribution and legal sanctions after
	  transmission

- They settle disputes in civil law including in relation to IPRs, competition issues such as interconnection, and reviewing—sometimes striking down—regulatory interventions. Decisions can often have a major impact on the shape of regulatory institutions.
- They hear criminal actions relating to content regulation, involving for instance defamation, obscenity, and pornography.[1]

The courts can impact powerfully on regulation, sometimes exposing weaknesses in regulatory instruments and obliging governments to take action on issues that they may, for one reason or another, be slow on which to move.

Governments, of course, are the key players in regulation, though the depth and scope of interventions varies from country to country. They design and pass legislation that determines the powers and responsibilities of most regulatory instruments, government or otherwise, and empower the police and judiciary to take action in certain areas. They also directly regulate some media activities from government departments or oversee regulation within quasi-autonomous but government-controlled regulatory entities.

Regulatory powers may also be distributed between different levels of governments, for instance between German Länder and federal structures, and the U.S. state and federal powers. Conflicts can arise between these, especially in the context of media convergence when boundaries separating different media are blurred.

Agencies dedicated solely to regulating provide the most visible forms of regulation. They act with varying degrees of autonomy from the executive government and have very different scope and levels of influence. They are ultimately, however, instruments of government policy, and hence cannot ever constitute a competing and fully independent power— their degree and form of autonomy is circumscribed by government legislation, sometimes firmed up by a constitution.

The best known agency is the Federal Communications Commission (FCC) in the United States, which is broad in scope and has a high degree of autonomy from executive government power. The European Commission has been promoting the separation of regulatory institutions from government departments into agencies or authorities, in telecommunications and media generally. However, few if any have the scope of the FCC, and although there is ongoing discussion of merging the responsibilities of broadcast, telecommunications, cable, and other media, it is a slow process. In the United Kingdom, for instance, a total of fourteen bodies claim jurisdiction over aspects of media delivery.[2]

There is also self-regulation, which is growing in importance. An association of professional practitioners, for instance a press council, is a widespread model. However, self-regulation invariably involves a relationship to government and cannot be seen as an alternative regime of regulation. Wielding significant influence will require at least recognition by the government, and self-regulation will usually cover only certain aspects of regulation, with public authorities retaining all legal sanctions and possibly other powers. Self-regulation has also sometimes emerged under the threat of direct regulation by the government, and thus does not imply a lack of interest by the government in the area. In effect, "enforced self-regulation" can be seen as an instrument of regulation that works through negotiation between sectoral actors and the state.

All the above, even the courts, can involve other agents in their deliberations and decision-making process. The general public, lobby groups, nongovernmental organizations, and individual firms or their associations may be permitted participation in the form of tribunals, consultation mechanisms, or public hearings. While some in themselves comprise little more than window dressing, effective use of these opportunities can sometimes lead to significant influence. Canada's regulator, the Canadian Radio-television and Telecommunications Commission (CRTC), uses a variety of public consultation instruments including:

- Public hearings—used for major decisions such as broadcast license renewals or important policy reviews. The public is invited to submit both oral and written submissions.
- Public notices—similar to the above, but only written submissions are accepted.
- Regional consultations, public forums, and town hall meetings—less formal processes aimed at gaining valuable information from the general public on specific issues. Submissions can be written or oral.
- Round table discussions and workshops—meetings held by invitation, involving, for example, representatives of public or consumer groups, industry players, and experts in particular areas.

These do not exhaust the instruments of regulation at the national level, but they do offer some idea of their diversity.

NOTES

1. Based on David Goldberg, Tony Prosser, and Stefaan Verhulst, *Regulating the Changing Media: A Comparative Study* (Oxford: Clarendon, 1998).
2. Quoted in Goldberg, Prosser, and Verhulst, *Regulating the Changing Media*, 25.

2

+

Global Governance Institutions

Governments "govern" countries. They have responsibility for devising and implementing public policy that balances the interests of society's different groups. Governments make laws and enforce them; provide and oversee maintenance of infrastructure for the economy; and to varying degrees undertake, support, and steer activities in a broad selection of areas, ranging from defense to healthcare, and from enterprise to education. Governments may perform these tasks well, badly, or practically not at all; they may involve the public and adopt policies in support of the public interest, or they may not. But governing is a responsibility of government—so where does "governance" come in?

Formal definitions of "governance" offer little illumination. In 1992, the Commission on Global Governance was established by Willy Brandt, the former chancellor of West Germany, "to articulate a vision of global co-operation that may inspire nations—leaders and people—to intensify their collective endeavours."[1] Laboring over three years, this independent commission of twenty-eight prominent world leaders had arrived by 1995 at a rather vague definition of "governance" as "the sum of the many ways individuals and institutions, public or private, manage their common affairs. It is a continuing process through which conflicting or diverse interests may be accommodated and co-operative action may be taken. It includes formal institutions and regimes empowered to enforce compliance, as well as informal arrangements that people and institutions either have agreed to or perceive to be in their interest."[2]

While governance usually involves institutions and rules, it is not reducible to these. Governance is fundamentally a set of processes that are employed to assess, weigh, and balance the different (and possibly competing) values and objectives inherent in societies' diverse interests and actors. And while governments are often at the center of this process, there are many examples of governance that do not involve government and some that come to life precisely because of the lack of involvement or ability on the part of government. A neighborhood organization of residents and local businesses that is formed to keep the streets clean when municipal authorities refuse to is one example of this. Other governance structures may be the result of hoping to exclude government involvement in a given domain, as in the case of a group of newspaper publishers that establishes a voluntary press code and a press council to deal with citizen complaints so that the government will not find cause to formally intervene.

At the global level, governance has primarily evolved as the responsibility of *intergovernmental* agencies, especially but not exclusively those that together make up the UN system. In fact, these agencies are no longer exclusively *intergovernmental* since both the private sector and nongovernmental organizations (NGOs) are increasingly involved in their structures.

The Imperative of Global Governance

Global governance structures have generally been motivated by two things: The avoidance of mutually destructive warfare and the enablement of mutually beneficial interaction.

Some objectives are better achieved through cooperation than individual action, and this holds true with small groups or large nations. For example, the eradication of highly infectious diseases is virtually impossible without ongoing cooperation such as coordinated immunization strategies, quarantines, border controls, and joint testing and research activities. Where a global good is at stake, and a common threat perceived, strong motivation exists for agreeing and adhering to global protocols. The environment may also be considered a global good, although one in which the mutual long-term interest is more prone to sacrifice on the alter of short-term self-interest. There is as yet little experience with concerted environmental protection and management at a global level. Nevertheless, as with infectious disease in a context of human mobility, protecting the environment does not readily permit opt-in or opt-out positioning. It is thus increasingly recognized that a cohesive approach including most nations is required for advancement in this area.

Coordination of spaces where many nations interact in the same manner, such as in the exchange of international post, likewise benefits from the adoption of overarching rules and conventions that apply to all participating nations. In the same vein, maritime law, space law, passport conventions, and so forth are all subject to bodies of rules that reside outside the realm of the individual nation-state. Certainly, these bodies of rules are not always equitable (in that existing imbalances may here be further entrenched) or designed to promote development. They are constructed, however, to ensure predictability and order within their designated space of jurisdiction and to ensure flows, transactions, and interactions that can be effected without friction and confusion. Without them, planes and ships could not be ensured safety of transit through international spaces, world travelers would have to assert their identity through means other than standardized documentation, and so forth.

Brief History of Global Governance and the Rise of the UN System

Prior to the nineteenth century, there were virtually no international governance structures. Relations between European states were worked out on a bilateral basis using tools that included everything from royal marriages to war. Colonies were not granted formal recognition other than as an extension of their colonizers.

By the early 1800s, relations between European states were beginning to collapse under the strain of their own volume and complexity. Improved communications and transport, the increasing importance of international trade, and the problems associated with defending far-flung colonies was bringing governments into regular contact that was increasingly marked by war. The Congress of Vienna (1814–1815) represents perhaps the first great international agreement. Called after the downfall of Napoléon I, the congress was mandated to establish a balance of power in Europe and thus bring an end to the wars that had been devastating the Continent. In addition to redistributing territories conquered by Napoléon, the congress established the Concert of Europe to enforce and review its decisions, laying down the foundations of modern international diplomacy and setting the stage for almost forty years of undisturbed peace in Europe.

Following the success of this early European multilateral exercise, the strategy was applied in other domains. Significantly, communications became the focus for the next stage of multilateralism. By the mid-nineteenth century, the bilateral agreements that had sustained the international postal system for decades were proving inadequate to deal with the growing demand brought about by the burgeoning commercial activity. Following an 1863 attempt to establish a model bilateral agreement that would streamline the existing complex of bilateral agreements, a German postal official drafted an idea for an international postal union that was implemented in 1874 as the General Postal Union (later the Universal Postal Union [UPU]). Originally formed by twenty-two states, all European except for Egypt and the United States, the union grew to fifty-five members in ten years and by 1914 almost all independent states were members.

A more recent communications innovation was even quicker to spark the creation of a multilateral organization. Invented in 1844, telegraphy was widely available in Europe by the mid-1850s. However, the bilateral agreements that made international telegraphy possible were even more complex than those of the postal service. Telegraph codes and technical standards varied from country to country and sending a message often required that it be transcribed at each frontier and then physically handed over to the next country for retransmission through its territory. By 1855, regional agreements started appearing and in 1865 a meeting of twenty European states was convened by France to work out a framework agreement and adopt common technical standards to facilitate interconnection. They also established common international tariff and accounting rules. The result was the International Telegraph Union, now known as the International Telecommunication Union (ITU).

A number of other specialized international organizations, such as the International Meteorological Organization (now the World Meteorological Organization [WMO]) appeared over the next few decades but it was not until 1919, after the "War to End All Wars," that the League of Nations was constituted as the first general permanent "global" forum. In 1945, immediately after World War II, the United Nations was established to mitigate the recurrence of major war, and the current era of global governance was launched in earnest.

With the preoccupation of peacekeeping and security,[3] much more than the League of Nations, the United Nations set about adopting an international coordinating role, with a greatly expanded number of member states, by bringing existing bodies such as the UPU, ITU, and WMO into the UN system as independent specialized agencies linked through cooperative agreements. Also created as specialized agencies were the World Bank, the International Monetary Fund (IMF), and the regional development banks. Efforts to establish an International Trade Organization failed but resulted in the General Agreement on Tariffs and Trade (see chapter 5). The United Nations' governance mandate also extends to social ideals encompassing fundamental human rights, development, and better standards of life. To this end, programs and funds, in addition to the body of specialized agencies, were established to address policy, research, and action in areas such as food, children, education, culture, and so forth. Figure 2.1 shows the current structure of the UN system.

The **UNITED NATIONS** system

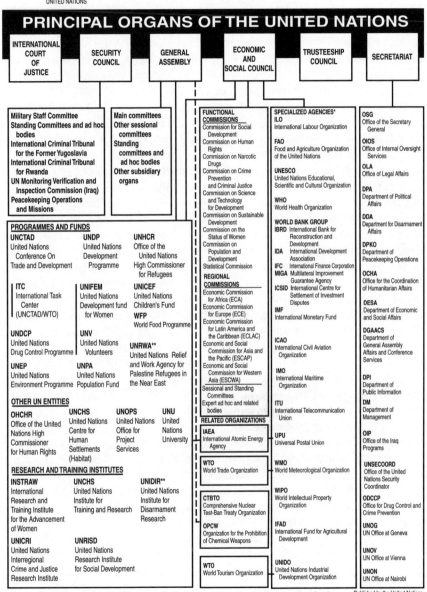

PRINCIPAL ORGANS OF THE UNITED NATIONS

INTERNATIONAL COURT OF JUSTICE	SECURITY COUNCIL	GENERAL ASSEMBLY	ECONOMIC AND SOCIAL COUNCIL	TRUSTEESHIP COUNCIL	SECRETARIAT

Military Staff Committee
Standing Committees and ad hoc bodies
International Criminal Tribunal for the Former Yugoslavia
International Criminal Tribunal for Rwanda
UN Monitoring Verification and Inspection Commission (Iraq)
Peacekeeping Operations and Missions

Main committees
Other sessional committees
Standing committees and ad hoc bodies
Other subsidiary organs

PROGRAMMES AND FUNDS

UNCTAD
United Nations Conference On Trade and Development

UNDP
United Nations Development Programme

UNHCR
Office of the United Nations High Commissioner for Refugees

ITC
International Task Center (UNCTAD/WTO)

UNIFEM
United Nations Development fund for Women

UNICEF
United Nations Children's Fund

WFP
World Food Programme

UNDCP
United Nations Drug Control Programme

UNV
United Nations Volunteers

UNRWA**
United Nations Relief and Work Agency for Palestine Refugees in the Near East

UNEP
United Nations Environment Programme

UNPA
United Nations Population Fund

OTHER UN ENTITIES

OHCHR
Office of the United Nations High Commissioner for Human Rights

UNCHS
United Nations Centre for Human Settlements (Habitat)

UNOPS
United Nations Office for Project Services

UNU
United Nations University

RESEARCH AND TRAINING INSTITUTES

INSTRAW
International Research and Training Institute for the Advancement of Women

UNCHS
United Nations Institute for Training and Research

UNIDIR**
United Nations Institute for Disarmament Research

UNICRI
United Nations Interregional Crime and Justice Research Institute

UNRISD
United Nations Research Institute for Social Development

FUNCTIONAL COMMISSIONS
Commission for Social Development
Commission on Human Rights
Commission on Narcotic Drugs
Commission on Crime Prevention and Criminal Justice
Commission on Science and Technology for Development
Commission on Sustainable Development
Commission on the Status of Women
Commission on Population and Development
Commission on Statistical Commission

REGIONAL COMMISSIONS
Economic Commission for Africa (ECA)
Economic Commission for Europe (ECE)
Economic Commission for Latin America and the Caribbean (ECLAC)
Economic and Social Commission for Asia and the Pacific (ESCAP)
Economic and Social Commission for Western Asia (ESCWA)
Sessional and Standing Committees
Expert ad hoc and related bodies

RELATED ORGANIZATIONS

IAEA
International Atomic Energy Agency

WTO
World Trade Organization

CTBTO
Comprehensive Nuclear Test-Ban Treaty Organization

OPCW
Organization for the Prohibition of Chemical Weapons

WTO
World Tourism Organization

SPECIALIZED AGENCIES*

ILO International Labour Organization

FAO Food and Agriculture Organization of the United Nations

UNESCO United Nations Educational, Scientific and Cultural Organization

WHO World Health Organization

WORLD BANK GROUP
IBRD International Bank for Reconstruction and Development
IDA International Development Association
IFC International Finance Corporation
MIGA Multilateral Improvement Guarantee Agency
ICSID International Centre for Settlement of Investment Disputes

IMF International Monetary Fund

ICAO International Civil Aviation Organization

IMO International Maritime Organization

ITU International Telecommunication Union

UPU Universal Postal Union

WMO World Meteorological Organization

WIPO World Intellectual Property Organization

IFAD International Fund for Agricultural Development

UNIDO United Nations Industrial Development Organization

OSG Office of the Secretary General

OIOS Office of Internal Oversight Services

OLA Office of Legal Affairs

DPA Department of Political Affairs

DDA Department for Disarmament Affairs

DPKO Department of Peacekeeping Operations

OCHA Office for the Coordination of Humanitarian Affairs

DESA Department of Economic and Social Affairs

DGAACS Department of General Assembly Affairs and Conference Services

DPI Department of Public Information

DM Department of Management

OIP Office of the Iraq Programs

UNSECOORD Office of the United Nations Security Coordinator

ODCCP Office for Drug Control and Crime Prevention

UNOG UN Office at Geneva

UNOV UN Office at Vienna

UNON UN Office at Nairobi

* Autonomous organizations working with the United Nations and each other through the coordinating machinery of the Economic and Social Council.
** Report only to the General Assembly.

Published by the United Nations
Department of Public Information
DPS1079 -January 2001

Figure 2.1

How the UN System of Global Governance Works

Members of the United Nations, and its specialized agencies, are sovereign countries that willingly accept certain obligations and agree to follow certain basic principles of international relations. For the United Nations and its agencies, these principles are outlined in the UN Charter,[4] an international treaty drafted when the United Nations was founded and ratified by each of its 189 member states.

While in theory the United Nations' highest body is the General Assembly, the reality is somewhat different and the United Nations provides an interesting study in controlled global democracy. The assembly, a sort of international parliament in which all member states are able to participate with voice and vote, can provide an indication of world government opinion, but it cannot force action by any state and has only minimal recourse to sanctions and other instruments to enforce its decisions. The Security Council has the most muscle in the UN system and under the UN Charter all member states are obligated to carry out council decisions. Of the fifteen members of the Security Council, ten are elected by the General Assembly and five—China, France, Russia, the United Kingdom, and the United States—are permanent members. The Security Council has the power to impose economic sanctions or arms embargoes, send troops to monitor truces and keep opposing forces apart, and even to authorize collective military activity, as it did in the 1991 war against Iraq. However, the rules give a veto to each of the permanent members, giving them significantly extra powers to influence world affairs in their own interests.

While sanctions and threats of military action may be effective for dealing with occasional and isolated situations, too frequent, or indeed too selective, recourse against them puts the moral authority of the United Nations and the Security Council in question. Moral authority is one of the main pillars on which global governance rests, and it is easily eroded.

There are many ways in which international law is distinct from national law. One important distinction is that national law applies to all people within a state, regardless of whether or not they are individually in agreement with it, while the legitimacy and effectiveness of international law is in virtually all cases rooted in and dependent on its acceptance by the nation-states that constitute the system. In other words, international law is enforceable only to the extent that states agree to adhere to it and, as a consequence, agree to surrender some of their sovereignty.

While reasons for doing this may vary on a case-by-case basis and may include various forms of coercion, such as the threat of sanctions, the offer of special trading privileges, or the conditionality of development aid, states generally choose to cooperate with global governance bodies because it would be costly not to do so and there is a perception of mutual benefit. Additionally, the very nature of national sovereignty is changing and receding in significance as a result of factors such as the decline of the nation-state, the globalization of environmental problems (highlighting the importance of the global commons), and the emergence of new types of alliances, including multinational economic and political alliances and federal states, with the accompanying notion of shared sovereignty.

New Actors in Global Governance Affairs

International governance organizations are designed primarily to do two things: to provide a *forum* for international debate and negotiation around policy formation and treaties, and to fulfil particular *services* that are of common benefit, such as setting standards or coordinating radio frequency use. Most international organizations engage in both, though, as argued later, their respective priority as inscribed in an organization's raison d'être will have a major impact on the initial design of its internal structure, formal powers, and establishment of, for example, decision-making processes. Perhaps most importantly, *who* is entitled to participate is also defined in these. Emerging from the tradition of bilateral negotiation and intergovernmental history of treaties, membership within the United Nations, and participation in formal proceedings is, as its name implies, restricted to nation-states.[5] Although there are also provisions for observer status, the issue of further expanding participation to civil society and the private sector is an important one.

In Kofi A. Annan's report to the UN Millennium Assembly, he stated, "[b]etter governance means greater participation, coupled with accountability. Therefore, the international public domain—including the United Nations—must be opened up further to the participation of the many actors whose contributions are essential to managing the path of globalization."[6]

A formal and limited mechanism for NGO consultation, mandated in the United Nations' founding charter, was established in 1968.[7] The rise in the number and influence of NGOs has been a phenomenon of the past century and especially the last few decades. Known previously and variously as charitable, community, independent, or professional associations, they have sprung up virtually everywhere and become international in scope, actively addressing issues in a diverse range of sectors. Their influence and role has likewise spread to participation within UN processes, first tangentially, and increasingly in formalized contexts. At the 1972 Stockholm Conference on the Human Environment, more than simply the environment was put on the agenda. With the emergence of an "environmental agenda," NGOs made their debut as forces with influence. Stockholm was also the impetus for subsequent UN global conferences held on topics of global concern.[8] These conferences were critical to establishing the participation of civil society (NGOs in particular) and the impetus to incorporate them within the UN system. The 1987 Brundtland Report also emphasized the participation of "civil society" in the management of sustainable development. Based on this report, the Rio Conference on Environment and Development took place in 1992 with the unprecedented presence of 27,000 NGO representatives. At the 1995 Fourth World Conference on Women in Beijing, NGO representatives numbered 35,000.

In 1996, following a three-year inquiry, the relationship and role of NGOs were redefined in the UN Resolution 1996/31,[9] updating and elaborating on provisions for NGO consultative status, in particular within the UN Economic and Social Council (ECOSOC) and in terms of access to resources maintained by the UN Secretariat. There are now 38,000 international NGOs, up from 6,000 in 1990. By 2000, about 2,500 NGOs had obtained formal consultative status with ECOSOC, additionally, many NGOs have official arrangements with other bodies of the United Nations. However, there is still a push for a greater access to information resources (that are either prohibitively expensive or UN protected for security reasons) and participatory roles for NGOs across the United Nations, beyond that already provided. In particular, it is a point of contention that NGOs are not granted consultative status within the General Assembly. Recommendations for further elevation of NGO status come both from outside and within the United Nations itself.[10] In the ITU, for example, the private sector enjoys almost full participation, i.e., it cannot vote on constitutional matters, but it has all other rights and privileges.

As these new actors are incorporated into the UN system, their different and sometimes incompatible visions of globalization and of reforming global governance will emerge to face each other, and governments, in the global arena. Their differential orientations and power bases, quantitatively and qualitatively, will demand the articulation of innovative structures of interaction if they are to assume responsibility "by the concept and practice of global citizenship," as called for by Annan in his Millennium address to the United Nations.

Summing Up

Global governance is a relatively new process, and yet the world has changed much since its initial manifestation. The UN Security Council created in 1945 with five designated members reflected a particular geopolitical reality that has lost much of its force today. Likewise, the implications on the balance of power of the entry and participation of newly independent colonies and smaller nations in the UN General Assembly were not fully anticipated. The newly recognised importance of global economic actors and of civil society exert further new influences on the global governance terrain, beyond the direct ambit of nations.

Successful adaptation and evolution of the United Nations, and of global governance, will focus on institutional change, participation and legitimacy. Its capacity to live up to and deepen its founding principles, to maintain credibility, and to resist powerful forces aiming to undermine and even, in effect, displace it, will be strengthened by enhanced transparency, the elimination of barriers to participation, and the opening out to other legitimate actors.

Notes

1. Commission on Global Governance, *Terms of Reference of the Commission on Global Governance* (Oxford: Oxford University Press, 1992), <http://www.cgg.ch/tor.htm> [last accessed: 26 November 2001].

2. Commission on Global Governance, *Our Global Neighbourhood: The Report of the Commission on Global Governance* (Oxford: Oxford University Press, 1995), <http://www.cgg.ch/contents.htm> [last accessed: 26 November 2001].

3. The full text of the UN Charter is available on the UN Web site at <http://www.un.org/aboutun/charter/index.html> [last accessed: 26 November 2001].

4. See note 3 concerning the UN Charter.

5. Article 4 of the UN Charter, "Membership in the United Nations is open to all peace-loving states which accept the obligations of the Charter and, in the judgement of the Organization, are willing and able to carry out these obligations."

6. Kofi A. Annan, *"We the Peoples": The Role of the United Nations in the 21st Century* (New York: United Nations, 2000), 13.

7. Article 71 of the UN Charter, "The Economic and Social Council may make suitable arrangements for consultation with non-governmental organizations which are concerned with matters within its competence. Such arrangements may be made with international organizations and, where appropriate, with national organizations after consultation with the Member of the United Nations concerned."

8. UN global conferences have been held on the topics of food, human settlements, women, social development, population and development, human rights, environment and development, children, natural disaster reduction, and so forth.

9. See <http://www.un.org/documents/ecosoc/res/1996/eres1996-31.htm> [last accessed: 26 November 2001].

10. UN Economic and Social Council, "Decision 1996/297" <http://www.hri.ca/uninfo/resolutn/dec297.shtml> [last accessed: 26 November 2001]: "At its 49th plenary meeting on 25 July 1996, the Economic and Social Council,

reaffirming the importance of the contributions of non-governmental organizations to the work of the United Nations, and taking into account the contributions made by non-governmental organizations to recent international conferences, decided to recommend that the General Assembly examine, at its fifty-first session, the question of the participation of non-governmental organizations in all areas of the work of the United Nations, in the light of the experience gained through the arrangements for consultation between non-governmental organizations and the Economic and Social Council."

3

Trends in Media

THE MEDIA CENTURY

During the past 100 years, the media have been transformed into one of modern society's most important institutions, exercising influence in virtually all aspects of social and political life, assuming a central role in the shaping of culture, and becoming one of the primary ways by which people learn about and interact with their world and between each other.

Important milestones mark the evolutionary path of today's mass media. An early one was the rise of cheap mass market newspapers at the end of the nineteenth century, but more significant were those of the growth of electronic media. These included the birth of broadcast radio in the 1920s, the introduction of television in the 1950s, the appearance of cable television and broadcast satellites in the 1970s, and, finally, the explosion of the Internet in the last half of the 1990s and continuing into the twenty-first century.

As the century wore on, the pace of change accelerated. Radio was around for thirty-eight years before 50 million radio listeners could tune in. Television achieved the same number of users in fourteen years. Four years after the privatization of the U.S. backbone in 1994, widely regarded as the moment the Internet became a public network, 50 million people were online. By the end of 2000 this number had risen to an estimated 400 million, with growth estimates exceeding 100 percent per year.[1] As an indicator of the growth of new multimedia, RealNetworks, the company that makes the most popular consumer software for streaming radio and video over the Internet, claimed 200 million unique registered users five years later.

However, the media century is more than a succession of momentous technological innovations in interactivity and dissemination. It is marked also by the emergence and consolidation of a number of trends that have changed, and are continuing to change, the nature of the media and of society itself, the last two decades witnessing a series of major institutional eruptions, and corporate and sectoral reshuffles. These are yet to abate as electronic media continue to reinvent themselves.

A few interrelated trends can be identified that are having significant impact on the media's social and political role and on governance of the sector, both at the national and global levels. These include privatization, technological change/convergence, concentration of ownership and control, and globalization of media markets and industries. Each of these trends poses challenges to the national regulatory systems described in chapter 1 and, taken together, enormously strain the current global governance practices and institutions described in Chapter 2. In this chapter we will identify and briefly explore these four trends with an eye towards the challenges they pose for governance.

PRIVATIZATION AND MARKET LIBERALIZATION

The basic ownership and financing models that were to dominate broadcasting for much of the twentieth century emerged only a few years after the introduction of broadcast radio in the 1920s.

In the United States the Radio Act of 1927 regulated broadcast radio as a primarily commercial enterprise, supported by advertising. While there were a few educational stations in the USA, they were owned by universities or foundations. At the root of this policy was the promotion of a market economy by almost all powerful interests, linked to a widespread distrust of the government's intentions–to this day, U.S. law explicitly prohibits the government from broadcasting in its own territory to its own citizens.

In Europe, the dominant trend was toward public broadcasting, at arm's length from government, paid for with public funds or with compulsory license fees on radio receivers collected directly by the broadcaster. Public broadcasting, it was argued, was the only way to guarantee that the radio spectrum would be put to use to promote social objectives (such as with educational and informational programing). In practice, the degree to which the public broadcasters were able to exercise independence from government varied significantly from country to country.

As Europe's colonies gained their independence, they generally adopted the public broadcasting model favored by their former colonial powers, although usually with more rather than less government influence. Less industrialized countries more influenced by the United States, notably the Philippines and most of Latin America, opted for private-sector ownership, although usually with some limited public broadcasting presence. Private-sector ownership did not, however, translate into abdication of government responsibility for the sector. Most countries with private-sector ownership also opted for a strong state presence in the form of licensing and regulatory bodies with the power to impose public service obligations on private-sector broadcasters (such as requiring private broadcasters to dedicate resources to production and distribution of national news, information, and cultural programs), to restrict anticompetitive practices (such as monopolistic ownership of media in a single market or country), and to limit or prohibit foreign ownership of national media.

The 1980s and 1990s saw the weakening of both European public broadcasting and U.S.–style regulation for public service broadcasting. In Europe, the challenge came first from illegal "pirate" broadcasters, some beaming their signals from powerful offshore stations and others openly operating unlicensed FM stations in urban centers. Unable to close them down, the European response was to license them, and thus at least to be able to regulate them. However, this offered only temporary respite; European public service broadcasting is still almost universally under attack—faced with reduction in subsidies and license fees and increasingly sophisticated competition, many of Europe's formerly great public broadcasters are resorting to commercial funding schemes and many that are not are offering programing that is increasingly indistinguishable from that of the commercial broadcasters.

In Europe's former African colonies, the change has been even more dramatic. In the mid-1980s, there were only seven independent broadcasters in all of Sub-Saharan Africa, but by the end of the 1990s there were literally thousands, most of them commercial and few of them producing any significant local programing. At the same time, in many countries, public broadcasters have become increasingly marginal, with their government subsidies being reduced or eliminated altogether.

In countries with a tradition of private-sector broadcasting, regulation for public service is becoming increasingly rare. Leading the trend is the United States, which in addition to eliminating most public service obligations has also loosened most restrictions on media ownership, while continuing to restrict foreign ownership, ostensibly for national security reasons. In Latin America, where already more than 60 percent of television programing comes from the United States, the elimination of public service obligations virtually guarantees the decimation of national television production in all but three countries.[2]

In the United States, recent steps in the same direction include a proposal that would see the radio spectrum fully privatized, developed by the Progress and Freedom Foundation, a Washington-based conservative think tank. At first dismissed, the proposal to allow the airwaves to be bought and sold like real estate later became the subject of congressional hearings. Less than a month after Republican president George W. Bush took office, it was endorsed in a letter to the Federal Communications Commission (FCC) by thirty-seven leading economists. While the proposal is unlikely to be implemented in the immediate future, full privatization of the radio spectrum, first in the United States but eventually imposed on all countries by the World Trade Organization (WTO) trade rules, can no longer be considered beyond the realm of the possible.

TECHNOLOGICAL CHANGE AND CONVERGENCE

The second trend is related to the pace and scope of technological change and especially to convergence.

Convergence is the merging of different technologies (especially computing and telecommunications) and industries to create new forms of cultural products and new modes for their production and delivery. Thus, for example, the discrete entities of music, film, and newspapers can now be offered over a variety of channels including satellite, cable television, and the Internet. Parallel to this technological convergence has been an industrial convergence, blurring the traditional distinctions between content producers and providers of hardware, software, and telecommunications services. AOL Time-Warner, Sony, and Vivendi Universal are only a few examples of companies with extensive activities in content production and distribution, telecommunications, and computing.

Convergence poses significant challenges for media governance. Regulation for distribution channels has historically treated different technologies, and hence distribution networks, as separate entities. At the national level, the primary separation has been the distinction between broadcast and telecommunications. Telecommunications service providers were regulated as common carriers, meaning that distribution rather than content was the focus of the regulation and the primary goals were to ensure access to the network and to coordinate the market and commercial practices of providing service at reasonable prices. Radio and television were regulated as broadcasters, with requirements for fairness, national content, and other social objectives being justified on the basis that the radio frequencies they use are a scarce public resource. However, technological developments and changes within the industries have challenged all this. Programs that once could only be delivered over the air can now use any combination of a variety of channels, including the Internet, over a wide range of technologies, including standard or enhanced telephone lines, cable, fiber optics, high-speed leased lines, satellites, and a variety of wireless digital technologies. The resultant new media have at least the potential to become de facto broadcasters, but they are regulated, if at all, as telecommunications services. Faced with this complex situation, even well-resourced and experienced regulators in rich countries have chosen not to regulate new media content for social objectives.[3]

In addition to competition for their markets, traditional broadcasters are also going to have to defend the radio frequencies they use to deliver their programing. Wireless voice and data telecommunications service providers, with deep pockets, are coveting the broad swath of the radio spectrum occupied by spectrum-hungry analogue broadcasters. While broadcasting is unlikely to be eliminated altogether in the near future, radio spectrum will undoubtedly be reallocated, with potentially severe implications for traditional over-the-air broadcasters.

CONSOLIDATION OF OWNERSHIP
AND CONTROL OF THE MEDIA

Concentration of ownership and control of media is not a new phenomenon. Indeed, more than 130 years ago control of the worldwide market for news was exercised by a media cartel consisting of three European news agencies that signed an agreement dividing the world news market among them, enabling them to eliminate competition and to enjoy significant economies of scale.[4] Some cultural and informational products and their distribution readily benefit from the economies of scale presented by mass audiences, and cultural producers can claim to produce large-budget products more efficiently if capitalizing on larger markets and/or audiences. Additionally, as with any industry, integration—owning or controlling access to different points of the production or distribution chain—also reduces competition and thus lowers costs and increases profits and possibilities for cross-subsidization of different branches of production.

During the latter part of the twentieth century, there has been an increase in concentration of ownership and control of national media, both in industrialized and less industrialized markets. This increased concentration can, in part, be explained by the maturing process of the market, with players simply taking advantage of the economies of scale mentioned earlier. Such is the case with European and North American newspaper markets, for example, that have seen a steady decline in the number of independent newspapers since the 1950s. The same was true of television in countries where it was dominated by the private sector. As early as the 1980s, three national networks, ABC, CBS, and NBC, had collectively 92 percent of television viewership in the United States. Other countries where private broadcasting has dominated for many years, such as Argentina, Brazil, and Mexico, exhibit even greater degrees of concentration.

However, privatization, liberalization, technological development, and convergence have combined to eliminate technical and regulatory barriers to vertical and horizontal integration of media, enabling the emergence of vast multimedia conglomerates with ownership both of entire chains of production and distribution (vertical integration) and control over various markets in the same sector (horizontal integration). In the United States—the current world leader in media concentration and integration—the result is that the three networks that once dominated U.S. television are now only parts of much larger multimedia conglomerates with vast holdings in cultural industries. ABC is part of the Disney empire, CBS is held by Viacom, NBC belongs to General Electric, and a new national network, Fox, belongs to News Corp.[5]

Admittedly, the United States is atypical, since its multimedia conglomerates are also the world's (add the other U.S. giant, AOL Time-Warner, Europe's Vivendi Universal and Bertelsmann, and Japan's Sony, all with major holdings in the United States, and the list of the giants of global multimedia is completed). Since so much of the world's media is produced in the United States, only a few regional media production hubs, such as Egypt, South Africa, Hong Kong, and India, offer similar opportunities for vertical integration of their media industries. There is, however, scope for consolidation of ownership of radio, television, and the press, and evidence shows that this is happening in much of the world. Between 1997 and 2000, the World Association for Christian Communication conducted an investigation into media ownership in central and eastern Europe, the Caribbean, the Pacific, Southeast Asia, South Asia, central and West Africa, southern Africa, and Latin America. While the report presents a variety and diversity of media situations, it concludes that media ownership patterns "are undergoing constant change as technologies and global economic imperatives combine to push forward the corporate agenda of greater media concentration."[6] The report also notes that, unlike in western Europe and North America, many countries of Africa, Latin America, and central and eastern Europe have high degrees of foreign ownership of their national print and broadcast media.

GLOBALIZATION OF MEDIA MARKETS AND INDUSTRIES

Capitalizing on the trends of liberalization, privatization, convergence, and consolidation is a final trend involving the massive restructuring of media institutions and of the way cultural products are produced, distributed, and consumed. The globalization of media markets and industries is marked by a number of developments, including increased foreign ownership of national media, the rise of global multimedia giants, and the increasing permeability of national boundaries to media products and channels, the latter providing global media with direct unregulated access to national audiences via direct satellite broadcasting and the Internet.

Significant challenges are posed by media globalization. Among the most salient are those related to the considerable economies of scale and the huge amounts of capital available to global media, which translate into almost insurmountable barriers to sector entry. Equally if not more important is the significant political influence wielded by the media giants in their home countries, in international fora, and in the countries in which they operate. Finally, the extraterritorial nature of global media keeps them beyond the reach of national media governance structures and practices. There are few policy options available to a government wanting to support development of national media in this environment, few business opportunities for underfinanced national media, and few meaningful fora for people who question this new world order to express their views. At the national level there is a growing governance vacuum, in which governments are excluded from shaping new media environments and in which market studies are the only form of public consultation.

In the remaining chapters of this book, we will look at some of the key institutions and instruments of global media governance and ask whether they will be capable of meeting the challenges posed by the new global media environment. Hanging in the balance is the potential of media for preserving ideals of human rights, cultural diversity, democracy, access to information, and universal service.

NOTES

1. For a discussion of methods to assess Internet growth, see: NUA <http://www.nua.ie/surveys/how_many_online/index.html>; and, Zook (2000), Internet metrics: using host and domain counts to map the internet, *Telecommunications Policy 24:* 6–7.

2. Argentina, Brazil, and Mexico have developed national markets and are exporters of television productions to other Latin American countries.

3. The Canadian Radio-television and Telecommunications Commission, for example, threw up its hands in 1999, becoming one of the first regulators in the world to admit that it could not regulate new media services on the Internet. See Canadian Radio-television and Telecommunications Commission, "Broadcasting Public Notice CRTC 1999-84, New Media" <http://www.crtc.gc.ca/archive/eng/Notices/1999/PB99-84.htm> [last accessed: 28 November 2001].

4. The three agencies were Reuters, Wolff, and Havas (now Agence France Presse). Their cartel remained in place until 1920, when it was challenged by the Associated Press from the United States.

5. For details on ownership of U.S. media, see the *Colombia Journalism Review*'s "Who Owns What," <http://www.cjr.org/owners/index.asp> [last accessed: 26 November 2001].

6. World Association for Christian Communications, *Media Ownership and Citizen Access: A Global Overview* (London: World Association for Christian Communications, 2001), 45.

II

4

✛

The International
Telecommunication Union

THE INTERNATIONAL TELECOMMUNICATION UNION AND MEDIA AND COMMUNICATIONS

The International Telecommunication Union (ITU) is the only special-ized agency of the United Nations devoted exclusively to a communi-cations issue. Formed in 1865 by national governments, it also claims the distinction of being the first truly international organization. Like all multilateral organizations, it is conceived as facilitating and admin-istering agreements between governments, involving also cooperation with others. The ITU's strategic plan for the period 1999–2003 sets out the purposes of the union:

"to provide a forum in which its members can cooperate for the rational use of telecommunications of all kinds in the following domains:

- a technical domain—to promote the development, efficient opera-tion, usefulness and general availability of telecommunication facili-ties and services;
- a development domain—to promote the development of telecom-munications in developing countries and the extension of the bene-fits of telecommunications to people everywhere;
- a policy domain—to promote the adoption of a broader approach to telecommunication issues in the global information economy and so-ciety."[1]

The ITU's main activities are:

- Allocating radio frequency spectrum and orbital slots for satellites to the various demand made upon it by governments and the private sector, from satellite television to mobile phones
- Developing common standards in communications equipment, operation, and services
- Facilitating agreement on sharing tariffs between international telecommunications operators
- Providing research, strategic advice, and training to developing countries, and the implementation of telecommunications projects to assist development.

The International Telecommunication Union
Location: Geneva
Established: 1865 (as the International Telegraph Union)
Membership: 189 countries, 656 sector members
Budget: Chf 327,000,000 ($200,000,000)
Secretariat staff:

- Head: Yoshio Utsumi, secretary-general (Japan)
- Head of the ITU Radiocommunication Standardization Sector: Robert W. Jones (Canada)
- Head of the ITU Telecommunications Standardization Sector: Houlin Zhao (China)
- Head ITU Development Sector: Hamadoun Touré (Mali)

Functions:

- Allocating radio frequency spectrum and satellite slots
- Developing common standards in communications equipment, operation, and services
- Facilitating agreement on sharing tariffs between international telecommunications operators
- Providing research, strategic advice, and training to developing countries and implementation of telecommunications projects to assist development

URL: <www.itu.int>

The ITU offers a forum at which governments and other key players exchange information and hammer out agreements on these matters. It works by consensus and has no enforcement procedures or sanctions to bring to bear against those contravening agreements.

Before describing these in more depth, it is worth asking: Why is there an international organization devoted to these in the first place? What is so special about telecommunications that it was the subject of such early international agreement?

A number of motivations can be found behind the ITU, and historically these intensified as the level and variety of communications between countries grew. Four main reasons can be discerned.

The first is the need for, and benefits of, standards and interconnection. Many manufactured goods benefit from some form of standardization, from standard screw sizes, to standard voltage for electricity. However, telecommunications is particularly dependent on standards because of its inherently transnational nature and because of additional benefits available to a fully interconnected communications system.

As we saw in chapter 2, early telegraphy and telecommunications systems were incompatible with each other. They were built using different standards and hence were unable to establish connection between competing companies and across different national boundaries. The benefits of interconnection became clear early on: Proprietary systems meant that those using one system could not communicate with users of another, and the inefficiency of this was plain to everyone. Either there would be massive duplication of the systems, with users being forced to subscribe to several, or the number of available cocommunicants would be very limited, greatly reducing the utility of the system and for each user.

In few other sectors is this problem so pressing and fundamental (the gauge of a railway track is somewhat analogous), and few can benefit as much from solving it. Furthermore, the standards problem was even more marked internationally where separate national industries had emerged.

Second is the problem of calculating tariffs and distributing revenue between different carriers. Telecommunications, like the postal system, faces a cross-border problem of how to share the income (postage stamps or telecommunications tariffs) between the *originator* of the traffic, who collects the tariffs, and those *completing the journey* on the other side of whatever border (not necessarily national) that is crossed. Indeed, several borders might have to be traversed, each charging different tariffs to their customers for similar journeys in different and fluctuating currencies, making the whole issue very complex.

Originally, first in the postal system then in telegraphy, a plethora of bilateral, trilateral, and quadrilateral relations were established. However, the complexity of creating and maintaining these relations was a heavy burden that had at various times threatened to slow the expansion of communications networks.

A third peculiarity of telecommunications is its extensive use of a "public good" in the form of radio frequency spectrum and later on, orbital slots in space. Electromagnetic frequencies used in radio represent a nondepletable natural resource. However, its value, to all classes of users, can be depleted through overcrowding, in that the use of the same frequency by different users leads to interference. Furthermore, because of its nature, no nation or company (despite some vigorous attempts) has been able to exert total sovereignty over the use of radio spectrum within its borders. Thus, the effective use of this resource demands an agreed allocation of slices of that spectrum to different uses and to different users. The agreement must cover both the rationing of this spectrum, splitting it up into different parcels, and the use of this spectrum by different parties. A similar task exists in relation to the allocation of satellite slots, especially in the geostationary orbit.

Fourth, telecommunications, as one element and a main conduit of the overall communications and media process of society, is usually regarded as more than simply conveying pieces of information from one place to another, analogous to the transportation of material goods. Rather, it is seen as vital to the dissemination—and control—of news and valuable information, as a strategic military and surveillance tool, as having a major social role in linking dispersed populations, as being a significant stimulant and facilitator of economic progress, and as entering into issues of culture and identity.

To the extent that these four factors are operative and recognized, there is a need for discussion, agreement, and regulation beyond what applies to conventional sectoral activities.

A BRIEF HISTORY

These four enduring factors largely account for the foundation and evolution of the ITU, its major functions and forms of organization. Of course, its history was, and still is, determined by other matters. As we shall see, telecommunications has undergone several major mutations that originated externally, caused for instance by the evolution of adjacent economic sectors and the rise and fall of various political and economic regimes. But these four factors allow us to isolate common threads, exerting their influence at different times over more than 135 years of ITU existence.

Early Days

The ITU was founded as the International Telegraph Union in May 1865 by twenty European countries that had also ratified the first International

Telegraph Convention. New members quickly joined, although, notably, not the United States, which preferred to negotiate agreements on a bilateral basis. The impetus at this stage came mainly from the first two factors mentioned earlier: the need for a simple multilateral agreement on tariffs and growing demands for common standards and interconnection.

For the first few decades, the ITU supported a modest permanent organization,[2] called ad hoc technical meetings, and held only administrative conferences. Telephony was first incorporated in 1903, initially merely as a supplement to telegraphic regulations.

Around the same time, the need for agreement on the radio spectrum was also emerging. This was separate from the activities of the ITU since the area was controlled by private operators in maritime communications among which the Anglo-Italian Marconi Wireless Company exerted near monopoly power. Partly motivated by worries about the Marconi practice of prohibiting users of their equipment to communicate with others— even where no technical barrier existed—a number of European countries got together in 1903 for the Preliminary Radio Conference held in Berlin. This later evolved into the International Radiotelegraph Union (IRU). Although thus sparked by a need for interconnection, the second conference, which was held in 1906, also saw the first agreement on the allocation of frequencies. The pace quickened as major technical advances and uses during the First World War revealed more clearly the commercial and propaganda potential of radio transmission.

From the beginning, the relationship between the two organizations was close, and by the late 1920s both the ITU and IRU had formed permanent consultative committees in their domains, respectively the International Telegraph and Telephone Consultative Committee (CCITT) and the International Radio Consultative Committee (CCIR). In 1932, a joint meeting of the ITU and the IRU was held in Madrid and the decision taken to merge into a new body, the International Telecommunication Union. This operational structure stayed in place until 1994, although some modifications and additions were made.

In 1947, the ITU voted to become a specialized agency of the United Nations and, modifying its structures and procedures accordingly, moved its headquarters from Berne to Geneva.

Pressures for Change

While the fundamental structures remained largely unchanged during this period, pressures did bring conflict and some modification. These derived from inherent tensions in the nature and organization of telecommunications, as well as from external forces. Although broadly agreed as indispensable, standard setting, tariff agreement, and allocation of radio frequencies and orbital positions inevitably faced difficulties, and periodic crises erupted for the ITU.

- The challenge for reaching agreement on standards was that those controlling dominant proprietary standards only reluctantly relinquish them for a common standard. They much prefer to force competitors to migrate to their standard, thus consolidating their dominant position. In the early decades of the twentieth century, for instance, standards became a concern of competition law in the United States, intent on forcing AT&T to end its anticompetitive use of standards. Even basic telephony was not resolved in favor of common standards and total interconnectivity until well into the twentieth century.[3] The issue of common standards can never be conflict-free in a situation of competing industries and carriers, and will tend to intensify as technological change opens up new possibilities and competition increases pressure to reach rapid agreement. Furthermore, the standards development process and outcome are by no means isolated from their commercial implications for the different actors—but this can also work to the ITU's benefit since it motivates large commercial concerns to devote considerable resources to developing and achieving consensus for ITU standards, hoping thereby to influence the outcome.
- By the late 1960s, the already difficult work of the CCIR, the invention and rapid take-up of communications satellites, and the need to allocate satellite orbital positions and associated radio frequencies became significantly more complicated and contentious. Matters came to a head when the ITU, now with a majority of less industrialized countries, voted to reserve orbital positions for use by countries not immediately in a position to take advantage of them—against the objections of more industrialized countries wanting to expand their services and area of control.
- The special character of telecommunications as a medium of economic and social development first exerted itself significantly during the 1950s, with the creation of the technical assistance function aimed at helping less industrialized countries to improve their networks. This evolved into a means to channel the UN Development Program (UNDP) and other resources to that end. In 1982, the ITU set up an Independent Commission for World Wide Telecommunications Development (also called the Maitland Commission), whose 1984 report spelled out some far reaching proposals to address the huge gap between telecommunications infrastructure in wealthy and poorer countries.
- The system of tariff sharing, initiated in 1865, also encountered ongoing problems, but it gradually evolved and extended to accommo-

date these by devising a framework governing the bilateral arrangements negotiated between countries, known as the accounting rate system. Over the past decade, this issue has become a central area of contention.

The ITU was, by design, a weak organization. Reluctant to cede sovereignty over a strategic communications area to a supranational organization, its founding members saddled it with a structure that was ill-prepared for innovation or for managing conflict. One of the most burdensome of these was that the ITU, unlike other multilateral institutions, was governed by a convention instead of a charter or a constitution. The difference is that a charter, while subject to amendment, is a more-or-less stable document that describes the objectives of an institution and the guidelines within which it can operate with a certain degree of autonomy. The ITU's entire convention, on the other hand, was subject to approval by each plenipotentiary and thus, at least in theory, the entire foundation of the organization could be scrapped by a simple vote of 50 percent of its membership. While in practice it has been relatively stable, the price of stability has been an institution unwilling to rock the boat and severely handicapped in its ability to plan. That the ITU has more elected positions than other multilateral organizations has had the same effect. Similarly, the requirement that decisions be made by consensus may have been appropriate fifty years ago when technology moved along at a predictable rate. By the latter years of the twentieth century, many believed it was becoming unworkable.

During the decades leading up to the mid-1980s, and despite occasional crises, the organization coped with these limitations and worked at a relatively leisurely pace, meeting at lengthy conferences and plenipotentiaries spread years apart to address substantive areas of work and to attempt to reduce slowly accumulating backlogs.

However, this was soon to change radically. The technical, political, and economic environment changed rapidly and decisively during the 1980s such that by the early 1990s, the ITU was forced to introduce its first major overhaul of structures and procedures since 1932.

The ITU Transformed?

External forces impacted on the four factors outlined earlier, intensifying their contradictions and leading to an urgent reappraisal of ITU structures and finally to a fundamental restructuring in 1994. Specifically, several strands of technological progress, first in microelectronics, then in space and satellite technology, in transmission media, and in several other areas, were beginning to merge through the implementation of digitalization.

This brought not only huge technological changes to telecommunications, including a range of new services and greatly increased capabilities and functionality, but also the potential for virtually total integration with computing. This in turn greatly increased corporate capacity to use telecommunications, creating in effect global management and production possibilities.

The massive potential of these technologies coincided with the rise of market liberalization policies, especially in the United States and the United Kingdom, but also in the European Union as a whole. The emerging orthodox position among the more powerful Western countries promoted the idea that the best way to harness these technologies was to privatize the telecommunications industries and liberalize trade and regulation. The wave of privatizations and liberalization that began in the 1980s left most of the world's telecommunications changed beyond recognition only a decade later.

The old procedures and structures of the ITU were thrown into disarray, under enormous pressure from all sides.

The standard setting system was threatened as giant corporations, investing vast sums in new technologies, could ill-afford to await the slow deliberations of the CCITT—and saw the potential to create their own de facto standards and thus to dominate new markets. New regional standards emerged as potential vehicles to further their aims, threatening to undermine the ITU's work.

The accounting system for agreeing on the division of tariffs began to crumble, with the United States forcing the pace of change. No longer was it a case of monopoly national carriers making gentleman's agreements to divide tariffs. Now, there were multiple carriers nationally, many emerging as multinational corporations and controlling networks in many countries; a wholesale "carrier's carriers" market began to appear; international private networks were put in place; new data and communication services emerged blurring the measurement of international exchanges; and ultimately the Internet seemed even to threaten traditional telephony altogether. Public-switched monopoly networks declined in importance with the rise of seamless global carriers, and the accounting rate system began to be replaced with more mechanisms that were ostensibly more market oriented.

Orbital and terrestrial spectrum allocation also became more problematic, as some countries began, in effect, to sell their slots to commercial concerns while others introduced various means to realize gain, such as auctions, from allocating the spectrum to users. The emergence of vast new private satellites systems, including low-orbital satellites, added further to the pressure.

Less industrialized countries also started to exploit their majority within the ITU, resulting in pressure for greater equity in the international regime and in criticism of the slow pace of convergence of telecommunications availability at a global level. Even Pekka Tarjanne, then the ITU secretary-general, raised the bigger picture in calling for an amendment to the Universal Declaration of Human Rights to include a Right to Communicate.

The ITU could see the writing on the wall. The choice was radical change or gradual disappearance. Finally, at a special plenipotentiary conference in 1992, after several high-level committees and expert groups had studied the problem, the ITU agreed to a reorganization of its structures. The main objectives of this reorganization were:

- To streamline and speed up the procedures and work
- To formalize a much more prominent role for the private sector
- To rationalize and focus the ITU's role in assisting less industrialized countries

Among the changes, which took effect at the Kyoto Plenipotentiary in 1994, was the adoption of a constitution and a thorough restructuring of the union, scrapping CCITT and CCIR in favor of three new sectors (which are discussed later in this chapter), introducing a new membership category, and offering the private sector a significantly heightened role in the restructured ITU.

Certain fundamentals remained unchanged, however, and it remains to be seen whether the continued commitment to practices like consensus decision making will restrict the ITU's ability to manage controversy or to conduct its work at the pace demanded by the telecommunications industry.

KEY ISSUES FACING THE ITU

Throughout the 1990s, the ITU continued its efforts "to establish the Union as the international focal point for all matters relating to telecommunications in the global information economy and society of the twenty-first century."[4] However, as the decade came to a close it became apparent that the forces of liberalization, competition, and globalization were stronger than anticipated, resulting in a change in the role of telecommunications and of the ITU itself. Other external factors also contributed to a changing role for the ITU, one of them being the World Trade Organization (WTO) and its new influence in telecommunications with the signing of the Agreement on Basic Telecommunication in 1997, which was part of the Uruguay Round. Although the ITU and WTO have very different functions and modes of operation, the rise of the trade paradigm in telecommunications in the context of liberalization will continue to have a major impact on the ITU. The more market mechanisms become the main mediators between telecommunications operators and countries, the lower the area of competence of the ITU.

The decline in importance of the accounting rate system offers an interesting example of the new rules of the game.

The Accounting Rate System

As we have seen, devising and agreeing to a method to divide income equitably and efficiently between originators of a message in one country and receivers in another, and any other in between, was a main impetus to the formation in 1865 of the precursor to the ITU. Since then, the ITU has continued to control and refine the accounting rate and settlement system, offering a multilateral forum in which the framework can adapt and evolve. Today, it is the concern of Study Group 3 of the ITU Telecommunications Standardization Sector (ITU–T) and has been teetering on the verge of collapse for some time.

The accounting rate system works on the basis of dual pricing to divide revenues between the originating telecommunications operator (where the phone call originates) and the terminating operator (where the phone call is completed). Irrespective of the difference in how much they charge their customers or what it costs to provide them, the two agree on a fictional price, called the accounting rate, as a common base by which to calculate how much the former pays the latter for completing the call. For many years, the actual amount paid out, the settlement rate, has been agreed to at half the accounting rate. That is, the originator pays half the accounting rate to the terminating operator. Annually, the totals are calculated and all operators pay out or receive a net hard currency payment in settlement. Thus, Study Group 3 provides the multilateral framework within which governments agree to the rules that their operators will follow. The precise level of the accounting rates are hammered out in bilateral agreements between the operators themselves.

The 1990s saw a growing imbalance in net total settlements between countries. By far, the greatest imbalance emerged between the United States and many other countries, as the Federal Communications Commission (FCC) reported net settlement rates rising steadily from below $2 billion in 1986 to over $5.4 billion by 1996. The actual causes of the increasing imbalance are numerous and complex—influenced by factors as varied as consumer prices, immigration patterns, and income levels, as well as service innovations such as call-back, that "falsely" reverse the originator and call terminator stations and the emergence of "private" networks that operate outside the normal international telephony accounting structure.

The areas where imbalances were taking place were highly selective. About 30 percent of the $5.1 billion deficit in 1995 went to other industrialized countries, while almost another 20 percent went to Mexico. But less than 4 percent ended up in Africa, and some of the poorest economies, like Somalia and Mozambique, were making net payments to the United States. Yet significant net transfers were flowing from the United States to certain poorer countries, mostly neighbors. The comparative weakness of economies and telecommunications sectors of many less industrialized countries resulted in a huge reliance on this transfer, for many amounting to between 30 percent and 70 percent of their total revenue and even more of their hard currency revenue.

Thus, historically, in addition to reflecting the higher cost of call completion in countries with less developed telecommunications infrastructures, these payments comprised, however imperfectly, the sole element of what might reasonably be termed a global universal service cross-subsidy, with the money generated by completing international calls being used to finance the maintenance and development of the national telecommunications infrastructures.

Early in 1997, with the accounting system on the verge of collapse, the FCC announced that it would unilaterally impose its own greatly reduced accounting rate, in effect setting the maximum amounts that it would allow U.S. carriers to pay out to others.

The ITU responded with a sharp criticism of the FCC proposal and, in 1999, issued its own counterproposal for a tariff schedule that, it argued, would both enable the poorest countries to collect the completion charges they needed to develop their national networks and offer more substantial reductions to most users. The ITU proposal was, however, too little too late, with many countries having already migrated to the FCC proposal even before it was announced. Furthermore, it has been argued, the ITU proposal amounted to an attempt to preserve a regime that, because of technological change and changes in the structure of the global telecommunications industry, could not be maintained.

Writing about the controversy at the end of 1999, Secretary-General Yoshio Utsumi of the ITU said:

> The process will be a test of whether or not there is still a will to use the ITU as a forum for collective, co-operative decision-making or whether special interests will engage in opportunistic strategic behaviour. Within the telecommunications sector, we have been fortunate to have a heritage of consensus and collaboration. If this spirit of co-operation no longer prevails, then perhaps it is time to move towards an alternative, confrontational regime, such as that which has evolved within the WTO. As a lawyer, perhaps I should not be sad to see the new business opportunities for my colleagues in the legal profession that international telecommunication disputes will bring. But as

Secretary-General of the ITU, I recognise that it would mark a sad end to a unique experiment in international collaboration.[5]

In recent years, the ITU has focused activities in a number of new areas. Among them, the high-profile TELECOM events, world and regional exhibitions, and conferences have been gaining importance as a major ITU activity. TELECOM 99, held in October 1999 in Geneva, attracted some 200,000 visitors, 3,000 media representatives, and more than 1,000 exhibitors. Another is planned for 2003, with regional TELECOMs to take place in Africa, Asia, the Americas, and the Middle East and Arab states. These are large and expensive events, with surpluses intended to finance projects in less industrialized countries. Also gaining in importance are the ITU's activities with regulators, especially those from developing countries. As a result of liberalization, more than seventy-five new independent regulators have emerged since 1990, most of them in developing countries. The ITU has been actively providing a forum for discussion of regulatory issues, as well as organizing workshops and conducting research.

The ITU is also taking a leadership role, in cooperation with other UN agencies, to prepare a World Summit on the Information Society "to develop a common vision and understanding of the information society and to draw up a strategic plan of action for concerted development towards realizing this vision."[6] The private sector and nongovernmental organizations (NGOs) are, according to the ITU, also to have a role in planning the summit. The summit will have two phases. Phase 1, which will take place in Switzerland in December 2003, is to adopt a Declaration of Principles and Action Plan addressing a broad range of themes related to the information society. Phase 2, which will take place in Tunisia in 2005, will assess progress and focus on themes related to development.

ITU'S STRUCTURE

The current structures of the ITU are still relatively new and continue to evolve slowly, with the occasional major leap. The ultimate success of the ITU in responding to its changing environment is still open to question.

The ITU is now organized into three sectors:

- ITU Telecommunications Standardization Sector (ITU–T), which also deals with tariffs
- ITU Radiocommunication Sector (ITU–R)
- ITU Development Sector (ITU–D)

All three sectors have a bureau and a director elected by the plenipotentiary, each of whom may convene an advisory group.

The formal hierarchy of authority, decision making, and implementation in the ITU may be sketched as follows, from the top down (somewhat simplistically):

- Constitution and Convention
- Plenipotentiary Conference, which meets every four years
- ITU Council
- Secretary-general
- World and regional conferences of each of the three sectors
- The three sectors, each with a director
- Study groups set up by these conferences to consider specific issues
- Program and actions supporting the study groups

The authority and functions of sectors are defined within the ITU Constitution supplemented by the ITU Convention, and the supreme decision-making body is the Plenipotentiary Conference, which normally meets every four years. As before, only member government nominees have the right to vote at these, although a number of states tend to identify entirely with the interests of their industries and include industry people among their delegates (see fig. 4.1)

Overall, plenipotentiaries are formal affairs, with the real work done elsewhere. They deal primarily with structural and legal matters that focus on the internal workings of the ITU and on rubber-stamping sector activities where required, but also occasionally they tackle major strategic issues such as the restructuring itself. In general, plenipotentiaries have little impact on the substantive business of the sectors except in so far as structural reform can hinder or facilitate their work, and bargaining over such structural issues tends to take place in corridors and behind closed doors involving a wider group than simply national governments. Elections are one area where there can be some controversy, and all the ITU officers are elected by the Plenipotentiary Convention, including the secretary-general, the deputy secretary-general, the directors of the three sectors, the members of the ITU Council, and the members of the Radio Regulations Board.[7]

The ITU Council comprises forty-six national delegates and meets periodically to review decisions taken at plenipotentiaries. It also has the right to exert certain limited powers between plenipotentiaries.

The secretary-general reports to the council and oversees the implementation of decisions taken at plenipotentiaries in relation to sectors, but also in relation to certain specific initiatives. For instance, in the mid-1990s, the Interagency Project on Universal Access to Basic Communication and Information Services was created on the initiative of the secretary-general and brought together a number of relevant UN agencies to debate this key issue.

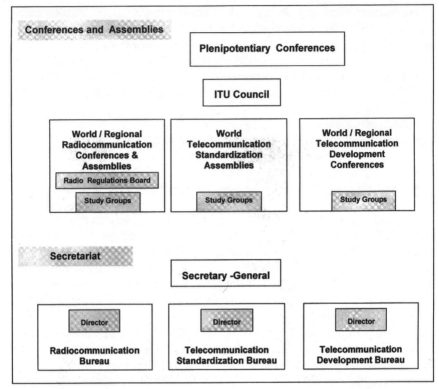

Figure 4.1

Beneath this are further different interconnected levels that, formally at least, are shared by all three sectors.

Broad guidelines for work in all three sectors are set by world and (if required) regional conferences, which occur between plenipotentiaries. They vary in frequency: the World Radiocommunication Conference meets every two years; while the World Development and World Standardization Conference meets every four years. Although last-minute hard bargaining can occur in some circumstances, these huge meetings involve much window dressing and diplomatic interaction, fulfilling the political requirements of an intergovernmental body.

Most of the work is done in study groups. Each world conference (and exceptionally, regional conferences) poses a set of issues to be resolved and sets up study groups to look into them. For instance, the tariff distribution issue is debated in Study Group 3 of the ITU–T; while Study Group 1 of the ITU–D considers policies, strategies, and financing of telecommunications.

Much of the real power of the ITU lies in these Study Groups, because it is here that consensus is achieved (if it is) on all the major issues of standards, tariffs, and radio frequency. They comprise technical experts meeting in a series of extended sessions, sometimes lasting months, and produce draft recommendations for consideration at regional and world conferences where, as mentioned, last-minute bargaining may take place. These recommendations, even when approved, are not legally binding and are only as strong as the consensus that developed around the drafting process. This is why effective participation in Study Groups may be considered a central axis of the power structure.

In relation to these Study Groups, the structural arrangements of 1994 also brought important changes to membership and influence. Until then, only governments could become members of the ITU. In 1994, a new, second tier, of membership was created to facilitate greater participation of the private sector and NGOs, recognizing officially the de facto influence they have exerted for years. The new members include telecommunications sector operators, scientific or industrial organizations, and financial or development institutions. The latter pay for the privilege, starting at about $30,000 annually for the ITU–T and ITU–R, and at about $4,000 for the ITU–D. However, this can pale in insignificance compared to the cost of keeping high-level technical experts in Geneva for weeks and months at a time, which members themselves must pay for. The 1998 Plenipotentiary further built on this by introducing the concept of associate members as a way for smaller entities and organizations to participate in the sectors, leaving the specifics of membership fees and privileges up to each sector. Both ITU–R and ITU–T established an associate membership category in 2000, setting an annual fee of about $6,000. ITU–D will make its decision at the World Telecommunication Development Forum in 2002.

Nongovernment members can fully partake in all ITU activities, with the exception of those relating to internal structures (i.e., the constitutions and voting in the plenipotentiaries and certain issues at world conferences) where they are limited to observer status. Thus, they play an equal role in Study Groups, including as rapporteurs and chairpersons, where key standards, tariffs, and other issues are debated and consensus established.

Worth noting is the fact that, unlike the UN Educational, Scientific, and Cultural Organization (UNESCO), the UNDP, and other UN organizations and contrary to the UN Economic and Social Council (ECOSOC) guidelines, the ITU has no specific arrangements to cooperate or liaise with development-oriented NGOs. An ITU–D Study Group was mandated to consider the question and reported in 1999, recommending that something be done, but nothing has yet come of it.[8]

The previously discussed structures are characteristic of all three sectors, but there are some variations between them derived mainly from the nature of their respective tasks. In particular, a separate part of the ITU–R is called the Radio Regulations Board, which develops administrative regulations (including the frequency allocations), that are treaty undertakings and hence binding on ITU signatories when adopted by the Plenipotentiary.

The influence of the three sectors, and the interest shown in them by major industrial players, also varies greatly. The ITU–T and ITU–R are taken most seriously (and have significantly larger budgets). The Study Group Recommendations in the ITU–D are also, in practice, of quite a different nature. Recommendations in the ITU–T and ITU–R are more substantial and influential, as they are the result of tough decisions and compromises between opposing and mutually exclusive options, forged by corporations with much at stake in the outcome. Recommendations coming from the ITU–D are "softer" and relate to national policy and investment areas. These are more likely to be ignored, or merely paid lip service, since the same pressures do not exist to come to a binding and permanent solution. Furthermore, these softer recommendations must make their mark in a policy sphere where they compete with the WTO, the World Bank, and other national and regional bodies.

NOTES

1. International Telecommunication Union (ITU), "Strategic Plan for the Union 1999–2003," <http://www.itu.int/osg/sec/strategicplan/sp9903e.pdf> [last accessed: 26 November 2001].

2. Until the ITU became a UN agency in 1947, the secretariat was provided by the Swiss government. In 1950, a Frenchman became the ITU's first non-Swiss secretary-general.

3. This, incidentally, was the first meaning given to the term "universal service": simply the technical ability of all users to call all others.

4. ITU, "Strategic Plan for the Union 1995–1999," <http://www.itu.int/osg/sec/strategicplan/sp95_99e.pdf> [last accessed: 26 November 2001].

5. Yoshio Utsumi, "Moving beyond International Accounting Rates," *Telecommunications Policy* 24, no. 1 (February 2000): 8.

6. From a promotional brochure produced following the UN Millennium Summit in 2000, <http://www.itu.int/wsis/> [last accessed: 26 November 2001].

7. Elections for senior positions can be hotly contested, with campaigns extending over months and even years. They can also be expensive. There is no requirement to declare campaign expenses, but some estimates put the cost of the current secretary-general's campaign at $10 million.

8. See the report and associated documents at <http://www.comunica.org/itu_ngo/> [last accessed: 26 November 2001].

5

The World Trade Organization and Trade in Media Products

The World Trade Organization (WTO) is the most powerful global[1] trade institution ever created. Its members—several governments around the world—have given it enormous powers to deliver sanctions should they breech its rules, sanctions strong enough to hurt even the most powerful government. No other global economic institution has been given more power. Why have governments done this?

The simple answer is that the WTO (like its predecessor, the General Agreement on Tariffs and Trade [the GATT]) is charged with eliminating international barriers to trade, and trade, in principle, should benefit both sides. If country A sells country B goods that the former can produce more cheaply and buys goods that the latter can produce more cheaply, then both are better off since they can concentrate their economic activities in areas where they enjoy a competitive advantage. In developing countries, the logic continues, the sale of basic commodities can yield the foreign exchange to purchase the technology needed to diversify the economy. The returns might therefore justify relinquishing some elements of sovereignty.

Reality, predictably, is rather more complex. The rules of the game tend to favor some of the players, and coercion, in more or less subtle forms, is woven in with the exercise of self-interest by governments, and with shifting alliances between government, business, and commercial interests. Many critics argue that the WTO is simply an instrument by which more powerful governments and corporations can govern international trade and economic relations to suit their own ends.

The WTO's primary activities are related to the negotiation, implementation, and administration of a set of agreements, known as the GATT, that

govern trade between its 140 member countries. These agreements are negotiated in a series of "rounds," and by joining the WTO countries agree to
provisions in the agreements that limit their right to pass laws, to tax, and
to regulate matters concerning international trade and economic relations.

During the first decades since its inception in 1947, the agreements negotiated during the GATT rounds focused on reducing tariffs on manufactured goods that, at the national level, were already subject to minimal
national regulation. However, by 1986, when the eighth or Uruguay
Round began, the GATT had succeeded in reducing tariffs on manufactured goods and turned its attention to new areas, including financial
services, transport and telecommunications infrastructure, intellectual
property rights (IPRs), and media.

The World Trade Organization
Location: Geneva
Established: 1995 (replaced the GATT, the temporary body formed in
1947 to negotiate and administer the trade agreement of the same name)
Membership: 143 countries accounting for more than 90 percent of world
trade (December 2001)
Budget: Chf 127,000,000 ($77,000,000)
Secretariat staff: 500
Main governance bodies: Ministerial Conference (meets every two years)
and General Council (implements conference policy decisions and respon-
sible for day-to-day administration)
Head: Mike Moore, director-general (Australia). Moore is serving the first
half of the position's six-year term. Supachai Panitchpakdi (Thailand) takes
over in September 2002 for the remaining three years.
Functions:

- Administering all the GATT and WTO agreements
- Negotiating and implementing new trade agreements
- Handling trade disputes
- Monitoring national trade policies
- Technical assistance and training for developing countries

URL: <www.wto.org>

A BRIEF HISTORY OF THE WTO

In the years of optimism after the Second World War, the UN Economic
and Social Council (ECOSOC) had been given the task of coordinating a
tripartite set of new bodies: the International Monetary Fund (IMF) to ensure stable exchange rates and balance of payments, the International

Bank for Reconstruction and Development (better known as the World Bank) to provide loans for development, and the International Trade Organization (ITO) to ensure a stable system in trade between countries. Their aim was to ensure a more balanced and equitable world development and to avoid the emergence ever again of global economic dynamics that fostered international tension and ultimately contributed to aggression and war.

Neither the IMF nor the World Bank have fully achieved their intended coordination roles, but the ITO failed even to get off the starting blocks. Its charter, which was adopted in 1948, included broad ranging aspects of commercial policy, employment, price stabilization, and even the flow of capital and know-how—all based on grounds of equity and balanced growth. However, it was not to be, because in 1950 the United States, and consequently some other countries, refused to ratify the charter. The main objection was its very comprehensiveness and the extent to which it could have regulated, supervised, and enforced international rules.

But one element of the ITO did get swiftly underway. In 1947, negotiations began on an agreement—the GATT—to deal with commercial policy, the reduction of tariffs and trade barriers, and the abolition of trade preferences among a limited number of countries. The GATT was to be applied on a provisional basis, in the form of a contract with legal rights and obligations between twenty-three countries or "contracting parties" that together with their colonies accounted for 80 percent of world trade.[2]

It is no coincidence that this ITO function alone survived and flourished.[3] Trade, then as now, was dominated by the rich countries, and the GATT, according to its critics, was used by them to maintain their position.

In the first decades since its inception in 1947, the GATT focused on reducing tariffs on manufactured goods that, at the national level, were already subject to minimal national regulation. However, the introduction of new sectors into the negotiation process did not pursue a balanced and reciprocal process of enabling each country to gain from its comparative advantage. In general, wealthier countries actively and successfully pressed for the inclusion of goods in which they held a significant advantage and had much to gain from exporting, while goods where poorer countries had an advantage, such as textiles and agriculture, were largely excluded. The inclusion or exclusion of sectors in trade negotiations was driven primarily by the needs of wealthier countries and by the competition and negotiations between them to the exclusion of others.

By the time the Uruguay Round began in 1986, the dynamics had shifted somewhat. Services now occupied an important position in wealthy countries' economies and they had a developed expertise in the sector, giving them an unassailable comparative advantage and resulting in pressure to extend the GATT's scope beyond traded goods toward services. At the same time, the target of agreements went beyond tariffs to "nontariff barriers," with an ever more open-ended definition.

Developing countries opposed the inclusion of any service sectors, since in many countries they were largely nationally owned but underdeveloped and ill-prepared to withstand competition from better-resourced foreign companies. The North realized concessions were needed to get these on the agenda. Trade in agriculture was brought to the table, as it had anyhow become very costly to maintain the system of subsidies.[4] The North also agreed to concede in the long term on textiles. Under pressure from their debts, and facing the refusal of the North to negotiate trade matters in any other forum, the less industrialized countries agreed. The round lasted eight long years, concluding in 1994 (though telecommunications took a few years longer) and it included the General Agreement on Trade in Service (GATS) and the agreements on Trade-Related Aspects of Intellectual Property Rights (TRIPS).

During the round, it became apparent that the ad hoc structures of the GATT were stretched beyond their limits. The GATT had grown from 23 signatories in 1947 to 128 in 1984. More importantly, world trade changed dramatically—increasing from $60 billion in 1948 to almost $6.8 trillion in 1999, including $1.35 trillion in services. In January 1995, the WTO was born as the GATT's successor and is now a permanent structure with considerably extended powers.

The WTO differs from the GATT in several important respects.

- It replaces the temporary and ad hoc arrangements of the GATT with a permanent institutional structure
- It stretches the meaning of trade to embrace services, including trade in banking, insurance, travel, and telecommunications, and trade in ideas (or IPRs) embodied in patents, copyrights, and other legal mechanisms
- It wields much more powerful sanctions than its predecessor, the imposition of which under the GATT had required, in practice, the agreement of the offender
- Its agreements apply to all members, whereas the GATT had allowed for plurilateral agreements, effectively allowing countries to opt out of agreements covering specific sectors

The WTO is likely to become the *sole* forum for future negotiations and agreements on ever more trade-related issues. Yet it operates outside the UN system and includes none of the instruments envisaged originally for the ITO that would bring it beyond its exclusive focus on free trade. While its domain spreads out and its power grows, its remit remains as narrow as ever.

MEDIA AND COMMUNICATIONS

The WTO is important in several areas of media, including telecommunications infrastructure and services and trade in media products and services.[5] Throughout most of the GATT's history, telecommunications infrastructures and services were usually the domain of nationally owned monopolies (public or private), the rationale for this ranging from "natural monopoly" economics to national security and a desire to maintain control of key communications infrastructures. The sector was governed by a web of legislation and regulation to serve the greater public good and there was little interest in opening it up to international trade or foreign investment.

There was a similar lack of enthusiasm for opening up mass media and cultural production. Like telecommunications, national regulations were also in place for a wide range of reasons, including to ensure diversity of content, to protect cultural integrity, and to restrict the free flow of information. Media products and services, as we have seen in chapter 1, are often highly regulated nationally regarding concentration of ownership, content, and diversity. Even newspapers and film, on the lighter end of the regulation scale, are seldom as free of control as most conventional goods and are recognized everywhere as a distinct feature and force in national culture and society.

Thus, measured by the degree of national market freedom, even in the early 1980s, media and communications would have seemed unlikely sectors to include in the round of trade negotiations that was soon to begin.

However, the 1980s and 1990s witnessed a major upheaval in these sectors at the national level, resulting in the introduction of market dynamics into telecommunications and the loosening of regulation of mass media outlets, content, and ownership. By the mid 1980s, powerful corporate telecommunications and media lobbies had succeeded in setting firmly in motion the liberalization of these sectors nationally in North America, Europe, and elsewhere, with the private sector and some degree of competition moving into areas previously prohibited. Attention then turned to the international arena, where prospects in the underdeveloped telecommunications and media sectors seemed limitless. Encouraged by the Uruguay Round's success at putting trade in services on the agenda, industrialized countries turned to the GATT, a multilateral trade agreement with significant enforcement potential and securely under their control, as the tool most suited to prizing open telecommunications and media markets.

The major drive by the industrialized countries to include media and communications in the GATT came primarily from the private sector, which had succeeded in breaking into previously prohibited or restricted markets nationally and now shifted its focus outside. The telecommunications sector, freed from comfortable but ultimately constraining national boundaries, was eyeing the rest of the world to invest very profitably in equipment sales, infrastructure purchase or development, and services provision, while mainly U.S.–based media companies recognized their advantages of scale and capacity over virtually any rival anywhere in the world.

The move was on, and, as we have seen, combined business and government lobbies succeeded in putting telecommunications and services on the agenda of the Uruguay Round, which culminated with the successful opening up of the telecommunications services sector. Efforts to open negotiations on audiovisual markets[6] in the WTO stalled, at least temporarily, as they, collectively, became a victim primarily of disagreement between the United States and the European Union. However, they are still on the agenda and will likely surface again during the Doha round of negotiations launched in November 2001.

Thus, the WTO now plays a major role in the global governance of telecommunications equipment, infrastructure, and services, and is the power "in-waiting" in the area of cultural products such as books, films, television, and other media. Combined with its decisive influence in IPRs,[7] the WTO can reasonably claim to be the single most powerful player in media and communications governance globally.

The next sections consider, respectively, the implications of the WTO's involvement in international trade and investment in telecommunications and media.

TELECOMMUNICATIONS

As mentioned earlier in this chapter, by the beginning of the 1980s, services had gained more prominence in industrialized countries' economies and there was enormous interest in gaining access to emerging service markets in the developing world. Among these services, telecommunications proved to be both one of the most attractive and difficult to negotiate.

On the table were voice telephony, data transmission, telex, telegraph, facsimile, private-leased circuit services, fixed and mobile systems and services, cellular telephony, mobile data services, paging, and personal communications systems. By the agreed completion date of the Uruguay Round of negotiations in 1994, sixty countries had committed themselves on value-added telecommunications services, but only eight on basic services such as telephony and the public data network. More negotiation was needed, and a special group, the Negotiating Group on Basic Telecommunications, was set up for a fixed period. When it failed, a second group was constituted to take it further.

Negotiations were difficult and marked by dramatic moments, such as when the United States almost collapsed them by temporarily pulling out in April 1996, claiming that the offers on the table were insufficient, both in terms of the overall number of countries participating and of the extent of liberalization that countries were willing to agree to. It is noticeable, however, that almost all major stumbling blocks arose out of disagreements between the United States, Canada, Japan, and the European Union, while less industrialized countries were marginalized in the negotiations.[8] It was not until February 1997 that agreement was finally reached on telecommunications, with a total of sixty-nine countries signing up to the Agreement on Basic Telecommunication (ABT). It came into force in February 1998.

Agreement would have been impossible but for huge gains in liberalization during the 1980s and early 1990s, outside the WTO, through the efforts of such organizations as the Organization for Economic Cooperation and Development (OECD), the World Bank, and the Group of Seven, as well as within the European Union, the North American Free Trade Agreement (NAFTA), and other agreements. In industrialized countries, liberalization of these sectors had only come about after considerable and often acrimonious engagement with government, trade unions, and other opposition to liberalization in basic telecommunications. In much of the rest of the world, liberalization came into being when governments signed the WTO agreement, committing themselves to it without the inconveniences associated with public debate over the future of key communications infrastructures.

The regulatory principles of the agreement, which had been agreed to in 1996 in a "Reference Paper" and subsequently endorsed by all but eleven[9] of the ABT signatories, cover, in principle:

- Opening markets to foreign investment in all areas of telecommunications, including voice telephony, leased lines, mobile, and satellite
- Ensuring that discrimination by dominant players is prohibited to ease market entry
- Ensuring fair, transparent, and nondiscriminatory interconnection with dominant suppliers
- Requiring a regulator independent of any telecommunications supplier
- Allocating frequencies, numbers, and other resources in a transparent and nondiscriminatory manner

Of course, no country signed up to full-scale liberalization in all areas. Even for those committing to the principles and to specific liberalization measures, the timescale for implementation was another matter, in some cases not specified at all. Thus sixty-one countries pledged to open their markets in basic voice telephony only at some time in the future, relinquishing monopoly and national ownership. Most also put specific limits on foreign ownership. South Africa, for instance, committed itself to a duopoly in most basic services from 2003 and to limit foreign ownership to 30 percent. Furthermore, most wealthy countries agreed simply to "standstill" commitments (i.e., measures that they had already adopted nationally).

But the agreement was nevertheless a major milestone. The national commitments to open telecommunications markets that had been made in industrialized countries in the 1980s and 1990s were now elevated to an international level. And there is no going back without risking possibly severe sanctions, the result being constant pressure to extend commitments.

At least as important as specific commitments made—these mainly added incrementally to a process that was well underway—was the fact that for the first time, all countries were brought under a single set of clearly defined and enforceable rules. For transnational capital in this sector, investment through purchase of foreign companies and other means is far more secure, transparent, and simple. Market access will be gradual, but steady. China, the fastest growing telecommunications market, pledged to allow foreign investment in joint ventures of up to 25 percent in 2002, 35 percent in 2003, 49 percent in 2004, and to eliminate all geographic restrictions by the end of 2005.

For some less industrialized countries, the telecommunications agreement may yield greater external investment than would otherwise have been the case. This in turn will lead to the growth of networks and of access to them. Although ownership will increasingly be external and profits are likely to be repatriated elsewhere, improved telecommunications services, as long as they are affordable, should lead to better performance of other sectors and contribute to the improvement of social services.

But there are risks associated with this strategy.

Investment will naturally seek out the most profitable areas first, which may not coincide with identified social or development needs such as improving rural access or implementing a universal access policy. The extent to which regulation can, in effect, divert some profits from the most lucrative areas to others less lucrative but socially important (e.g., through implementing a universal service policy) may be constrained by the agreement. The wording on this is somewhat ambiguous: "Any member has the right to define the kind of universal service obligation it wishes to maintain. Such obligations will not be regarded as anti-competitive per se, provided they are administered in a transparent, non-discriminatory and competitively neutral manner and are not more burdensome than necessary for the kind of universal service defined by the member."[10]

One commentator spells out the risk in the terms "not more burdensome than necessary":

Thus, if national policy promotes access to telecommunication services on the basis of a cross-subsidization scheme (charging higher rates for international calls, and requiring that these resources be used to ensure lower rates for local calls in rural areas, for example), this exception to the practice of purely cost-based tariffs might be considered by foreign market entrants to be more burdensome than necessary. In consequence the policy would be perceived as a violation of international trade law. It would be up to the (largely obscure) arbitration mechanisms of the WTO to judge the legitimacy of the national policy proposal.[11]

If social policy were constrained in this manner, it would constitute a clear case of WTO imperatives restricting national social and development policy. Precise interpretation of this clause, and its implications, will emerge in time.

MEDIA PRODUCTS AND SERVICES

During the last two decades of the twentieth century, a number of interlinked factors bolstered trade in audiovisual products. First, technological developments greatly eased the bottleneck of spectrum availability and transmission capabilities. Second, liberalization and privatization of broadcasting resulted in more radio and television broadcast outlets. Combined with other changes, this meant that demand was shifting toward more content to fill the available channels. Third, for a number of reasons the prominent, sometimes dominant, public involvement in television and radio was challenged and a process of liberalization swept through most industrialized countries. While media regulation for societal and cultural development was retained everywhere, usually somewhat watered down, the role of the private sector was greatly enhanced and the number of media enterprises multiplied. Finally, media corporations embarked on a long and sustained process of concentration of ownership and of convergence of previously discreet media sectors.

In practice, these private-sector media enterprises greatly reduced the political and technical barriers to trade in audiovisual products. In terms of both media ownership and of content, national and international commercial interactions multiplied. Local television, cable networks, and radio stations were taken over by foreign companies (notwithstanding foreign ownership restrictions in many countries, including the United States), and the market in television programs, films, music, and other areas expanded rapidly, with the United States being the main beneficiary globally, followed by a few countries that established themselves as suppliers of regional content, such as South Africa and Mexico.

This was well underway when the Uruguay Round negotiations on audiovisual products—which were included as part of the GATS package—reached a head in the early 1990s. However, despite, or perhaps partly because of, the recent growth in international audiovisual commercial activity, it proved to be among the most contentious issues, delaying agreement well beyond the anticipated date. The main rift was between the United States and the countries of the European Union, particularly France. The latter were arguing for an exception by which the protection of culture would constitute a legitimate cause to support and subsidize national cultural production, even if such measures gave them a market advantage over imported products. After marathon rounds of negotiations in Geneva, in the end they could agree only to disagree, and the audiovisual sector was in effect omitted from the WTO deal.[12] Cable and satellite television were also kept out of the telecommunications agreement, which took even longer to complete.

However, the issue is by no means settled—in practice, only a temporary truce, at least on this battlefield, was declared.[13] The audiovisual sector was included on the list of "mandated sectors" (i.e., those automatically on the agenda for a new round), and discussions began in 2000 as part of the ongoing GATS negotiations. The United States has signaled its determination to pursue the issue to the end, and the Doha round set to conclude by the end of 2004, may offer the opportunity.

The tension between culture and commerce, as it is depicted, arose in *nonaudiovisual* media as a dispute in the WTO. The best known ruling has been in relation to magazine trade in a case brought against Canada by the United States. Canada had imposed an 80 percent tax on advertising in split-run magazines (magazines such as *Time*'s Canadian edition that are foreign-owned and feature primarily foreign editorial content but carry local advertising) and a quota on the number of magazines entering the country. It also maintained postal costs that favored Canadian-produced magazines. Canada justified its measures as necessary for defending Canadian culture. However, the WTO ruled against Canada, and the country, which had very much helped to shape the WTO, was forced to drop or amend the contentious provisions and to recognize that its participation in the WTO made it difficult to sustain its pursuit of certain social and cultural goals.

The effective exclusion of audiovisual products from the Uruguay Round added no new obstacles to trade in audiovisual products, nor did it prevent regional and bilateral agreements being struck. Cultural issues have been included in most major regional trading agreements, and the outcomes offer insights into the parameters of the issues and possible solutions (see textbox).

Regional Trade Agreements and Cultural Products
The issue of whether cultural industries, including broadcasting, publishing, and film, has been arising in regional trade negotiations, where, unlike in the WTO, agreement has been reached.

NAFTA

A double standard exists within NAFTA (established in 1994) in regard to the audiovisual sector and the testimony to the different circumstances of the negotiating parties. The United States had predictably gone for open markets, but the approach of Canada and Mexico differed.

The cultural industries' agreement between the United States and Canada in NAFTA was a "grandparent" clause brought forward from the earlier 1989 Free Trade Agreement between the two. It was the result of months of vigorous and intricate negotiations, but it came at a price. The controversial section states that "cultural industries are exempt from the provisions of this agreement." The price is then spelled out. Retaliation "of equivalent commercial effect" is permitted in response to use of the exception. This means that the United States could respond to Canadian cultural protection measures by imposing its own restrictions, or other measures, to the same value as that lost by U.S. companies.

Mexico declined to go down this route, with the main exception of a limit of 49 percent ownership of audiovisual industries, maintaining that it had little cause for concern. The relative strength of Mexican media, the opportunity to address Spanish-speaking markets in the United States, the cultural and language distance from the United States that appeared to offer some protection, and the general lack of resources available to pay for retaliatory measures all probably played a part. By contrast, Canada had long expressed grave concern over domination by cultural products from the United States, and its own industry was relatively weak.

EUROPEAN UNION

The EU audiovisual policy, having a remit well beyond trade, attempts explicitly to reconcile the cultural and economic sides. It does not exist in a single agreement, but is spread between, for instance, the 1989 Directive on Broadcasting, the 1992 Treaty of Maastricht, and the 1997 Treaty of Amsterdam. The task is complicated by the need to consider both internal trade between EU member states and external trade primarily with the United States. The solution was seen initially to be liberalization within the European Union and protectionism, only very gradually relaxed, at the EU borders. But this worked only if, on the one hand, internal liberalization was seen as nonthreatening to EU national cultures by bringing a "common European heritage" to the fore, and on the other hand, the single internal market would eventually yield the economies of scale needed to compete globally. Yet, the factors that rendered intra-European liberalization non-threatening—language and cultural barriers—were also going to prevent those economies of scale being reached. Put another way, the economies of scale could have been attained only through the dominance of one cultural model, which would have meant the reduction of all to a low common denominator and not the flowering of a common European culture. U.S. audio visual producers, by contrast, already had the advantage of economies of scale from their own market and had long reduced much content to a portable level of homogeneity.

The policy could not be coherently sustained, under pressure from a number of sides, and the net outcome was the commercialization of European media but with no corresponding EU level regulation for diversity and without significant protection from non–EU products.* The huge increase in broadcast hours and channels following liberalization was not at all matched by an increase in EU program production, despite the MEDIA Program funded by the European Union to support a trans-European industry. Low-cost U.S. content flooded into fragmented national markets, and the European Union's audiovisual trade deficit with the United States grew enormously during this period. Within Europe, public service broadcasters with a commitment to diversity lost out heavily to a few emerging European media conglomerates serving mainly local markets. A Protocol to the Amsterdam Treaty of 1997,** however, did establish the important principle that public service media are exempt from the rigors of liberalization and may receive state subsidization in the general public interest. The coming to the fore of the "Information Society" in more recent years has further complicated the issues, with the convergence of telecommunications and audiovisual policy. Debate and discussion continues, especially within the European Parliament, and will remain very relevant to EU approaches on the global stage.

MERCADO COMÚN DEL SUR

The Mercado Común del Sur (MERCOSUR; Southern Cone Common Market) is a trading bloc and common market comprising Argentina, Brazil, Uruguay, and Paraguay. It has not been very active in the cultural field but what policies it has adopted combine the European Union's desire to promote the cultural integration of member states and Canada's desire to keep its cultural industries nationally owned. There are two main references to cultural industries and policies in MERCOSUR protocols. The first is in a 1994 agreement to liberalize cross-border investments in which Brazil, Paraguay, and Uruguay all exempted broadcasting. Argentina did not make any exemptions in the audiovisual sector. The other reference is in the Cultural Integration Protocol approved in 1996 that, like the EU legislation, attempts to build on the idea that "culture constitutes a fundamental element of integration processes" and thus establishes that "member-states will seek to promote cooperation and trade between their cultural institutions and agents." However, while the protocol explicitly mentions the audiovisual sector as one of those to receive attention, the activities undertaken as a result of it have mostly been concerned with promoting artistic exchanges (performing arts, fellowship programs, and young writers exchange programs), rather than mass market audiovisual production.

Despite the lack of official attention given to the sector, a form of integration has been taking place, as Argentina and Brazil, two countries with large (and highly concentrated) audiovisual industries, have both become net exporters of television programs, while Paraguay and Uruguay have replaced some of their U.S. imports with programs from their larger MERCOSUR partners. Clearly, this change has been facilitated by cultural similarities of the four countries, which are much more apparent than in the European Union or even the NAFTA countries. However, MERCOSUR has not helped develop audiovisual activities in the smaller countries. Nor has it significantly contributed to the diversity of content, since most production is controlled by O Globo in Brazil, the largest media conglomerate in Latin America, and by the Argentinian oligopoly of Grupo Clarín and Telefé.

* Article 4 of the 1989 directive states that "member-states shall ensure, where practicable and by appropriate means, that broadcasters reserve for European works . . . a majority proportion of their transmission time."

** The Protocol on the System of Public Broadcasting in the Member States says that "[t]he provisions of the Treaty establishing the European Community shall be without prejudice to the competence of Member States to provide for the funding of public service broadcasting insofar as such funding is granted to broadcasting organizations for the fulfilment of the public service remit as conferred, defined and organized by each Member State, and insofar as such funding does not affect trading conditions and competition in the Community to an extent which would be contrary to the common interest, while the realization of the remit of that public service shall be taken into account."

Source: This is loosely based on Hernan Galperin, "Cultural Industries Policy in Regional Trade Agreements: The Cases of NAFTA, the European Union and MERCOSUR," *Media, Culture and Society* 21 (1999): 627–648.

The NAFTA solution gives some protection to culture against commercial trade pressures, but only at the expense of, in practice, defining it as a commodity. By permitting retaliation to the same level as the commercial cost of cultural protection measures, this solution already puts a market price on culture—even if one is not obliged to sell.

The EU approach exposes the conflict between commercial and cultural goals by dealing with both internal and external markets. The MEDIA

Program demonstrates the difficulty of building up a sector, through public subsidy, that is globally (or even regionally) competitive at the same time as striving to enhance cultural diversity. Direct political agreement to protect public service broadcasting from the assaults of commercial media appears to be more effective in at least offering a breathing space to diversity while the debates rage on.

The French position adopted during the WTO (and other) negotiations, as well as the Canadian position, hinges on the right to cultural self-defense. While meeting some degree of success as a strategy, this argument has been criticized as in some respects static, inward looking, and exclusive.[14] It focuses narrowly on existing cultural specificity, rather than on a regime most appropriate to supporting a variety of cultural dynamics within a society by encouraging diverse and vibrant media and cultural evolution. While it does prevent a rapid destruction of aspects of national cultural traits and the homogenization from "culture-free" commercial productions, as a negatively defined measure it is unlikely to endure.

The impact of an exclusively trade-driven regime in audiovisual products could be catastrophic. National legislators might be unable to implement measures relating to the media that support cultural diversity or political pluralism. The prospects for an open, critical public sphere would be greatly diminished, existing only in the interstices of a media controlled by the dictates of the market.

The premise of a market-driven international audiovisual trade regime is basically the same as for other sectors—people should be offered a wide selection and can choose by paying for what they want. However, a mitigating issue is whether media products are supply, rather than demand, driven. If that which is available is in fact dictated by dominant suppliers, then "choice" is somewhat illusory.

Many factors have been moving the sector in this direction. The huge numbers of stations must find content. For the fragmented markets in many regions of the world (Latin America and part of Asia may be an exception here), the lowest-cost content comes from the United States where the costs of production are already largely if not entirely recouped on the home market. Vertically controlled and horizontally integrated audiovisual sectors offer such products significant economies of scale and scope and favor their own content over others. The net effect is that the sector has become, in practice, driven by what is available.

THE WTO'S STRUCTURE

The WTO currently has 143 member governments, and nearly 30 queuing up to join (December 2001). The latter include Russia, former Soviet

Union, and eastern bloc countries, less industrialized countries such as Cambodia, and very small countries like Andorra. Its staff of 500 is based in Geneva, and its main functions are:

- To provide a forum for trade negotiations between governments
- To administer the trade agreements reached
- To handle trade disputes
- To review national trading policies and to assist poorer countries to implement agreements

At its simplest, it is a mechanism to facilitate governments to come to binding agreements that limit their sovereignty in the area of international trade.[15] Through protracted, complex, but ultimately power-based negotiations, governments agree to selectively reduce barriers to trade and introduce measures to smooth the way for the movement of goods and services across borders, while protecting the interests of the producers and traders.

The secretary-general is appointed by consensus—a decision-making process that was adopted when the GATT was a relatively small organization. The growing number of WTO members and the widely diverging views within the organization make consensus building difficult and time consuming—with the selection more accurately described as a process of bartering between the major powers and geographical regions.[16] It is unlikely that the consensus system will be replaced with a voting system. However, making the consensus system more efficient is a priority and currently under study, in particular, in terms of the possibility of introducing an executive committee—which might impact favorably on developing country participation.

The top body is the Ministerial Council, comprising all members, which meets at least every two years. Beneath it is the General Council, which also meets as the Trade Policy Review Body and the Dispute Settlement Body. Three sectoral councils report to the General Council: the Goods Council, dealing with traditional commodities; the Services Council, set up to work on GATS; and the Intellectual Property Council, established to work on the TRIPS agreement. Beneath these are numerous Specialized Committees, Working Groups, and Working Parties, focusing on specific agreements as well as on sectoral issues such as the environment and the membership (see fig. 5.1). Some countries maintain representation in Geneva, with their representatives permanently employed in the various levels of activities. Many of the poorest countries, however, cannot afford to have such representatives.

As a multilateral organization, the WTO has little formal decision-making powers, though it can sometimes greatly influence outcomes.

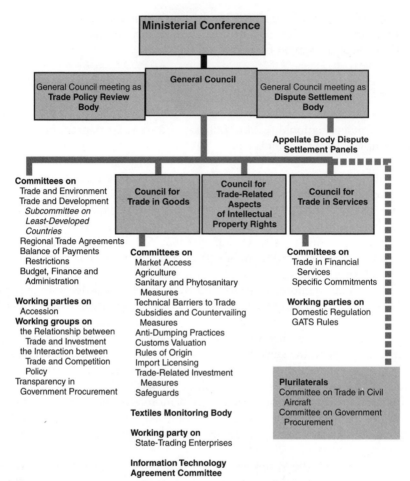

Figure 5.1

The real action takes place in the negotiations between governments, which occur in successive rounds.

Eight rounds have so far been completed, with the last one, the Uruguay Round, concluding in 1994 after eight years with the addition of the GATS and TRIPS agreements and the formation of the WTO in January the following year. The Doha round began in November 2001 and is to be concluded by the first of January 2003. In general, agreements cover a broad set of goods and each country decides when and to what extent it will sign up for individual items. When countries do sign, sometimes with a period of grace for poorer countries, there can be no going back—the "ratchet effect" means that no country is permitted to backpedal on its agreement or to renegotiate its terms, under threat of very severe sanctions.

Thus, the Dispute Settlement Body is especially important and is stronger, quicker, and more predictable than its predecessor in the GATT. Any country can claim another is in breach of the agreement, setting in motion a succession of stages that, unless there is a consensus not to do so, continues through to the end of the process and the resolution of the dispute. The process can take no more than fifteen months, from the time an aggrieved country files a complaint, allowing even for an appeal by the loser. If the losing party does not change the practice, then the winning country may, with the approval of the WTO, apply sanctions that can cost large sums of money.

However, some extreme and sustained criticisms have been leveled against the structure of the WTO in recent years. Critics have argued that the more powerful countries reap the benefits of the growing world trade, while many poorer countries are actually worse off, and that this is the fault, in major part, of the structure of the organization (and of its predecessor) as it is deployed in real world politics.[17] Problems identified for poorer countries include the following:[18]

In the Doha round, less industrialized countries, many confronting horrifying numbers of AIDS related deaths, won a major political battle against the drug companies of wealthy countries that will relax patent rules on medicines. Yet in other key areas, such as agriculture, no concessions were made. And less industrialized countries must add to their already demanding agenda high-speed negotiations on investment, competition and industrial tariffs. Little support was offered to prevent a total overload of their negotiating capacity.

1. Although less industrialized countries comprise a majority of WTO members, almost all are in one way or another already greatly dependent on the more powerful nations, such as on the United States, the European Union, or Japan, in terms of imports, exports, aid, and security. Justified by experience, poorer countries fear that failure to comply with the wishes of these powerful countries in the WTO may result in wider threats to their overall well being and security.
2. Trade negotiations proceed on the basis of concessions by one country in one area, in return for concessions by the other in another. Such bartering benefits large, diversified economies, as they can gain more by giving more.
3. Poorer countries have fewer human and technical resources, are often poorly briefed and prepared, and are unable to afford up to fifty meetings a week in Geneva.

As Nelson Mandela commented, rules applied uniformly are not necessarily fair, given the different circumstances of members.[19] Even where concessions are finally extracted from the powerful, as in agriculture and textiles, creative calculations and interpretations may largely negate the potential benefit to poorer countries, who are furthermore often reluctant to enter into a dispute.[20]

The huge influence of transnational corporations on the WTO has also come in for criticism.[21] Transnational corporations are understandably concerned about the rules of trade, as a means to access potentially profitable markets. They determine their freedom to move anywhere in the world, to source the lowest-cost materials and labor, and to sell in the most profitable markets. They can strongly influence profitability through, for instance, prohibiting expensive licenses and eliminating excise duties.

They pursue their interests in the WTO through highly organized, well-resourced lobby groups. Corporations, more usually competing with each other, come together in long-term cooperation to influence the agendas and outcomes of trade rounds. Their influence on governments is enormous, with some governments equating their interests with those of their corporations. There are also close personal and personnel links between the WTO and corporations—the normal route for retiring director-generals is into top-level management positions in industry, and many industry directors are on key WTO dispute panels. No other nongovernment sector has a significant say.

Furthermore, the secrecy through which it conducts its business is also heavily criticized as undemocratic and in the interest of more powerful members. The practice has been for the major trading blocs first to come to agreement behind closed doors, and then to present this to others for rubber stamping, or at best slight revision. Also, unlike in other UN organizations or national legislatures, no record is kept of the rationale for and debates surrounding particular decisions, records that would allow those not participating directly in discussions to understand the issues and engage them later on.

NOTES

1. Only with the accession of China in December 2001 could the WTO really lay claim to being a global institution. However, Russia remains outside.

2. One of the consequences of GATT being established as an agreement rather than as an institution alongside the IMF and the World Bank, as the ITO would have been, is that GATT was not part of the UN system and thus not subordinate to the UN Charter and the Universal Declaration of Human Rights. When the WTO was established as a permanent institution forty-eight years later, it continued outside the UN system, while the IMF and the World Bank have always been in it. Repeated calls to bring the WTO within the United Nations are unlikely to receive much attention within the halls of the WTO.

3. The UN Conference for Trade and Development struggled into existence in 1964, but has always been severely restricted in what it can do, with all its negotiating functions finally being stripped away in favor of GATT in 1992.

4. Trade in agriculture was brought to the table, but it was not resolved. In March 2001, Secretary-General Kofi A. Annan of the United Nations called on industrialized countries to open their markets to agricultural products, saying that the minimum net gain for developing countries would be $100 billion a year, more than twice the amount of annual aid flows. The WTO says that agricultural products are high on its list of priorities, but there will be strong resistance to this, particularly from the United States.

5. The third major area of WTO influence is in IPRs, through the TRIPS agreement. The World Intellectual Property Organization, which is discussed in chapter 7, was specifically set up to govern this area.

6. The audiovisual services in the WTO negotiations comprise: motion picture and video tape production, distribution, and projection; radio and television production and transmission; and sound recording. The definition is gray at the edges especially in radio and television, but a general suggestion by the WTO Secretariat is that "commitments involving programming content are classified under audiovisual services, while those purely involving the transmission of information are classified under telecommunications." See WTO Council for Trade in Services, "Audiovisual Services: Background Note by the Secretariat," S/C/W/40, 15 June 1998.

7. See chapter 7.

8. This is not atypical of WTO negotiations. The best-known dispute to date is the one between the United States and the European Union over import restrictions on bananas, despite the fact that neither party grows bananas.

9. Bolivia, India, Malaysia, Morocco, Pakistan, the Philippines, Turkey, and Venezuela did not endorse the entire document, while Bangladesh, Mauritius, and Thailand eventually agreed to adopt it.

10. WTO, "Negotiating Group on Basic Telecommunications," reference paper, April 24, Geneva.

11. Cees Hamelink, *ICTs and Social Development: The Global Policy Context* (Geneva: UN Research Institute for Social Development, 1998), <http://www.unrisd.org/infotech/conferen/icts/icts.htm> [last accessed: 26 November 2001].

12. Although the text of the agreement makes no reference to audiovisual products, thirteen countries had made commitments in the sector by the end of the round, with the number rising a little since with the accession of new members.

13. The ill-fated 1997 Multilateral Agreement on Investment deal, which was to be struck behind the closed doors of the OECD before opposition caused its abandonment, had already excluded the audiovisual sector from its terms at the insistence of Europe.

14. Shalini Venturelli, "Cultural Rights and World Trade Agreements in the Information Society," *Gazette* 60, no. 1 (1998): 47–76.

15. "WTO agreements are little more than extensive lists of policies, laws and regulations that governments can no longer establish or maintain." See Steven Shrybman, *The World Trade Organization: A Citizen's Guide* (Toronto: CCPA/Lorimer, 1999).

16. A squabble broke out regarding who should succeed the first secretary-general, who served until the end of 1998. The consensus that emerged involved splitting the current six-year term in half, with the Australian Mike Moore serving until September 2002, at which point Thailand's Supachai Panitchpakdi will take over. The delay left very little time to prepare for the Seattle meeting, which ended in disarray, but it also made the successive occupants of the post, in the words of Brazil's ambassador, "capitit diminutio"—of diminished capacity.

17. The least industrialized countries, with 10 percent of the world's population, have only 0.3 percent of world trade, half the share they had twenty years ago. Sub-Saharan Africa is expected to be $1.2 billion worse off as a result of the Uruguay Round. See the UN Development Program, *Human Development Report, 1997* (New York: UN Development Program, 1997).

18. Alieen Kwa, "WTO and Developing Countries," in Foreign Policy Briefs 3, no. 37 (1998), <http://www.foreignpolicy-infocus.org/briefs/vol3/v3n37wto/html>, 1998 [last accessed: 26 November 2001]. See also Oxfam Briefing Paper 9, "Eight Broken Promises: Why the WTO Isn't Working for the World's Poor," <http://www.oxfam.org.uk/policy/paper/8broken/8broken.html>, November 2001 [last accessed 30 November 2001].

19. Kwa, "WTO and Developing Countries."

20. Kwa, "WTO and Developing Countries."

21. Panos Institute, "More Power to the World Trade Organizations?" Panos briefing, <http://www.oneworld.org/panos>, November 1999 [last accessed: 26 November 2001].

6

✛

The UN Educational, Scientific, and Cultural Organization

The governance structures of media and communications might look very different today if a debate that stormed through the UN Educational, Scientific, and Cultural Organization (UNESCO) in the late 1970s and early 1980s had played itself out differently. Dubbed the New World Information and Communication Order (NWICO), in the end it had little enduring impact on media and communications. But, as we shall see, its impact on UNESCO is still felt today.

UNESCO, of course, is about much more than communication. Its objective is to contribute to world peace by promoting international collaboration in education, science, culture, and communication, in order to further "universal respect for justice, for the rule of law and for the human rights and fundamental freedoms which are affirmed for the people of the world, without distinction of race, sex, language or religion, by the Charter of the United Nations."[1] In contrast to the practical origins of many governance institutions, the fundamentally humanist impulse behind UNESCO is evident in its founding constitution: "Since wars begin in the minds of men, it is in the minds of men that the defences of peace must be constructed. . . . A peace based exclusively upon the political and economic arrangements of governments would not be a peace which could secure the unanimous, lasting and sincere support of the peoples of the world, and the peace must therefore be founded, if it is not to fail, upon the intellectual and moral solidarity of mankind."[2]

UN Educational, Scientific, and Cultural Organization
Location: Paris
Established: 1945
Membership: 188 countries plus 5 associate members
Budget: $544,000,000
Secretariat staff: 2,200 (plus 500 in 73 field offices and units around the world)
Head: Koichiro Matsuura, director-general (Japan)
Functions: The main objective of UNESCO is to contribute to peace and security in the world by promoting collaboration among nations through education, science, culture, and communication in order to further universal respect for justice, for the rule of law, and for the human rights and fundamental freedoms that are affirmed for the peoples of the world, without distinction of race, sex, language, or religion by the UN Charter. To fulfil its mandate, UNESCO performs five principal functions:

- Prospective studies: what forms of education, science, culture, and communication for tomorrow's world?
- The advancement, transfer, and sharing of knowledge: relying primarily on research, training, and teaching activities.
- Standard-setting action: the preparation and adoption of international instruments and statutory recommendations.
- Expertise: provided to member states for their development policies and projects in the form of "technical cooperation."
- Exchange of specialized information.

URL: <http://www.unesco.int>

Such lofty aspirations in a world dominated, but for brief moments, by geopolitical struggles and economic expansionism were bound at certain points to resolve into existential crises. UNESCO never had clear authority over a distinct and essential domain of economic, social, or scientific applications. While in one sense claiming to be nonpolitical by building directly on the intellectual and moral solidarity of humankind, in another its deeply political intent could never hope to remain aloof from the global political and economic fray. And so it proved to be, especially in the area of communications.

Although UNESCO has a broader mandate, media and communications feature strongly as means for realizing its objectives. Of the three points in its constitution, the first is to: "Collaborate in the work of advancing the mutual knowledge and understanding of peoples, through all means of mass communication and to that end recommend such international agreements as may be necessary to promote the free flow of ideas by word and image."[3]

This wide-ranging mandate in media and communications, however, lacks a compelling material base in a specific domain of action. The International Telecommunication Union (ITU), for instance, has clear responsibility for spectrum allocation and standards in telecommunications, while the World Intellectual Property Organization (WIPO) has an undeniable mandate in intellectual property rights. UNESCO, by contrast, had by the early 1950s surrendered its jurisdiction over the substantive areas of freedom of information and news and press content to the UN General Assembly (where a committee continues to oversee it), on the pragmatic basis of protecting itself against negative publicity that already surrounded the issue in the context of the emerging Cold War. Thus, the issue here is not UNESCO's need to act through government consensus and agreement—this it shares with most UN agencies. Rather, it is the absence of a specific mandate in an area of media and communications in which there is a compelling and practical need for international agreement.

UNESCO's broad but vague domain can be both an asset and a liability in terms of having an impact on its objective: an asset because it can in principle engage in a wide range of activities; a liability because it has limited clout in any essential area. Its checkered history demonstrates both its potential and its limits, as a quick look shows.

A BRIEF HISTORY

Origins to the 1970s

UNESCO can claim some predecessors. The International Committee of Intellectual Cooperation, and its executing agency, the International Institute of Intellectual Cooperation had existed in Geneva since the 1920s and merged into the new organization on its foundation. The International Bureau of Education, also based in Geneva since the 1920s, also became part of UNESCO in 1969.

The proposal to create the organization came from a Conference of Allied Ministers of Education, which had begun to meet in November 1942. Borne on a wave of revulsion at the inhumanity of the Second World War, UNESCO's founding conference was in London in June 1945, with twenty founding signatories. UNESCO was far more than a merger of its forerunners, incorporating much wider goals in cultural, educational, and scientific matters.

A high degree of consensus has reigned internationally on the desirability of preserving and sustaining culture, in particular. The Hague Convention for the Protection of Cultural Property in the event of Armed Conflict (1954), the Convention on the Means of Prohibiting and Preventing the Illicit Import, Export, and Transfer of Ownership of Cultural Property (1970), and the Convention for the Protection of the World Cultural and Natural Heritage (1972) were widely adopted without major disagreement. Given that enforcement mechanisms are limited or absent, however, implementation of their wide range of instruments is often difficult and patchy.

In a similar vein, in 1968 a UNESCO conference of experts debated the issue of cultural rights as "human rights," concluding in the conference statement that "[t]he rights to culture include the possibility for each man to obtain the means of developing his personality, through his direct participation in the creation of human values and of becoming, in this way, responsible for his situation, whether local or on a world scale."[4] Rights to participation in culture were further grounded and extended, in the 1978 Declaration on Race and Racial Prejudice,[5] to the protection of cultural identity, thus implying the need for conservation, development, and diffusion of culture within the context of international cultural cooperation.

For educational and scientific matters, UNESCO has been instrumental in many conventions, international conferences, and congresses in international cooperation. Major ones in education include the Congress on the Eradication of Illiteracy (1965), the Convention against Discrimination in Education (1960), the World Conference on Books (1982), and the World Conference on Higher Education (1998); and in scientific cooperation, the Intergovernmental Conference for Rational Use and Conservation of Biosphere (1968), the Conference on World Science Information System UNISIST (1971), and the World Science Conference (1999).

Media have featured in UNESCO activities from the earliest times, and not only under the direct communication remit. International educational, cultural, and scientific exchange was seen as a central defense of peace in the "minds of men," and various media were recognized as a means to facilitate this. In 1948, the Beirut Convention adopted the Agreement for Facilitating the International Circulation of Visual and Auditory Materials of an Education, Scientific, and Cultural Character. Its main effect was to exempt such material from all customs duties and quantitative restrictions. This was followed in 1950 by the Florence Convention's Agreement on the Importation of Educational, Scientific and Cultural Materials, which did the same for books and other publications.

Satellite as a means of transmission of cultural content has also long been a concern of UNESCO. By the late 1960s, direct satellite broadcasting was becoming an issue in terms of the control of foreign cultural and commercial flows. Most countries felt that there should be express obligations for the operation of such broadcasts, requiring some form of consent by those receiving the signal (see chapter 4). In 1972, UNESCO adopted the Declaration on the Use of Satellite Broadcasting for the Free Flow of Information, the Spread of Education and Greater Cultural Exchanges. It included relatively strong provisions on the matter, making reference to Article 19 of the Universal Declaration on Human Rights and stressing the free flow of information and news between all countries, developed and developing, but also affirming the prior consent principle: "it is necessary that states, taking into account the principle of the freedom of information, reach or promote prior agreements concerning direct satellite broadcasting to the population of countries other than the population of origin of the transmission (Article 9). It was passed by fifty-five votes in favor, seven against, and twenty-two abstentions. As a declaration, it had little binding impact, but already the lines were becoming clear: the seven against were Australia, Canada, Costa Rica, Denmark, West Germany, the United Kingdom, and the United States.

In 1974, UNESCO, along with WIPO, oversaw a further convention on satellites, but this time with somewhat opposite intent—to provide protection for the copyright owners of satellite broadcast signals. The Convention Relating to the Distribution of Programme-Carrying Signals Transmitted by Satellite obliges member states to "take adequate measures to prevent the distribution of programme-carrying signal by any distributor for whom the signal emitted to or passing through satellite is not intended." It entered into force in 1979. In some respects, these two main actions of UNESCO in relation to satellite communication are indicative of a broader shift—from balancing the sovereign rights of nations against the free flow of information doctrine, to a greater emphasis on the property rights of information owners including a refinement (indeed, ironically, a restriction) of free flow.

UNESCO was also active in other areas of copyright, in the context of broadening access to education and cultural material. It created a system whereby wealthier countries could pay the copyrights of poor countries for their own authors; meanwhile, a joint UNESCO/WIPO consultative committee on Access by Developing Countries to Works Protected by Copyright (1979) continues to engage in awareness raising and facilitates negotiation of publishing and translation contracts.

All of this, however, was merely a prelude to what many consider UNESCO's high, or low, point, depending on your point of view, in the arena of media and communications. This began in the 1970s with the NWICO.

New World Information and Communication Order

The debate on NWICO represented the first time that media and communications were argued in a truly global way. It raged (with varying titles) inside and outside the United Nations from the mid-1970s through to the mid-1980s. It is important less for its outcome—there are few tangible effects today—than for the fact that such key issues on media and communications were actually debated at all. In today's climate of dominant orthodox positions, it is important to recall that a diversity of views did exist and that until very recently there was still widespread and serious discussion and division on what a future media and communications regime should look like.

The NWICO debate did not appear from nowhere and can be understood only in its broader context. The growing power of the less industrialized countries following decolonization, and the resulting new balance of power in the United Nations, provide the starting point. By 1974, less industrialized countries had succeeded in formulating and asserting an economic philosophy in the United Nations, against the resistance of the more powerful nations. The New International Economic Order (NIEO) had five main axes:

- Improved terms of trade for less industrialized countries to address current imbalances
- More indigenous control of productive assets in less industrialized countries, thus enhancing national control of development strategies
- More interaction between less industrialized countries in trade and other forms of cooperation
- Greater "counterpenetration" by poorer countries of the richer country markets
- More influence of less industrialized countries in the Bretton Woods organizations (World Bank, the International Monetary Fund, the General Agreement on Tariffs and Trade, and so forth) and on the activities of transnational corporations

A declaration on the NIEO was approved by the UN General Assembly on 1 May 1974, along with a (limited) program of action. The declaration encouraged member states to:

Work urgently for the establishment of a NIEO based on "equity, sovereign equality, interdependence, common interest and cooperation among states," irrespective of their economic and social systems which shall correct inequalities and redress existing injustices, make it possible to eliminate the widening gap between developed and the developing countries and ensure steadily accelerating economic and social developments and peace and justice for future generations.

Most of the concerns that gave rise to the NIEO were very relevant also to media and communications:

- The "free-flow" doctrine of information flow, in place since the 1940s, was reinforcing the dominance of Western media and news content

- The growing concentration of the media and communications industry was translating into more foreign ownership of media in smaller and poorer countries
- The growing importance of Western-controlled technologies to media production and dissemination was making it difficult for others to keep up

Against a backdrop of the crucial role of media and communications in the context of nation building and decolonization, many countries became seriously concerned about the impact on national identity, cultural integrity, and political and economic sovereignty. Doubts about trends in cultural and media "imperialism," and its long-term implications, were heard not only in less industrialized countries, but also in many others including France, Canada, and Finland.

NWICO was spearheaded by the Non-Aligned Movement (NAM) of UN countries. As the only UN body equipped to debate in a coherent manner the range of issues raised regarding media, communications, culture, news distribution, and so forth, it was inevitable that the action would primarily be staged in UNESCO. The NAM constituted a large group of countries defined by their independence of the Cold War protagonists, led initially by the Organization of Petroleum Exporting Countries and relying on their new-found oil-based power. At a series of meetings between 1973 and 1976, the NAM progressed from a simple critique of transnational corporations and powerful governments, to a much more sophisticated plan for a New World Information Order (as it was known then).

At the same time, responding to movements within the United Nations as a whole, UNESCO was convening a number of expert groups and commissioning background papers on issues such as direct broadcast satellites, which many countries feared would beam unwanted messages with impunity, and on the development of national communication policies.

Both strands met at the 1976 UNESCO General Assembly, under Director-General Amadou Mahtar M'Bow, and a wide gulf became apparent between the views of the NAM and the Western countries including the United States, the United Kingdom, and several others. A showdown was avoided only by the creation of an International Commission for the Study of Communication Problems, generally called the MacBride Commission after its chair, Seán MacBride. But NWICO was now firmly on the UNESCO agenda, explicitly linked by M'Bow to the NIEO, and would stay there for a decade.

The 1978 UNESCO General Assembly saw further acrimonious debate and furious diplomatic battles. Nevertheless, there was a significant outcome, at least on paper, in that agreement was reached on a Declaration on Mass Media.[6] This contained a diluted version of the original, much broader, proposal, and the free-flow doctrine supported by the United

States, the United Kingdom, and others was amended to one of a "free-flow and wider and better balanced dissemination of information."

The MacBride Commission reported to the 1980 General Assembly. The *Many Voices, One World* report was comprehensive (with a notable exception in relation to gender), wide ranging, and came with a long list of recommendations. For the first time, NWICO had a general framework, a detailed justification, and a set of proposals. Inevitably, the report was couched in ambiguous language on key issues to accommodate divergent views, and recommendations were often weak and based on reciprocal concession. The most difficult issues were earmarked to be explored in more depth in the future. After teetering on the brink of collapse, the commission's findings were endorsed. One tangible outcome was agreement to set up an International Programme for the Development of Communication (IPDC), seen by some as an instrument to coordinate a huge range of resources into realizing NWICO aims. It continues in existence today, and although it does useful work, its budget has been small in relation to the size of the problem and indeed in relation to the hopes of many in less industrialized countries.[7]

The veneer of agreement, however, was thin. Instead of bringing the sides together, the entire process exposed the gulf between them and entrenched the positions especially of the West. A counteroffensive was not long in coming.

The United States led the attack on UNESCO, supported strongly by the private media industry and lobbies such as the World Press Freedom Committee. With a background argument that UNESCO should be a technical agency and steer clear of political issues, the main charge was that less industrialized countries were attempting to impose government control of the media and to suppress freedom of the press—despite the fact that freedom of the press was strongly endorsed at every turn by NWICO. M'Bow came under particular attack, often personalized, but UNESCO continued to support the NWICO concept and resolutions until well into the 1980s by sponsoring meetings, promoting dialogue, and trying to disentangle the especially knotty and contentious issues. The NAM also continued its work by holding a large conference in late 1980 that called for an intensification of efforts to promote NWICO.

At the end of 1983, however, the United States notified UNESCO of its intention to withdraw from UNESCO, carrying out the threat a year later. Its strongest ally, the United Kingdom, left the following year. The decisions were taken partly because of NWICO, but probably represented also the United States' and the United Kingdom's broader rejection of multilateralism for which UNESCO was a key component. NWICO managed to stay on the UNESCO agenda, though with little action, until 1987. The replacement of M'Bow in that year by Federico Mayor of Spain, and the changed overall mood, led to its final disappearance. UNESCO's medium-term plan for 1990 to 1995 made only cursory mention of NWICO and reinstated the free-flow doctrine at the center.

The imbalances underlying the NWICO movement were not so easily disposed of, and in some respects continue to worsen. However, for many the main lesson of NWICO was that the way forward would have to be through the democratization of media and communications, rather than through state- or industry-led efforts to create new global orders. The MacBride Round Table, for instance, met annually from 1989 to 1999 to continue the spirit of the MacBride Commission but in a wider context, bringing together nongovernmental organizations (NGOs), academics, as well as governments to debate the issues. The People's Communication Charter[8] also promotes the same principles of democratization of media at all levels, as do a number of other emerging civil society organizations.

UNESCO SINCE NWICO

After NWICO and under its new director-general, Federico Mayor, UNESCO generally steered clear of controversial issues, among them media governance. Although UNESCO was hoping to woo the United States and the United Kingdom back into the fold, the former in particular probably judged that it could exert greater influence by remaining outside. The loss of 25 percent of its budget left UNESCO weakened, and its efforts to reengage led it to shy away from anything it perceived to be against the interests of the United States, ironically giving the United States more influence as a nonmember than it had as a member. The United Kingdom finally returned in 1997, when a Labour government was elected to power. The United States still remains outside.

UNESCO continues to support media and communications initiatives and programs in practical ways, aiming both to ensure that free flow does not mean simply a free hand for corporate and private interests, but also the information to promote "the progress of societies and their democratic functions democratic functioning" and to "strengthen communication capacities, particularly in developing countries."[9] For example, it promotes a nonpartisan press through IFEX, the International Freedom of Expression Clearing House, a mechanism to mobilize a rapid international response to press freedom violations, and through training, exchanges, and resource centers for journalists; it has run meetings and congresses, for instance on the ethical, legal, and societal challenges of the Internet and cyberspace, and on telematics to promote development; and it produces and disseminates electronic libraries and archives. Its activities in capacity building for developing countries include supporting an academic network of UNESCO chairs in communications (ORBICOM), IPDC grants to dozens of communications projects including community radio and the Internet, and assistance to news agencies from developing regions.

In governance of media and communications, however, perhaps the main UNESCO intervention was the World Commission on Culture and Development. This was set up jointly by the United Nations and UNESCO to develop "proposals for both urgent and long term action to meet cultural needs in the context of development."[10] Chaired by Javier Pérez de Cuéllar, the former UN secretary-general, it presented its report *Our Creative Diversity*, to the UN General Assembly in 1995. It put forward some important proposals relating to media, which it covered in some depth. Arguing for a switch of emphasis from the national to the international level in efforts to channel the world's media capacity to "support cultural diversity and democratic discourse," it raised issues about concentration of media ownership internationally, and argued for a global "public sphere in which there is room for alternative voices." Among its most radical proposals was a global subsidy for public service and community media:

> The Commission regards the airwaves and space as part of the global commons, a collective asset that belongs to all humankind. . . . Nationally, community and public broadcasting services require public subsidies. Just as a major portion of funding for existing public services could come from within the national television system itself, internationally, the redistribution of benefits from the growing global commercial media activity could help subsidize the rest. As a first step and within a market context, the Commission suggests that the time may have come for commercial regional or international satellite radio and television interests which now use the global commons free of charge to contribute to the financing of a more plural media system. New revenue could be invested in alternative programming for international distribution.[11]

To follow it up, it proposed that UNESCO, in consultation with other UN agencies such as the ITU, undertake a feasibility study on the issue without delay.

This was an independent commission, giving it the freedom to make such proposals but also absolving its sponsors of responsibility or commitments regarding its recommendations. UNESCO was careful to underline the latter aspect.[12] In March 1998, the report finally resurfaced at a UNESCO–sponsored Intergovernmental Conference on Cultural Policies for Development, in Stockholm. This particular recommendation was not included in the draft Action Plan presented to the meeting. The conference did, however, gain the endorsement of 140 countries to the Action Plan that included specific requests to member states to:

- Consider providing public service radio and television and promote space for community, linguistic, and minority services
- Adopt or reinforce national efforts that foster media pluralism and freedom of expression

But even these were weaker versions of the Draft Plan, which was far firmer in encouraging states to provide public radio and television, rather than merely to "consider" their provision, and in calling for international, as well as national, legislation to promote media pluralism. A further proposal that such legislation foster "competition and prevent excessive concentration of media ownership" was changed to refer instead to fostering "freedom of expression." Another proposal in the draft Action Plan, to "promote the Internet as a universal public service by fostering connectivity and not-for-profit use consortia and by adopting reasonable pricing policies," disappeared altogether.[13]

These changes are indicative of the global political environment in which even a hint at the dangers of media concentration and the need to regulate commercial activity is considered risky.

UNESCO'S STRUCTURE

UNESCO's main decision-making body is the General Conference, with a membership of 188 countries. Any member of the United Nations may join, and non–UN members need approval of two-thirds of UNESCO membership—a rule rapidly reaching redundancy. It meets every two years and determines the policies of the organization, approves its main lines of action and budget, and appoints the director-general. It also "summons international conferences" of members on specific issues and can adopt member recommendations on diverse topics by simple majority and international conventions by two-thirds majority approval.

Its Executive Board has fifty-eight members. The director-general is appointed by the General Conference for a six-year term, on the recommendation of the Executive Board. The director-general appoints the staff of the Secretariat, and prepares the draft program, the budget, and proposals for action. Currently, five program sectors, along with the administrative and support services, implement the work. The five are: education; natural sciences; social and human sciences; culture; and communication, information, and informatics. The Secretariat has about 2,200 staff, about

500 outside its Paris headquarters, in its 60 field offices and units around the world (see fig. 6.1).

The large presence outside headquarters is not the only reflection of its aspiration to impact on ordinary people, on civil society, and on nongovernmental institutions and organizations involved in education, culture, and communication. In addition to its global superstructure, it has established UNESCO National Commissions, encourages UNESCO Clubs, Associations, and Centers, and has developed particularly strong relations with NGOs.

- A total of 189 countries have set up National Commission's, comprising education, scientific, and cultural experts
- A total of 4,800 UNESCO Clubs, Associations, and Centers are spread around the world to promote the ideals of UNESCO and actions at the grassroots level

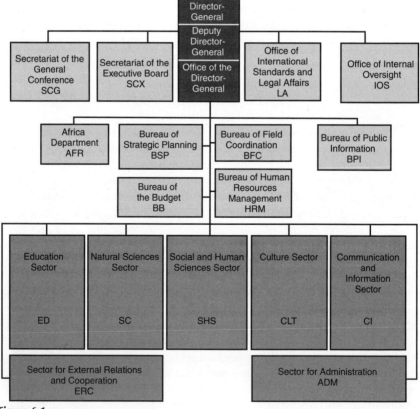

Figure 6.1

- Almost 600 NGOs maintain official relations with UNESCO, at different levels according to their remit and level of organization.

Most of UNESCO's influence is exercised through more than 100 advisory and consultative committees, International Commissions, and Intergovernmental Councils for the management of UNESCO's major programs.

The IPDC has a unique structure within UNESCO. The IPDC Intergovernmental Council, comprising thirty-nine members elected from UNESCO's General Conference, guides and oversees the grants program.

NOTES

1. See the UNESCO Constitution, <http://www.unesco.org/general/eng/about/constitution/> [last accessed: 26 November 2001].

2. Preamble of the UNESCO Constitution.

3. Article 1, Section 2(a) of the UNESCO Constitution.

4. UNESCO, "Cultural Rights as Human Rights" (Paris: UNESCO, 1970). (The conference was held 8–13 July 1968.)

5. Declaration on Race and Racial Prejudice, adopted and proclaimed by the General Conference of the United Nations Educational, Scientific and Cultural Organization at its twentieth session, on 27 November 1978: "Article 5, 1. Culture, as a product of all human beings and a common heritage of mankind, and education in its broadest sense, offer men and women increasingly effective means of adaptation, enabling them not only to affirm that they are born equal in dignity and rights, but also to recognize that they should respect the right of all groups to their own cultural identity and the development of their distinctive cultural life within the national and international contexts, it being understood that it rests with each group to decide in complete freedom on the maintenance, and, if appropriate, the adaptation or enrichment of the values which it regards as essential to its identity."

6. Declaration of Fundamental Principles Concerning the Contribution of the Mass Media to Strengthening Peace and International Understanding, to the Promotion of Human Rights and to Countering Racialism, Apartheid and Incitement to War, 20th Session of the UNESCO General Conference, Paris 1978.

7. Between 1980 and 2000, IPDC spent some $85 million on over 900 projects, with funds donated from many countries. Its aims are to strengthen mass communication in developing countries, to develop technical and human resources, to promote the transfer of technology, and to foster pluralism and independence of the media, democracy, and human rights.

8. See <http://www.pccharter.net> [last accessed: 2 February 2002].

9. UN Educational, Scientific, and Cultural Organization, *Medium Term Strategy, 1996–2001* (Paris: UN Educational, Scientific, and Cultural Organization, 1995).

10. UNESCO, "Our Creative Diversity: Report of the World Commission on Culture and Development" (Paris: UNESCO, 1995); see "Appendix: The Commission and Its Work."

11. UNESCO, "Our Creative Diversity: Report of the World Commission on Culture and Development."

12. Marc Raboy, "Challenges for the Global Regulation of Communication" (contribution to the Vidéazimut Virtual Conference on the Right to Communicate and the Communication of Rights, 1999), <http://commposite.uqam.ca/videaz/wg1/0007.html> [last accessed: 26 November 2001].

13. Raboy, "Challenges for the Global Regulation of Communication."

7

+

The World Intellectual Property Organization and Intellectual Property Rights

The World Intellectual Property Organization (WIPO) is the organization specifically set up to promote and protect intellectual property rights (IPRs). Although the World Trade Organization (WTO) has more recently come to the fore in this area, WIPO remains the only organization whose exclusive concern is with IPRs.

IPRs are rights relating to creations of the mind—ideas—and bestow a monopoly over or restrict access to their use. Historically, IPRs emerged in the industrialized countries in specific forms, the main ones being copyright, patents, and trademarks. Copyright protects the right to control the use or expression of creative works, such as writing, songs, music, drawings, and sculptures.[1] Patents and trademarks focus on ideas relating to industry, the former covering new inventions and processes, the latter the use of signs or symbols that identify goods and services. Copyright is the most relevant in the present context of media governance.[2]

IPRS AND MEDIA GOVERNANCE

Creations of the mind differ from other creations in ways that mold the nature of associated rights. Some, such as works of art, writing, and media productions generally tend to be associated very closely with the author, embodying the intellectual personality as represented to society. This gives rise to a *moral* right to choose to publish or not, to be recognized as the author, and to prevent unauthorized modification.

World Intellectual Property Organization
Location: Geneva
Established: 1893 as the United International Bureau for the Protection of Intellectual Property; it became the World Intellectual Property Organization (WIPO) in 1970 and, in 1974, WIPO became a specialized agency of the United Nations.
Membership: 175 countries
Budget: Chf 410,000,000 ($250,000,000)
Secretariat staff: 760
Head: Dr. Kamil Idris, director-general (Sudan)
Functions: Administers twenty-one treaties (two of those jointly with other international organizations) and carries out a rich and varied program of work, through its member states and secretariat, that seeks to:

- Harmonize national intellectual property legislation and procedures
- Provide services for international applications for industrial property rights
- Exchange intellectual property information
- Provide legal and technical assistance to developing and other countries
- Facilitate the resolution of private intellectual property disputes
- Marshal information technology as a tool for storing, accessing, and using valuable intellectual property information

URL: <http://www.wipo.int>

They differ from material creations not only because of their immateriality per se, but also because this aspect allows for their reproduction at a tiny fraction of the cost of their original development. This poses a problem for those investing in the creative process who also seek a fair return. Thus, copyright protects not the idea itself or any particular material embodiment, such as a book, film, or computer program. It rather extends to the *use* or *expression* of the idea, and hence its reproduction, in any material form whatever. This is based on an *economic* right of return on investment.

Conversely, the very reproducibility of an idea gives it its special value. It is social in its very nature, ideally adapted to sharing. Much of human history can be seen as the transmission of good ideas between people, cumulated from one generation to the next. Ideas, unlike material things, never wear out, though they may be lost or lose their current value. The notion of a monopoly over the use of ideas is therefore inherently in tension with the very nature and the *social* value of ideas.

Between the creator and users of an idea there will always be a trade-off. As with any goods, innovation and intellectual creation is promoted through ensuring that those who put in the effort and investment are adequately compensated. In contrast to material goods, however, IPRs lapse beyond a period of time and enter the public domain to be used by anyone.

IPRs are thus fashioned by tensions between competing rights claimed, broadly, by three groups:

- Authors, who can claim a moral right over content in so far as it is associated with them
- Owners (originally the authors), who can claim an economic right to a fair rate of return as an incentive to invest in the creative process
- Users, or society in general, who can claim a public interest right, since ideas are inherently social in nature and the entry of ideas into the public domain is a core dynamic of social evolution

IPRs must balance these often contradictory values, the moral, the economic, and the social.

The central relevance of IPRs to media and communications, especially that of copyright, is obvious. Media content of all kinds comprises ideas that are embodied in forms specific to each medium, for instance, aural or visual, fleeting or fixed. Laws and agreements that define and enforce these rights are thus a key factor in determining who gets to use ideas—including media content—and the terms under which they gain access to them. Internationally, too, the governance of IPRs is critical to the nature and extent of interaction of ideas between societies, via the media, and therefore to the use and impact within societies of ideas coming from outside.

A BRIEF PREHISTORY

Basic Building Blocks

In some respects, the history of WIPO parallels that of the International Telecommunication Union (ITU). Almost as old, it emerged from the urgent need of governments to cooperate to eliminate obstacles to economic and technological development and trade, and found its feet through the merger of two related but independent strands of activity.

WIPO traces its early origins to the Paris Convention for the Protection of Industrial Property, which came into force in 1884 with fifteen signatories. Its aim was to provide protection for industrial inventions and ideas in countries other than those of the originators. Action had been demanded for some time to counter what was claimed to be widespread copying of new inventions and subsequent commercial exploitation in other countries. Foreign exhibitors had, a decade earlier, even refused to participate in an international inventor exhibition in Vienna. The Paris Convention covered rights already formulated at the national level in Western countries, including patents, trademarks, and industrial designs, and created the framework for entities from one signatory country to pursue its rights under the national law of other signatory countries.

Around the same time, artists, writers, and performers faced a similar problem regarding the sale or use of their work in other countries. The Berne Convention for the Protection of Literary and Artistic Works was agreed in 1886, covering everything from novels and poems to operas, drawings, and sculptures.

The small bureau set up by each to administer the agreements combined in 1893 and formed an organization called the United International Bureau for the Protection of Intellectual Property (known by its French acronym, BIRPI) that was based in Berne, Switzerland. The two treaties, amended and supplemented over the years, remain cornerstones of global governance of IPRs.

The initial focus of these two treaties was on the economic rights of IPRs and the trade-off with the public interest. The moral rights of living authors were recognized only in the 1928 Rome revision of the Berne convention, when a revised Article 6 was introduced. These rights were extended beyond the death of the author in a later Brussels revision of 1948.

Evolution through Technology Change

Waves of new media and communications technologies from early in the twentieth century, in particular reproduction and dissemination technologies, posed successive challenges to the balance and stability of IPR regimes.

An early outcome was to enhance the economic role of publishers, distributors, and sellers, who transformed the ideas into forms suitable for mass consumption and enabled their mass distribution. IPRs became big business. Ownership rights migrated from their creators, consolidating into the hands of these intermediaries who were intent on establishing and expanding their own distinct rights. The emergence of broadcast radio and television, phonograms, and films led to the creation of "neighboring rights," which extended copyright to cover certain uses of the copyrighted works. In effect, this was a major boost to economic aspects of IPRs. It was confirmed internationally with the signing of the Rome Convention for the Protection of Performers, Producers of Phonograms, and Broadcasting Organizations (1961) and the Geneva Convention for the Protection of Producers of Phonograms against Unauthorized Duplication of Their Phonograms (1971).

Commercially driven technology continued in the 1970s to put international agreements under pressure on the issue of copyright of satellite transmission, which fell outside the conventional definition of broadcasting. Satellite transmission had several complex international dimensions to it, and ITU, the UN Educational, Scientific, and Cultural Organization (UNESCO), and WIPO were all implicated. These were resolved for the most part with the Brussels Convention Relating to the Distribution of Programme-Carrying Signals Transmitted by Satellite (1974).

By this time BIRPI was also evolving institutionally. It moved from Berne to Geneva in 1960, the home of many key UN and multilateral agencies. In 1970, when the Convention Establishing the World Intellectual Property Organization, signed in Stockholm in July 1967, came into force, BIRPI became WIPO, undergoing structural and administrative reforms. In 1974, WIPO became a specialized agency of the United Nations.

The Era of Copyright Industries

The economic importance of intellectual property of all kinds was growing rapidly, but especially in the burgeoning copyright industries of the Northern countries. By the 1980s, the U.S. film, television, print, and other copyright industries had assumed major proportions in the economy. Many developing countries recognized their importance in the development process, and during the 1970s and largely based on work by WIPO and UNCTAD, a diversity of IPR forms adapted to the need of different levels of development were deployed. Not all followed established Western models, a fact that was soon to pit them against the copyright industries of the North. The trend toward greater flexibility was forced into reverse by the industrialized countries during the 1980s, and a tightening of the system began.

Economic growth of the sector was greatly facilitated by the electronics revolution, but also challenged by it. Reproduction technology, including photocopiers, tape recorders, and video cassette recorders gave rise to a parallel "pirate" industry, especially in Asia with their looser or absent laws. The industry in industrialized countries believed it was costing them dearly in lost revenues; by 1988, it calculated that it was losing $1.3 billion annually. A further effect of the electronics revolution was to exacerbate the tension between copyright owners and reproduction for legitimate social use, such as education, an issue carefully circumscribed under the Berne Treaty and balanced to maintain a public interest. Reproduction of music and television for home use also raised a set of complex legal and practical issues.

The main, but very limited, outcome in WIPO was the Geneva Treaty on the International Registration of Audiovisual Works (1989) that set up a WIPO register for audio and video, thus facilitating national attempts at curtailing the pirate industry in a voluntary manner. The question of piracy, however, was far from resolved to the satisfaction of the industrialized countries, and the tension between copyright owners and public interest use simmered on.

The Shift to Trade

Around the mid-1980s, a second major international forum for IPRs was emerging in the form of the General Agreement on Tariffs and Trade (GATT). As copyright industries grew, so too did international trade. As media industries in the North began to concentrate into larger conglomerates and look ever more to international markets, trade issues came more to the fore. The copyright industries were on the brink of becoming truly global.

Strictly speaking, the role of a trade organization in IPRs could be construed as very limited. Until the mid-1980s, GATT was concerned almost exclusively with lowering trade barriers to manufactured goods. The sole provisions relating to IPRs were designed to ensure that they could not be used illegitimately as nontariff barriers to trade—for instance onerous or expensive "marking requirements" for foreign goods. WIPO, however, was explicitly created to promote IPRs and so was the natural terrain for further strengthening of IPRs sought by the copyright industries and their governments. The question arises, therefore, as to how IPRs ended up on the agenda of GATT's Uruguay Round, beginning in 1986 and culminating with the Trade-Related Aspects of Intellectual Property Rights (TRIPS) agreements of 1995, with GATT by then having evolved into the WTO. What caused this decisive shift in the forum in which IPRs were negotiated?

By far the strongest proponent of the introduction of IPRs into GATT was the United States. The motivation for its position was twofold. On the one hand, it had for decades consistently opposed developing country positions in the Paris Convention concerning patents and trademarks that argued that the conventions were skewed in favor of already industrialized countries.[3] The United States feared that revising the Paris Convention would force it to yield concessions. The clean slate offered by GATT suited its interests.

The other, and probably more important, reason was the issue of enforcement. Under WIPO conventions, as under the Universal Copyright Convention of UNESCO to which the United States was a signatory, rights are enforced through national law, including civil or criminal penalties for violations of these rights. Where a dispute arises between states, there is a provision in some cases for settlement in the International Court of Justice, a long and often inconclusive process. However, GATT had its own international enforcement procedures, with the power to impose very significant penalties. GATT also opened the door to unilateral retaliatory action by more powerful countries across a range of areas.

Thus, the United States, later joined by the European Union and Japan, led the shift away from WIPO to GATT and later the WTO. Although under an agreement signed between WIPO and the WTO in 1995, they jointly administer the TRIPS agreement, and in practice, the WTO is the driving force. Their cooperation is mainly on the shared access to WIPO technical resources and databases and on the provision of assistance to less industrialized countries to implement the TRIPS obligations (the subject of a separate joint initiative agreed in 1998).

The inclusion of IPRs in the Uruguay Round, culminating with the TRIPS agreement, was a watershed in the relative weight given to the competing rights in IPRs. The balance tipped decisively in favor of the rights of the owners and investors, who engaged in trade, over those of creators and of the public. The full implications of the TRIPS agreement have yet to emerge.

THE PROVISIONS AND IMPACT OF TRIPS

The TRIPS agreement was, as mentioned, a watershed in IPR evolution and is generally recognized as a major victory for the industrialized countries and the transnational copyright industries. While imposing IPR standards and patterns of the industrialized countries on the rest of the world, it also greatly limits the freedom of countries to shape their systems according to national objectives and degrees of development.[4]

It was controversial from the beginning of the Uruguay Round, having been initially approved for inclusion in 1986 only on a restricted set of issues concerning counterfeit goods. The industrialized countries gradually turned up the pressure, with the United States going as far as threatening unilateral trade sanctions under Section 301 of the U.S. Trade Act. The less industrialized countries eventually accepted in principle a broader remit, in 1989, and then capitulated in practice at the negotiating table. The main concessions won by the less industrialized countries concerned timing. Transition periods until 2000 for developing countries, and 2007 for the least industrialized, were permitted so that they could bring their legislation into line.

The most controversial aspects of the TRIPS agreement, from the perspective of developing countries, had little to do with media and communications. The most serious reservations, persevering today, were expressed regarding patenting of life forms and of pharmaceuticals, with critics arguing that the agreement supports "biopiracy" by facilitating patenting by firms in industrialized countries of plants and other living organisms whose medical and other useful attributes have been known and used for generations in traditional societies. It makes little provision for the recognition of traditional knowledge. The transfer of enormous royalties for pharmaceuticals needed to combat widespread diseases among poor populations, even where locally produced, and the restrictions on reverse engineering are other key points of contention. (The launch of the WTO's Doha round of negotiations in November 2001 saw significant concession with regard to the former.)

The implications in developing countries for media and communications have, understandably, been overshadowed by these burning issues. The longer time horizon on media issues, as perceived by many governments, may also play a part. Nevertheless, the stakes are high. And they are not solely the concern of developing countries. The TRIPS agreement on media and communications, when seen in the broader context of trends in media and communications generally, has global ramifications and virtually nowhere will be left unaffected.

TRIPS begins by committing all signatories to a minimum standard of IPRs as laid down in the Berne and Paris Conventions. The only exception, interestingly, is the Berne Convention Clause on moral rights in copyright, which at the insistence of the United States is not obligatory. The agreement operates on the basis of granting "national treatment" and "most-favored-nation" status, thereby eliminating discrimination against (and between) foreign nationals. In relation to copyright and related rights, the main provisions are:

- The extension of copyright to software as a literary creation
- The creation, for the first time, of "rental" rights to copyright owners, which means that the owner may prevent commercial rental even after the legitimate purchase of a copy[5]
- Protection enduring the lifetime of an author and then fifty years further, or for works belonging to corporate bodies, a total of fifty years
- Strengthened enforcement rules through an obligation to instigate criminal proceedings and to prescribe penalties against piracy

In themselves, these appear as merely incremental changes to the existing situation. However, in the broader context of the media and communications industry globally, their impact is greatly magnified. Trends toward concentration of ownership of media, ever wider geographical penetration, and growing vertical and horizontal integration gathered pace during the 1990s and into the twenty-first century. More than merely bolstered by the TRIPS agreement, there are concerns that they herald a new and potentially dangerous era in the social, economic, and cultural role of media and communications in society. To many, in developed and developing countries, the long-term implications are so far reaching as to be literally unimaginable—which, they argue, in itself is an adequate case for fundamental reconsideration. Such concerns include:

- The gradual but inexorable transformation of what was hitherto treated as public domain information into privately owned information, while simultaneously ensuring that access to information created digitally is tightly circumscribed. Immediate concerns are on shrinking applications of "fair use" for education and on the expropriation of indigenous and traditional knowledge for private profit.
- The narrowing of the internationally recognized legal forms of ownership to copyright, patent, trademarks, and similar rigid concepts as distinct from other, more open social forms that include collective use rights, development rights, and so forth. The economic rights of owners are increasingly valued over the moral rights of creators and the social rights of the public interest. There is a countermovement to this that includes the Open Source Initiative, OpenContent, and CopyLeft initiatives that inherently recognize the importance of both collective work (e.g., open source software that encourages innovative use and development by a "community" of users) and free use and distribution of information resources providing that authorship is acknowledged (e.g., as provided by the OpenContent licensing conditions).[6] The Linux operating platform and early Netscape versions are examples of open source software; for information and document distribution, there is a strong education and library movement advocating fair-use policies.
- Continuous reinforcement of these legal forms and their impact through extending the lifetime of IPRs, ironically in an era in which the useful lifetime of much information is contracting.
- Greatly fortifying policing and enforcement of the economic aspect of IPRs, which is becoming one of the most severe systems of enforceable penalties in international agreements ever conceived, combined with the neglect of social and moral aspects.

Taken together, the trend is toward the transformation of the communication between people according to the rules of the market. Media content and productions of all kinds are increasingly produced and consumed as commodities, subject only to the same regulation and control as other commodities.

It is not commodification of media industries per se that is feared. Rather, it is the impact this could have on other critical functions performed by the media, in particular its role in cultural identity formation and sustenance and the capacity of society to engage in democratic discourse and decision making.

PROGNOSIS FOR IPRS AND MEDIA

The driving force in IPRs, and hence of central concern to WIPO even as it risks being overshadowed by the WTO, continues to be a struggle between competing rights. At the forefront is the tussle between economic rights of copyright owners and social rights of users. Although not necessarily an intended outcome, the enlargement of one area of IPR rights is inevitably at the expense of another. For instance, a lengthier period before copyright exhaustion is, at the same time, a delay in entry into the public domain, and the imposition of the Western model of IPRs simultaneously excludes other forms geared toward maximizing the development potential of poorer countries.

Insight into whether these trends will continue, or have already peaked, can be gained from positions pursued by the most powerful actors in various arenas in recent years. Not just international fora are relevant here, but also those at the national and regional level, since they very often are driven by the same dynamics, anticipating positions to be pursued internationally.

Events around or since the time of the TRIPS agreement point in certain directions.

A major WIPO conference at the end of 1996 saw the agreement of two treaties, the WIPO Copyright Treaty and the WIPO Performance and Phonograms Treaty,[7] effectively updating the Berne Convention on Copyright. The positions adopted there remain central in the IPRs arena.

- The European Union and the United States, the latter taking the lead, worked together to introduce strict copyright provisions for digital databases, including temporary digital copies. Since this could cover downloading data from the Web, it became a highly contentious issue pitching one set of industries against another. Powerful telecommunications and Internet companies combined with libraries and others to face up to publishers, the film industry, and software companies who supported the U.S.–EU stance. After much wrangling, a group of African countries, who had little immediate self-interest, put forward and secured support for a proposal that was so watered down as to be ineffective and the effort of the United States and European Union failed.
- The European Union and the United States attempted to use the negotiations to extend economic rights beyond that contained in the Berne Treaty, that would impose more restrictive definitions of the "exhaustion" of rights (extending their period of applicability) and the extension of rights to all kinds of rental. Against strong resistance from a large number of countries and interest groups, this, too, failed.

These and other positions of the European Union and the United States were attempts to achieve long-term goals they had failed to secure in the TRIPS agreement. They are now reflected in the national legislation in the United States and the European Union, which suggests that attempts to internationalize them will continue. In 1996, the European Union had introduced a database directive of its own, which codified and considerably extended database ownership rights in the direction of including not just the originators of the data, but also those who compile the databases. Many argue that this significantly curtails databases in the public domain. Under pressure from copyright industries such as Disney, which would have seen its copyright on Mickey Mouse run out in 2004, the United States in 1998 passed the Sonny Bono Copyright Term Extension Act, thereby lengthening the period of copyright in the case of pre-1978 copyright to some ninety-five years.

During the late 1990s, less industrialized countries were preparing to implement the TRIPS agreement, which for most of them came into force in January 2000. Here, the same pressures could be seen at work. The United States was accused by several countries, including Thailand, Ecuador, Argentina, and India, of using strong-arm unilateral tactics, including threats of severe trade sanctions, to force them to modify their domestic laws to become TRIPS compliant in directions that suited the United States.

Thus, wealthier countries are likely to continue to exert strong pressure, in whatever fora they can, to extend and strengthen the economic aspects of IPRs. Likely goals are:

- A longer period of time for which economic rights can be claimed
- Extending the domain of IPRs to more countries through accession to existing treaties
- Deepening of IPRs to include all forms of existing cultural activity, and further into electronic and Internet communication and other emerging forms
- Further strengthening of the mechanisms of enforcement

WIPO'S STRUCTURE

As with other international organizations of the UN family, WIPO's membership comprises states that are represented by governments. By March 2001, there were 175 member states.

WIPO is a "convention of conventions," meaning that it is an agreement by which members allow it to administer other agreements that concern IPRs. "Administering" a convention means providing and running the mechanisms that enable its terms, in practice, to be applied. WIPO offers a forum for signatories to come together and make decisions, it provides technical assistance in various issues that require it and has a center of expertise for those who want to avail of it, it facilitates mediation and arbitration, it helps poorer countries to implement their commitments, it oversees enforcement mechanisms, and it generally implements any actions that members believe are necessary to achieve their agreed aims.

WIPO pulls together under a single framework a total of twenty-one different conventions (or treaties), fifteen on industrial property and six on copyright. Of these, eleven concern IPRs.

Five of the industrial property treaties relate to IPRs:

- Paris Convention for the Protection of Industrial Property (1883)
- Madrid Agreement for the Repression of False or Deceptive Indications of Source on Goods (1891)
- Nairobi Treaty on the Protection of the Olympic Symbol (1981)
- Washington Treaty on Intellectual Property in Respect of Integrated Circuits (1989)
- Trademark Law Treaty (1994)

And all six copyright treaties are relevant to IPRs:

- Berne Convention for the Protection of Literary and Artistic Works (1886)
- Rome Convention for the Protection of Performers, Producers of Phonograms, and Broadcasting Organizations (1961)
- Geneva Convention for the Protection of Producers of Phonograms against Unauthorized Duplication of Their Phonograms (1971)
- Brussels Convention Relating to the Distribution of Program-Carrying Signals Transmitted by Satellite (1974)
- WIPO Copyright Treaty (1996)
- WIPO Performance and Phonograms Treaty (1996)

Each convention creates, in WIPO terminology, a "union" of its signatories. The formation of WIPO did not alter the conventions already signed, but rather enveloped them, along with their respective unions, unchanged into the broader structure of WIPO.

Because of this, there are two levels of participation for countries, those who are members of unions (i.e., signatories of the Berne, Paris, and other conventions), and others who may be invited to become party to the WIPO convention as members of the United Nations and specialized agencies— though they have not signed up to any specific conventions. Although all are equal signatories of the WIPO convention, the difference comes out in the right to participate in the main decision-making instruments: the General Assembly and the Conference. However, given that so many have now signed conventions, the distinction is becoming redundant.

The General Assembly comprises members of unions, each with one vote (others have only observer status). The General Assembly appoints the director-general; invites into WIPO new members and observers, including nongovernment organizations; and also decides (by a three-quarters majority) whether WIPO will administer other conventions. The General Assembly currently has 163 members.

The Conference brings together all members of WIPO, a total of 175. It can make recommendations regarding IPRs but its main power is to amend the WIPO convention. Here, voting rights are again different, with nonunion members entitled to vote only where the issue concerned affects their rights and obligations.

The General Assembly and the Conference are held every two years, back to back.

Much of the real power lies with the Coordination Committee. This committee nominates the director-general for appointment by the General Assembly, and, if it is refused by the latter, continues to nominate further candidates until agreement is reached. A two-thirds majority is required of the General Assembly, but also of the Berne and Paris Unions (which have 144 and 160 signatories, respectively). The committee also prepares the agendas for the General Assembly and the Conference and approves the deputy directors-general. The committee currently has seventy-two members, selected in a peculiar process that again gives prominence to the Paris and Berne signatories. All WIPO members, however, may have observer status on the Coordinating Committee and take part in discussions. It meets once a year in Geneva.

The International Bureau is the executive arm of the organization, led by the director-general, who reports to the General Assembly, and two or more deputy directors-general. It has a staff of about 700 people. The director-general is appointed for a six-year term and is its chief executive.

WIPO is mostly self-financing, which is unusual for a UN organization. Its three major registration systems, for patents, trademarks, and designs, generate about 85 percent of its budget, with most of the rest coming from member states.

Although WIPO is concerned exclusively with international aspects of IPRs, unlike the WTO it has no dedicated international enforcement procedures, a fact that significantly influences how members view its efficacy. Its agreements are policed through national legal systems, which are obliged to be brought into line with the conventions to which the country has subscribed (though the Paris Convention can also settle some disputes through the International Court of Justice).

NOTES

1. Modern copyright law is based on a 1710 British law that had quite different intentions. While the Statute of Anne recognized certain rights of copyright holders, its purpose was to break the almost complete control of the English book trade that had been exercised by the Stationers' Company of London for over 150 years. The law's most important contribution was to limit the length of time copyright could be exercised before the works entered the "public domain," thus ending Stationers' monopoly control of published knowledge. The law also restricted copyright holders' rights to printing, publishing, and selling, thus preventing them from controlling the use of a work once purchased.

2. For a discussion of WIPO's role in the current domain name system debacle, which is grounded in debates over governability of trademarks, see chapter 8.

3. The United States did not accede to the Berne Convention until 1989. Aspects of national legislation preventing it prior to this included a refusal to acknowledge the moral rights of authors long opposed by the film industry and a policy that required first publication in either the United States or Canada to qualify for U.S. copyright protection, ironically a piece of protectionist legislation of over 100 years' standing. Before 1989, the United States was the signatory of the Universal Copyright Convention of UNESCO. By withdrawing from UNESCO in 1984, the United States had left itself without a platform from which to influence policy, and this was also a factor in signing the Berne Convention. The acting commissioner for the U.S. Patent and Trademark Office supported in testimony the accession to Berne since WIPO "was not as politisized as UNESCO, and the influence of the developing countries in WIPO is not so disproportionate as in UNESCO." See Ronald V. Bettig, *Copyrighting Culture: The Political Economy of Intellectual Property* (Boulder, Colo.: Westview, 1996), 221–222.

4. South Centre, *The TRIPS Agreement: A Guide for the South* (Geneva: South Centre, 1997), <http://www.southcentre.org/publications/trips/tripsmain.pdf> [last accessed: 26 November 2001].

5. This amounts to a reversal of the provisions in place since the Statute of Anne (1710), which had sought to prevent a publisher's control of the use of a work once purchased.

6. See OpenContent License, <http://www.opencontent.org/opl.shtm> [last accessed: 26 November 2001]; Open Source Initiative, <http://www.opensource.org> [last accessed: 26 November 2001]; and CopyLeft, <http://www.gnu.org/copyleft/copyleft.html#whatiscopyleft> [last accessed: 26 November 2001].

7. Neither has yet entered into force. The WIPO Copyright Treaty has fifty-one signatories, but just fifteen countries out of a required thirty have so far ratified the treaty. The WIPO Performance and Phonograms Treaty has fifty signatories, with just thirteen ratifying out of the thirty needed. The United States has ratified both, while the European Union has ratified neither.

8

The Internet Corporation for Assigned Names and Numbers and Internet Governance

That a new and rapidly growing communication network poses challenges for both national and international governance should come as no surprise. As we saw in chapter 3, barely ten years after its invention in 1844 the telegraph encountered comparable challenges in Europe, quickly resulting in the creation of the International Telegraph Union (now known as the International Telecommunication Union [ITU]). The outcome, as it was for telegraphy, will be strongly marked by its specific historical circumstances. First, international Internet governance became a pressing issue during a period of strong liberalization and privatization, and suspicion among the major powers and big business regarding whether existing UN governance organizations would adequately serve their needs. Second, in contrast with telegraphy, telephony, and broadcasting, most countries implemented the Internet first as a system for international communication and only later used it for national or local communication. The important exception was the United States, where it was at the outset designed as a national communication system. In practice, as we shall see, this has meant that as the rules for global Internet governance are being written, they are inescapably shaped by the United States' early decision to liberalize, privatize, and commercialize the new medium.

Some of the issues raised for governance internationally of the Internet are described in this chapter. As the Internet evolves through successive reconfigurations, driven by shifting dynamics and embracing new sets of users, its regulation and governing entities have diversified. This chapter begins by mapping out the key issues and briefly describing

various bodies involved in Internet governance. After this lengthy introduction, we turn to the Internet Corporation for Assigned Names and
Numbers (ICANN), the most prominent governing organization among
them.

Internet Corporation for Assigned Names and Numbers
Location: Marina del Rey, California, United States
Established: 1998
Membership: 76,000 at-large members
Budget: $6,500,000
Secretariat staff: 17
Head: Dr. M. Stuart Lynn , president and chief executive office (United
States)
Functions: Responsibility for the Internet protocol address space alloca-
tion, protocol parameter assignment, domain name system management,
and root server system management functions
URL: <http://www.icann.org>

Need for Global Governance

At the center of media convergence, with a rapid rate of growth and
sudden central position in the "new economy," the Internet has already
reconfigured itself several times. Originally a network linking a hand-
ful of researchers, new capabilities—e-mail, the World Wide Web, Internet telephony, and peer-to-peer networking and exchanges (see
textbox)—successively altered the way it is used and introduced new
spheres of regulatory contention from intellectual property rights
(IPRs) to long-distance call completion regimes. The sudden globalization of reach (though not of "depth" in most less industrialized countries), the recurring urgent need for technical standardization, and the
emerging contradictions between the social and developmental role of
the Internet and the growing commercialization of content and use all
point to the need for governance. Thus, the core tension between regulating for societal development and regulating for the sector as an industry applies to the Internet as well.

Furthermore, since the Internet can be used to watch films, make telephone calls, and read newspapers and books, its regulation clearly has implications for enforcement of regulation of the other media—several of
which have already sprung regulatory leaks via the Internet.

Napster

Founded in May 1999 by the then nineteen-year-old college student Shawn Fanning, Napster is file-swapping software that uses an integrated browser and communications system to facilitate free sharing of music files over the Internet. Users can access a chat program, an MP3 audio player (for those who do not have an external player), and a tracking program to bookmark specific MP3 libraries for future use. Using Napster, individuals can locate specific tracks of music that are available in MP3 and WMA format and download them from other individuals' MP3 collections to their hard disks. In this regard, Napster differs from other illegal MP3 sites, in that it only provides information regarding the location of MP3 files, rather than brokering them via the Napster site. Napster would not have been so controversial had it not spread so enthusiastically. During the month of January 2001 alone, three billion songs were downloaded.

A U.S. lawsuit, which was initiated by the rock band Metallica and major record labels for copyright infringement, was issued against Napster in April 2000 by the Recording Industry Association of America. An initial ruling led to the order that Napster be shut down. This was appealed and the case culminated in the February 2001 order that Napster must prevent its subscribers from gaining access to content on its search index that could potentially infringe copyrights.

Music consumers via Napster altered the distribution, form, and access to a cultural product—thus divorcing music recording from the producers in terms of a chain of remuneration, rendering the traditional compact disc (CD) product into a new format and challenging existing copyright laws that allow for a certain degree of sharing of cultural products. The Napster phenomenon demonstrated that there was a significant (and still untapped) market for different forms of consumption of individual tracks of music, especially if instantaneously available, rather than a unique and entire CD purchase. Whether this preference will in fact be profitable to the music industry is soon to be tested. During the U.S. court case, Napster formed an alliance with Bertelsmann to develop a subscription-based service. This joint venture, now entitled MusicNet, also includes AOL Time-Warner and EMI, and plans to offer digital music download subscription services by the end of 2001.

Social Issues

Soon after the 1994 transformation of the Internet in the United States from a relatively small publicly owned academic network to a fast-growing primarily commercial one, came a growing awareness of its social potential and of the importance of policy development in the area.

From the mid 1990s, the question of supporting universal Internet access arose in the industrialized countries, with calls for measures to provide availability, especially in rural and disadvantaged areas, in schools, community centers, and in the home. Policy responses such as flat-rate or reduced-rate telephone billing,[1] universal service obligations on network operators, and community-level access were implemented to facilitate wider take-up. By the late 1990s, however, the term "Digital Divide" emerged as a description of the huge gap in access, usage, and content opening between the wealthy countries and the rest of the world, and especially within poorer countries, between urban areas and business users and rural areas. Accessing the Internet was becoming a development issue with global political implications, though solutions were usually framed within the dominant paradigm of liberalization and privatization. Barriers to the Internet are especially acute in poorer countries and regions, beyond the paucity of network infrastructure. Unlike basic telephony, Internet use requires literacy (preferably in English or another major European language), availability of computers, and knowledge of how to use them.

To date, there has been far more talk than action concerning the Digital Divide. Most measures, such as assistance with liberalizing national telecommunications and Internet policy, coincide fully with the liberalization agenda in general (no doubt a major factor in their motivation), though others believe this agenda to be part of the problem, not of the solution. Substantive measures outside this paradigm, such as the creation of mechanisms to subsidize access, have tended not to go beyond limited pilot projects.

The accessibility and visibility of noncommercial uses of and *content* on the Internet are also becoming a matter of concern. Currently, there exist more than two billion Web pages, with several million added daily, creating an explosion of available content. This content must be classified in order to be accessible, and classification inevitably involves selection. But ordinary search engines, which typically index only 15 percent of available pages, tend to give much higher profile to commercial sites due to the latter's marketing and technical savvy. There is thus an argument to increase the visibility of noncommercial sites and content on the Web.[2]

Conversely, an early and still continuing focus for regulation is to keep certain content off the Internet. Systematic and concerted attempts to censor politically unwelcome Internet messages and information are confined to a number of highly controlled societies and have never proved fully effective. However, there is much widespread concern over the inability to prevent the use of the Internet to distribute and exchange sexually explicit, pornographic, and violent material—regarding which social norms vary enormously—and of universally condemned pedophilic and other grossly abusive material. The very nature of the Internet makes it extremely difficult to control its flow across national boundaries.

The Internet also brings with it a host of issues concerning privacy, such as the potential for misuse of online databases of personal information such as e-mail addresses and credit card numbers, the right to refuse commercial material and advertisements, and the dangers of governments and companies intercepting private correspondence. "Cookies," which are small bits of information stored on a users computer by Web servers, are one of the predominant ways of collecting information about visitors to Web sites, ostensibly to facilitate interaction with the user. However, information about shopping habits, personal preferences, and personal data can be combined for direct marketing and other perhaps more pernicious uses. Cookie files can be left on the user's hard drive to be accessed for future sessions. While users can "opt out" of the cookies system by simply turning them off, most do not know the relevant steps to do this, and more to the point, typical Internet users do not know what cookies are, why they are collected, and how they might be employed to ends that the user might find controversial. While some users may be happy to receive information tailored to their specific profile, others may prefer to not be part of a database that could be resold or unintentionally disclosed.

Another aspect of privacy issues concerns technology-enhanced eavesdropping. Technology now permits efficient monitoring practices—such as workplace monitoring of keystrokes, Web surfing, and e-mail; and at a different level, the U.S. Federal Bureau of Investigation developed Carnivore technology that when hooked into an Internet service provider is capable of scanning the online activities of millions and flagging "unusual" activity for closer surveillance.

The requirements for Internet privacy legislation are in the early stages of being understood. With the increase of online transactions of all kinds, policies will need to address under what conditions information can be collected and how it may subsequently be used. To date, many Web sites that collect information about users provide a privacy policy statement, outlining how collected information will—or will not—be used.

Many privacy issues overlap with security issues and, to some degree, if privacy issues are adequately addressed, then by default security issues are covered as well. Responsibility and requirements for ensuring security of databases; guidelines and criteria for collecting, processing, and handling information; and liability for not adhering to practices that protect individuals' right to privacy in all respects, including the online environment, all work to make for a stronger and more secure network. Conversely, from the security perspective, secure server identification provides the dual function of providing authentication of identity and of ensuring the security of confidential transaction information. However, confidentiality and other information about the transaction is still prone to subsequent misuse and also needs to be covered by privacy legislation. In recent years, the United States and Europe have been sparring to have competing policies adopted in this area.

Industry Issues

When the huge potential of the World Wide Web was just becoming apparent in the early 1990s, the Internet was still predominantly noncommercial and much speculation focused on how deployment and management of the infrastructure would be paid for. In the United States, and in effect therefore for much of the rest of the world, privatization was the answer. Within two years, there was an explosion of infrastructure, of content, and of course advertising; and doing business over the Internet for both electronic and nonelectronic goods began to take hold.

With digitization and media convergence, IPRs were inevitably heading into troubled waters and have sent tremors through the legislative and regulatory fronts. Potentially, software, music, books, film, and other digitizable products could be duplicated and shared over the Internet virtually for free. The music industry, with the sudden and explosive growth of Napster, which allowed people anywhere in the world to share music between their own hard disks, fought a high-profile battle to stem the free flow between music lovers. But it also opened up new horizons in what customers want in terms of immediate access and control and exposed how the industry was failing to address these. An analogous process has been taking place in telecommunications, where Internet telephony offers the same service at a small fraction of the price of conventional networks for international calls. Many of the issues were different for Internet telephony,[3] but both challenged, at least momentarily, the market dominance of major players in media and communications industries as well as some of the most powerful companies in the world.

Finally, shifts in market and market structures with increasingly larger mergers and corresponding dangers of oligopoly and predatory practices, and the globalization of media industries, raised in the Internet sector as well the need for a corresponding level of governance.

Technical Standards and Architecture

Technical choices for Internet architecture and design may also have economic, political, and social implications. The architecture—the underlying technology and technological configuration of the Internet—is of key importance to what can be done online and to the limits and possibilities for regulating and governing the online environment.

For instance, simple to use and more attractive user interfaces have been developed in order to enhance ease of use. However, as user interfaces become simpler, the technology behind them becomes more complex and the operation more opaque to the user. Early Internet software was typically open source software, that is, it was free and available to all to refine to their needs and develop further. But with the commercialization of the Internet, "private" networks such as AOL promoted their proprietary networks and interfaces. Internet standards and protocols have become more deeply embedded and entrenched, defining much more than technical infrastructure. The trade-off is a general difficulty in assessing the risks concerning privacy and surveillance, ever increasing vulnerability to viruses, and interfaces and software that inherently encourage a passive acceptance of packaged offerings. Examples of this include the default page that the browser is programed to take users to and cookies used to store and gather user information that can be turned to commercial advantage.

A further area of considerable dispute, based initially on what appeared to be merely a technical question, arose in relation to domain names and the right to use specific Internet addresses. Domain names acquired significant commercial value when it was realized that in the absence of a coherent online directory, they could effectively be used to provide reliable and simple means for people to locate the specific sites they were seeking—or conversely misdirect them to others that they were not. Cybersquatting practices involve acquiring domain names to resell them at an inflated price to someone who has a specific connection with the name, or to acquire a name with the intention of capitalizing on the reputation of the name in order to, for example, sell a similar product or service. In neither case does the cybersquatter have a legitimate claim to the domain name. And, in fact, demonstration of a claim has not been required to reserve or purchase a domain name, but can only be contested after the fact. Strategies to stem the incidence of cybersquatting are being implemented—in part by the introduction of new generic top-level domains (gTLDs; see textbox), through new reservation procedures, and by creating guidelines for who can apply for the different categories of gTLDs.

Issues of naming and numbering are no longer handled by domain name system (DNS) allocations, but rather by an increasingly entangled collection of economic and political disputes around domain names and trademarks, individual and corporate identities, and Internet administration and national jurisdictions. Thus, the framework within which technological standards and policies are formulated and implemented may also, in principle, be a matter for governance.

Governance Organizations

Before a more detailed consideration of ICANN, it is important to stress that it by no means stands alone in governing the Internet. The complexities of a global network of hundreds of millions of users, and innumerable systems and languages, requires coordination of policies and standards on a very grand scale and with great attention to detail. Although issues relating to content have the higher profile, the technical coordination of the system's plumbing and architecture has seen the creation of several new organizations and forced adaptation in others implicated in the plethora of standards required for the different and overlapping layers of Internet architecture.[4] ICANN's current importance and profile justifies its inclusion here, but at any time, others among these organizations could very quickly come to the fore in governance issues. The Internet has some way to go before its governance structures stabilize.

Many organizations are now concerned with different aspects of Internet management and functioning. Some have been formed specifically to address Internet issues such as the Internet Society (ISOC), created in 1992 by the Internet Architecture Board (IAB; known as the Internet Activities Board until 1992) as an independent, international organization of Internet professionals that provides coordination for the Internet and its internetworked technologies and applications. The IBA now oversees Internet administration and technical development activities. In 1986, the IAB created the Internet Engineering Task Force (IETF), which forms ad hoc working groups to address specific problems or technical issues such as standards and protocols. The International Organization for Standardization (ISO) accredited the IETF as an international standards body at the end of 1994. And, the Internet Research Task Force, like the IETF, is concerned with topics related to Internet protocols, applications, architecture, and technology, but focuses on long-term research concerning the Internet's future development.

In addition to the bodies formed under the ISOC umbrella, a number of sector-specific organizations have also been formed, the most prominent of these are the World Wide Web Consortium, a closed membership organization created in 1994 to develop common protocols that promote Internet evolution and ensure its interoperability, and finally the body of main concern to us here, the Internet Corporation for Assigned Names and Numbers, a nonprofit organization created in 1998 to oversee and manage Internet Assigned Numbers Authority (IANA) functions.

Existing world-level and regional organizations are also involved in various aspects of the global Internet order. These include the ITU, which is concerned primarily with physical and transport standards; the World Trade Organization for existing and emerging trade issues including many relating to IPR content; the World Intellectual Property Organization (WIPO; see textbox) in its advisory capacity for naming and trademark disputes; the UN Educational, Scientific, and Cultural Organization for cultural issues; and standards organizations such as the ISO, the American National Standards Institute, the European Telecommunications Standards Institute, and the International Trademark Association (INTA)—all of these organizations provide authority for particular layers of the network that fall within their expertise.

The Root Server System and the DNS

The root server system refers to a master list of all top-level domain (TLD) names (such as .com, .net, and .org, and the individual country codes—such as .ca and .nl). This root server is regularly updated and referred to by servers linked to the Internet. A key feature of DNS registration is ensuring that all names are unique—this is no small feat as there are currently in excess of 35 million registered domain names.* Uniqueness of naming is imperative for routing and because the Internet to date has yet to benefit from the development of an effective directory system. Often, corporate names are also the online corporate address, such as <www.cocacola.com>.**

The root system consists of thirteen file servers, maintained in separate geographical locations (ten in the United States, two in Europe, and one in Japan) for both security and efficiency of routing purposes. The central or "A" server is operated by VeriSign (who acquired Network Solutions Inc. [NSI] in 2000) under the administration of ICANN. VeriSign maintains and updates the master list of TDL names (in the form of a small data file), which in turn is replicated to the other twelve root servers on a daily basis.

The data file at the core of the root server system is known as the *legacy root* because it is the definitive official list of domain name registration. The legacy root comprises 244 country code TLDs; seven gTLDs (new ones are to be added; see further on), and one four-letter TLD (.arpa). However, creating TLDs outside of this system is technically possible. It is less well known that there exist a large number of alternative TLDs that are simply not recognized by most domain name servers.*** For these TLDs, individual users direct their software to use an alternate domain name server, thus having access to both the legacy root and whatever additional TLDs are also supported by that name server.

Previously, only standard letters and numbers from the Roman alphabet could be used for DNS registration. However, recently VeriSign has provided for registration in more than seventy languages, allowing for a new range of accents and characters.

Prominent current DNS issues concern the appointing of new TLDs by ICANN and further opening the DNS market to competition.

* For up-to-date statistics, see <http://www.domainstats.com/> [last accessed: 26 November 2001].

** Research is currently underway to develop an Internet-wide WHOIS directory. Offering a related service is RealNames, an entirely private name registration business, which sells keywords that can be used instead of domain names. Keywords are routed by RealNames to the licensed user of that word (e.g., "coke" is licensed to Coca-Cola). Unlike domain names, RealNames keywords cannot be resold, which prohibits cybersquatting.

*** For example, see <http://www.name-space.com> [last accessed: 26 November 2001], which offers 546 TLDs.

ICANN

ICANN evolved as a resolution to the conflict of how to assign Internet protocol (IP) addresses for the Internet in the new privatized context. Given the various strands of its roots and its course of evolution, governing the Internet on a global level inevitably became a hotbed of contention and passion. At one end of the spectrum is a strong coalition of users who feel that the Internet should not be regulated—but that as in the past, standards, practices, and applications should be allowed to evolve organically. At the other end are others whose use of the Internet puts a premium on security, total reliability, and constant innovation and expansion, and who thus demand centralized concerted governance efforts (though of varying kinds). In between these two poles, there is room for negotiation—and in one instance, this resulted in the creation of ICANN. Not surprisingly, views regarding the legitimacy of ICANN's claim to represent all Internet users range from the cynical to the utopian.

As its name suggests, the Internet Corporation for Assigned Names and Numbers is responsible for managing the process of assigning names and numbers for the Internet. Formed in October 1998 as a nonprofit private-sector corporation, ICANN coordinates the DNS, the allocation of IP address space, and manages the root server system. At the most fundamental level of Internet architecture is the DNS, which is the means to control routing of Internet traffic. The DNS relies on a single data file (the legacy root—see textbox) that contains all the Internet naming and numbering information. With the privatization and explosion of the World Wide Web in the mid-1990s, corporate presence very quickly became both an imperative and a new site of contention. The possibility of using names to designate a Web site—rather than a numerical IP address—now meant that companies expected to be able to claim trademarked words and phrases in cyberspace in addition to the rights already held for exclusive commercial use. The mandate of

ICANN is predominantly technical. However, decisions it takes for future naming and numbering architecture will have profound social and economic consequences for some and benefits for others. In its self-representation, ICANN has focused on its technical mandate—and does not formally acknowledge the political mandate inherent in this.

ICANN's very brief history has from the start been the subject of much controversy. Most of the issues that plague and define it as an organization have their roots in the acrimonious history between the ISOC and NSI. In part, this can be understood in terms of decentralized and organic evolution of the Internet and tension introduced by calls for a more centralized and controlled approach. A similar problematic was the intent of the U.S. Department of Commerce to retain U.S. control over the legacy root. Thus, we begin ICANN's brief history at the point when naming and numbering could no longer be fulfilled under the direction of one computer scientist, and plans for transition to a more formal body fell under the scrutiny of previously uninvolved parties.

A Brief Prehistory

Until 1994, most of the IANA functions were administered by Internet pioneer Jon Postel and supported by funding from the Defense Advanced Research Projects Agency. However, there was an increasing need to institutionalize the process, as domain name registration was growing at an exponential rate (from 300 per month in 1992, to 45,000 per month by late 1995[5]). Postel proposed that IANA administration be privatized under the auspices of ISOC, but this was contested on the grounds that ISOC had no authority to either own or control the IANA process. Concurrent to this, NSI had been contracted by the U.S. National Science Foundation (NSF) to handle domain registrations for a fixed payment of $1 million per year. This agreement was revisited based on the exponential increase in registrations, and beginning in 1995 NSI was allowed to charge yearly fees to end users. Needless to say, with the Internet doubling its user base each year, these registration fees turned the administration into an attractive business.

NSI's profiting from Internet administration activities was problematic to much of the Internet community, including ISOC, which was intent on undermining NSI's monopoly in domain name registration. Postel drafted another plan for decentralization that included the implementation of 150 new gTLDs to be administered by registries around the world and overseen by ISOC.

In response to strong private-sector opposition and lacking the legitimacy and clout to mobilize action based on Postel's second proposal,

ISOC brought together an International Ad Hoc Committee (IAHC) to continue pressure to introduce competition for domain name registration. The IAHC initiative was more strategic in that it called on the participation of WIPO, INTA, ITU, NSF, and ISOC technical expertise. Ultimately, its proposal to recognize domain names as a public resource, and to create the Council of Registrars under the auspices of the ITU, was opposed by the U.S. government. The U.S. government supported industry self-regulation and was wary of the proposal to subject Internet administration to Swiss law. Furthermore, the IHAC proposal returned ultimate control to national governments, sending up red flags to the business sector, which preferred a position of control over development and implementation of standards setting.

Because of the publicity and debate generated and new alliances initiated in the IHAC process, the U.S. government responded with its own series of interventions, most notably the Clinton administration's eCommerce Paper,[6] the Notice of Inquiry on domain name policy,[7] the White Paper[8] outlining the proposal to move the naming and numbering administration to private-sector self-regulation, and the subsequent International Forum on the White Paper that detailed a proposal for a nonprofit, private-sector corporation that would work in concert with the NSI and the Commerce Department.

Thus, in 1998, ICANN was established as a private, nonprofit, California corporation, and was officially recognized by the Commerce Department as responsible for the Internet naming and numbering process. In the short term, this diffused some of the Commerce Department's fears of losing control of the DNS, and aspirations for a framework for a global governance institution were realized.

Initial and Current Structure and Main Activities

In addition to its designated function, much of ICANN's initial preoccupation has been with consolidating its organizational structure and posts (see fig. 8.1). The first nine members of the ICANN board were chosen by Postel. By September 2000, this interim board[9] was to be replaced with a board comprising nineteen directors of which nine would be elected by three supporting organizations, nine elected by the at large membership, and the chief executive officer, hired by the elected board members.[10] Although the interim board was also intended to be replaced at the time of election, in 1999 its members controversially redefined themselves as "initial" members, with an extended term and with four of these continuing an unelected second term, only leaving five of the directors to be elected by the at-large membership.

ICANN Organizational Chart

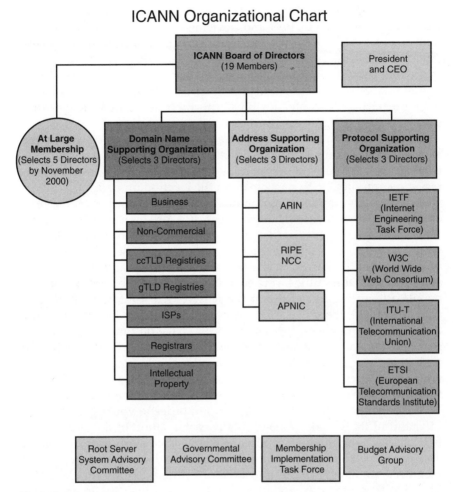

Figure 8.1

Characteristics of who would formally constitute the "at-large membership" was not defined in the White Paper beyond the requirement that the organization be "representative of Internet users around the globe" and that policies "will depend on input from the broad and growing community of users."[11] In fact, whether ICANN would be a *membership* (or *user*), rather than a *professional*, organization was one of the more contested issues during the International Forum on the White Paper process. As a result, provisions for membership were written only into ICANN's bylaws, rather than into the more permanent articles of incorporation, and thus have been vulnerable to weakening and potentially to elimination. In 1998, ICANN's interim board began the process of concretizing the provision for membership, creating the Membership Advisory Committee in 1999 and devising the subsequent online election process. A proposal for indirect elections was strongly opposed. Thus, as a first real attempt of a form of decentralized global governance, the call for an at-large voting membership provided users with the semblance of an opportunity to govern the Internet, and with elections purporting to confer legitimacy to the organization, it was in a sense recalling the grassroots origins of the Internet.

Candidates for the five ICANN director positions to be elected by the at-large membership were first identified by an ICANN nominating committee, and subsequently nominations were accepted from the "Internet community."[12] To participate in the election process, individuals were required to complete an online application, supplying an e-mail address and a verifiable postal address. ICANN then sent (by normal post) a personal identification number (PIN) to each applicant, who would in turn confirm by e-mail to register his or her entitlement to vote. Between the launch of the registration process and the elections, some technical difficulties were encountered due to the sheer volume of people attempting to register at the ICANN site; and having successfully registered, there was no certainty that ICANN's letter containing the would-be member's PIN code would arrive on time—especially in regions with unreliable postal service. Analysis of the demographics of registrants indicates that there were membership drives within various regions and sectors.[13] In the end, there were only 158,000 online registrations from an estimated pool of over 400 million online. Of these, only 76,000 activated their membership in order to vote by using their PIN; and of those, only 34,035 actually cast a ballot. In the end, the official ICANN–nominated candidate was elected with only 130 valid votes cast for all of Africa. North America and Europe alone elected member-nominated candidates—both of whom are committed to fighting what they see as excessive corporate control over the Internet and to reforming ICANN around issues of transparency and accountability from within.

Achieving representative democracy at an international level is a formidable task, especially in such a new context where there exist few tried and tested formulae. In addition to procedural shortcomings, however, the at-large membership elections have also been criticized as not involving a wide enough constituency. ICANN's mandate to ensure only that Internet users are represented already embodies the Digital Divide by excluding those who do not yet have access to the Internet from decisions pertaining to its design and administration. Nonusers and would-be users are thus reliant on other bodies to lobby for the representation of their interests.

Uniform Dispute Resolution

All DNS registrants must agree to adhere to ICANN's Uniform Dispute Resolution Policy (UDRP), which directs disputes to ICANN arbitration providers. When registering a domain name, registrants accept, in the fine-print terms and conditions, to commit themselves to this process. The procedure is a method to resolve disputes out of court, can be initiated by any registrant, and is primarily limited to cyberpiracy and cybersquatting cases. ICANN can revoke the right to use a domain name or transfer it to its "rightful" owner. Other forms of redress must be sought through legal action, and likewise, decisions under the UDRP are subject to challenge by court action. WIPO reports that of the cases completed to date, about 65 percent involved a transfer of domain name.

WIPO's Role in ICANN

In the U.S. White Paper that established ICANN, WIPO was called on to write a report to advise ICANN on IPR issues. This report would:

1. Develop recommendations for a uniform approach to resolving trademark/domain name disputes involving cyberpiracy (as opposed to conflicts between trademark holders with legitimate competing rights)
2. Recommend a process for protecting famous trademarks in the gTLDs
3. Evaluate the effects, based on studies conducted by independent organizations, such as the National Research Council of the National Academy of Sciences, of adding new global gTLDs and related dispute resolution procedures on trademark and intellectual property holders

The final version, "Report on the First WIPO Internet Domain Name Process," issued on April 30, 1999, was the starting point for ICANN's subsequent Domain Name Dispute Resolution Policy. Additionally, WIPO is key in the UDRP process and was the first of four "dispute resolution service providers" to be approved.

The "Report on the Second WIPO Internet Domain Name Process," which is expected to be published in mid-2001, will address issues that arose during the first consultation, but that were deemed to be outside of its scope of inquiry. These issues include personal names; international non-proprietary names for pharmaceutical substances, recommended by the World Health Organization to protect patient safety worldwide; names of international intergovernmental organizations, such as the United Nations; geographical indicators; and trade names.

Competition for Domain Name Provision

The introduction of a Shared Registration System has meant the end of VeriSign's monopoly over TLD registration (.com, .net, and .org) and registry administration. In spite of a transition to competition in registration provision that began in late 1998, the incumbent positioning of VeriSign and recent backroom machinations have caused major crises of confidence in ICANN's governance abilities. At present, ICANN is accepting applications for registrar accreditation on a "rolling basis." There are currently about 170 registrars, however VeriSign still retains approximately 40 percent of the business.

New gTLDs

The key reasons for proposing new gTLDs, according to VeriSign, include the overcrowding of the .com space; the intention to reflect the Web's global nature; to be able to reinforce the meaning of the original gTLDs, and subsequent gTLDs as well, by providing new categories that confer more information; and to decrease the potential for cybersquatting by making attractive domain names less scarce.[14] By adding new gTLDs, companies and organizations intent on preserving their identity in the online environment would be required to police against use of their names for all gTLDs, buy new gTLDs, and undergo some form of arbitration for perceived contravention of use of proprietary names. Because of the costs this would incur to individual businesses and organizations, during the proposal's first year ICANN faced significant opposition to introducing new gTLDs.[15] However, the decreasing pool of available names in the existing gTLDs—particularly for .com and the new domains—contributed to changing the climate. The new gTLDs were accepted and more are expected.

Summing Up

The U.S. "national" Internet began with restricted access, then opened up to educational and research institutions. In both of these contexts, content—and regulation of content—was limited to a text-based environment. There were no real regulation hurdles, as most contraventions (or perceived ones) could be dealt with using existing local laws. Technical evolution has required new bodies to coordinate change and to ensure effective and efficient Internet operations—especially as the private sector is ever increasingly entrenched in the functioning of the Internet and as governments are increasingly cognizant of the Internet's inherent economic growth potentials. Evolving from informal self-regulation of a small community of users, regulation of the Internet has spread to different levels and bodies of governance. With the pending arrival of the third generation of Internet—which will involve new architecture, protocols, interfaces, and possibilities for content—there is and will continue to be a need for much higher levels of coordination and negotiation of different sectors of user groups than currently have been created.

The governance model represented by ICANN is radically different from the other institutions examined in this book. Most importantly, ICANN is positioned as a nongovernmental alternative to the intergovernmental system that is the norm. If this were the only difference, it would be a relatively simple matter to compare ICANN with any of the others and draw conclusions about ICANN's model. However, the very narrow scope of its mandate and its limited budget ($6.5 million as opposed to, for example, the ITU's $200 million) make it more readily comparable to a single technical committee of the ITU, for example, without the competence, the mandate, or the legitimacy to take on a broader and more political agenda.

Nevertheless, ICANN does provide a model for a new way of practicing global governance of media and communications. Clearly, ICANN constitutes a unique model of global governance; however, it is too early in the Internet century to predict whether the model will work. At present, for the very limited mandate of technical coordination of naming and numbering, there is still a lacuna of legitimacy and a corresponding façade of participation at the individual user level. Internet governance will need a much broader global vision, whether from ICANN or elsewhere.

Notes

1. The United States and Canada are virtually unique in the world in their adoption of a flat-rate billing regime that gives consumers unlimited local telephone calls for a low monthly fee. Flat-rate billing is often cited as one of the reasons why the Internet was adopted much earlier in North America. Many European and a few developing countries have introduced reduced-rate calls for Internet access.

2. E. Hargittai, "Standing before the Portals: Non-profit Websites in an Age of Commercial Gatekeepers," *info* 2, no. 6 (December 2000).

3. See International Telecommunication Union, *ITU Internet Reports: IP Telephony* (Geneva: International Telecommunication Union, 2001).

4. These different layers of standards include physical, transport, server and routing, security, presentation, and content.

5. Milton Mueller, "ICANN and Internet Governance: Sorting through the Debris of 'Self-Regulation,'" *info* 1, no. 6 (1999): 500.

6. "A Framework for Global Electronic Commerce," The White House, <http://www.ecommerce.gov/framewrk.htm>, 1 July 1997 [last accessed: 26 November 2001].

7. U.S. Department of Commerce, "NTIA, Request for Comments," 62 Fed. Reg. 35896, 2 July 1997 (Washington, D.C.: U.S. Department of Commerce, 1997).

8. U.S. Department of Commerce, "Statement of Policy, Management of Internet Names and Addresses," 63 Fed. Reg. 31741 (Washington, D.C.: U.S. Department of Commerce, 1998), <http://www.ntia.doc.gov/ntiahome/domainname/6_5_98dns.htm> [last accessed: 26 November 2001].

9. The original board consisted of four Americans, three Europeans, one representative from Japan, and one from Australia.

10. As provided in the White Paper, ICANN would "appoint, on an interim basis, an initial Board of Directors (an Interim Board) consisting of individuals representing the functional and geographic diversity of the Internet community. The Interim Board would likely need access to legal counsel with expertise in corporate law, competition law, intellectual property law, and emerging Internet law. The Interim Board could serve for a fixed period, until the Board of Directors is elected and installed, and we anticipate that members of the Interim Board would not themselves serve on the Board of Directors of the new corporation for a fixed period thereafter." See U.S. Department of Commerce, "Statement of Policy, Management of Internet Names and Addresses."

11. U.S. Department of Commerce, "Statement of Policy, Management of Internet Names and Addresses."

12. See ICANN, "Call for Recommendations and Expressions of Interest," <http://www.icann.org/committees/nomcom/call.htm> [last accessed: 26 November 2001].

13. Member count by region: Africa 315; Asia and Pacific 38,246; Europe 23,442; Latin America and the Caribbean 3,548; and North America 10,632. See ICANN, "At-Large Membership," <http://www.members.icann.org/activestats.html> [last accessed: 26 November 2001].

14. VeriSign, "Journey to the Right of the Dot: ICANN's New Web Extensions," VeriSign, Inc., <http://newdomains.networksolutions.com/gtld/tm_landingpage.jsp>, 2001 [last access: 26 November 2001].

15. The new TLDs are .aero, .biz, .coop, .info, .museum, .name, .pro.

III

9

Global Media Regulation

Part II outlined the activities of the main global governance institutions, analyzed their relevance to the media, presented the main media related issues on their respective agendas, and described their governance structures. This chapter takes a cross-cutting look at these, framing the individual institutions in a broader picture. It addresses the following questions:

- At different historical times, what has been the main rationale behind the emergence of media regulation on the world stage?
- What currently is the scope of international regulation?
- Who are the main actors in governing these, and how do they exert influence inside and outside the institutions?
- What are the main instruments used for regulating media at the global level?

Part III draws conclusions regarding just how effective the current and merging institutions are and in whose interests they operate.

THE EVOLVING RATIONALE FOR GLOBAL REGULATION

The desire to regulate media and communications at the international level, then the global level, has arisen historically in three broad phases as characterized by their rationale:

- The initial phase justified primarily by the economic logic of the industrial revolution, but accommodating the societal concerns of the time.

119

- A second phase marked by the emergence of the UN system, the expanded presence of developing countries as they gained their independence, and the increasingly vocal participation of these countries' global governance bodies. Societal and human rights aspects came to prominence at the international level.
- The current phase, coinciding with a weakening of the UN system and in which the economic, and specifically the trade, rationale is emphasized, now directly challenging regulation for the societal role of the media.

Phase One: Industry-Driven Internationalization

The initial impulse for international regulation and institutional development came from the media's role in economic development and internationalization, specifically in communication and intellectual property rights (IPRs).

A pressing need for multilateral cooperation was first felt by governments in the telecommunications sector. The International Telegraph Union was founded in 1865 to enable nationally owned telegraph networks to interconnect and communicate efficiently across national boundaries, with agreement on compatible standards and on sharing revenues from tariffs between national carriers for the leg of the service provided in each country. Forty years later, wireless communication received the same attention. A desire to support interconnection and reduce private monopoly power led to the first agreements on the allocation of radio frequencies in Berlin in 1906 and, indirectly, to the establishment of radio frequencies as a public good. The International Radiotelegraph Union was formed soon after and the two merged in 1932 to become the International Telecommunication Union (ITU).

Alongside but independent of these developments, concern was rising about the economic rights of industrial inventors on the one side, and creative artists on the other. IPRs, including patents and copyright, had evolved at the national level since the early eighteenth century, driven by print technology and the Enlightenment, and were relatively sophisticated. Internationally, however, they were very weak. In industry, this led to unauthorized replication of industrial inventions across borders without compensation for the inventors, which in turn was holding back investment and innovation. In the creative arts and media, especially books, widespread reproduction and plagiarism were causing similar problems.

Thus, two intergovernmental conventions, the Paris Convention on the Protection of Industry Property, covering patents and trademarks, and the Berne Convention on Literary and Artistic Works, covering copyright, were agreed to during the 1880s and were soon to share a common administration and, in effect, become a single institution—much later evolving into the World Intellectual Property Organization (WIPO).

By the early part of the twentieth century, key regulatory pillars of the media were in place. IPRs were secured, the sharing of radio spectrum became the subject of intergovernmental agreement, and a forum existed to agree to technical standards for international interconnection and general compatibility. This system proved relatively robust in adapting to economic and technical change and containing internal tensions up until the middle of the century. The appearance of public radio then television caused little disturbance to this international structure, since they were largely confined to national boundaries. Trade in media products continued along traditional lines or was relatively unproblematic such as in the film industry, which was initially dominated by Europe and later by the United States.

Although the driving force in setting up the international regulatory structures was economic, and their rationale was to secure an economic environment in which the media industry could operate internationally, there was at the same time a strand of concern for the societal aspects and the public sphere. The Berne Convention, for instance, established the moral rights of authors. There were disagreements, however. The United States refused to accede to the Berne Convention partly because of the moral rights granted to authors, which it saw potentially as a constraint on its media industry, especially film. (It signed only much later, when the overall climate had shifted decisively.)

In general, issues pertaining to societal regulation arose only rarely. However, only a relatively small number of industrialized and mainly European countries in the West was involved. Their colonies—which comprised much of the world—were included in the agreements, though the impact, if any, was indirect. Social, political, and cultural issues, and the public sphere generally, were relatively segregated from each other behind national barriers and were matters for only national concern.

Phase Two: New Issues, New Players

The Second World War marked a watershed in the thinking of the major powers, who had unleashed such destruction on the world. The international agenda was forcefully imbued with a normative and human rights aspect fuelled by the horrors and destruction of the war. International regulation of isolated sectoral matters as they arose was clearly inadequate, and the failure of the League of Nations formed after the First World War underpinned the case for a system of global governance much broader and deeper in scope. A suite of international governance organizations was hastily designed and drafted under the umbrella of the United Nations that attempted to create systematically a comprehensive framework within which economic and social cooperation could be pursued at the global level. Not all of these institutions were to survive the realpolitik that soon set in, particularly in the area of economic cooperation, but those that did contributed to a new agenda for media and communications.

The Universal Declaration of Human Rights, adopted in 1948, set down a normative context for international cooperation. Article 19 states: "Everyone has the right to freedom of opinion and expression; this right includes freedom to hold opinions without interference and to seek, receive and impart information and ideas through any media and regardless of frontiers."

In media and communications, the UN Educational, Scientific, and Cultural Organization (UNESCO) added a new dimension to international cooperation. For the first time, the value and diversity of cooperation on culture was recognized. Cooperation in education and science, a concern of precursors to UNESCO, was given fresh impetus including actions to support greater availability of educational and scientific materials and media. By 1950, just five years after its foundation, agreements were in place that promised to lubricate international circulation of media materials of all kinds, based on their cultural and educational value. UNESCO also introduced early on a concern for the safety and professionalism of journalism and of the news media.

However, the Second World War was a catalyst not only for global institutional development, but also for the geopolitical landscape in two further crucial respects: it provided a major impetus to struggles for independence by European colonies, which eventually led to a more active participation by developing countries in world affairs, and it began the slide toward the Cold War and the political and economic division of most of the world into two camps. These had a huge impact on the evolution of international relations and institutions in media, the former partially sustaining the impetus toward human rights and equity, the latter obscuring the core issues and polarizing and entrenching positions.

Technological developments, capitalizing on wartime- and Cold War–inspired innovations, were posing new challenges. The use of satellites for communication, with transmission footprints covering huge parts of the globe, raised to new heights the challenge of radio spectrum allocation and introduced the need to share out orbital slots between countries. This coincided from the late 1950s with the liberation of one colony after another, each in turn taking its seat at the United Nations and in its specialized agencies. For example, the ITU had only 70 members in 1945, compared to its current 189. Only a few years after the war, less industrialized countries accounted for a majority and by 1971 voted, against Western opposition, to reserve orbital slots on the basis of equal rights for all countries, even where countries were not likely to be in a position to utilize them for some time—the circumstance of most of them. Although this decision has yet to be tested in the important geostationary orbit (most less industrialized countries lack the technical and financial capacity to claim their slots), the rejection of a first-come first-served allocation prevented, at least in principle, the establishment of what in effect would have been permanent occupation by the wealthy countries.

However, potentially the most far-reaching movement of this phase was the New World Information and Communication Order (NWICO) debate during the 1970s and 1980s. As part of wider demands for a restructuring of the world economy with intergovernmental intervention to secure development goals, the NWICO debate, as pursued by the Non-Aligned Movement of nations in UNESCO and elsewhere, brought a fundamental normative issue to bear on media and communications. NWICO argued on the basis of equity and human rights for changes in international communications flows, support for communications infrastructure development, democratization of communications structures, and action to address cultural domination by the media. Perceived as threatening by Western media and many governments, and manipulated by both the United States and the Soviet Union in Cold War skirmishes, the movement was defeated in the end, culminating with the withdrawal of the United States and the United Kingdom from UNESCO (depriving it of 30 percent of its budget) and the realignment of UNESCO with Western interests. While UNESCO continued to support various media programs in less industrialized countries, it no longer offered a forum for debate on the fundamental aims and means of international media governance and regulation.

Other international institutions promoted a broadly development oriented agenda in media. In 1984, an ITU independent commission, the Maitland Commission, proposed a set of far-reaching interventions to improving telecommunications in less industrialized countries, including the creation of a fund for infrastructure development from international tariff settlements. The ITU also decided to restructure, creating a third sector, the Development Sector, alongside radio communications and telecommunications standardization. The new sector was devoted specifically to telecommunications in less industrialized countries.

During this time the issue of IPRs was also rising in importance, as information came to play a more central economic role and the use and value of copyright grew. WIPO and UNCTAD, working with the Berne, Paris, and subsequent agreements, began to work with less industrialized countries to design IPR regimes suited to their development needs.

However, since the early 1980s, the normative, human rights, and societal aspects of international media regulation have been increasingly silenced. The reinstatement of a narrow "free-flow of information" doctrine at UNESCO, the failure of the ITU Development Sector to deliver what many less industrialized countries had hoped it would in terms of accelerating telecommunications development, and the omission of social and cultural considerations in the emerging trade agreements on media and communications all contributed to a climate in which commercial concerns would come to the fore.

The experience of the UN/UNESCO offspring, the World Commission on Culture and Development, is instructive. In 1995, it called for reinforcement of international-level cooperation on the media's capacity to support cultural diversity and democratic discourse. Concentration of media ownership at the international level was raised, and the case was made for a global public sphere in which there is room for alternative voices and for a global subsidy for public service and community media. These proposals never made it to the subsequent UNESCO conference in 1998 and have since sunk without a trace.

Phase Three: Tilting to Trade

The third phase is characterized by the rise and consolidation of the liberalization agenda in media globally. The General Agreement on Tariffs and Trade (GATT)—and, decisively, its successor the World Trade Organization (WTO)—became the single most powerful intergovernmental actor in media and communication, despite—or rather because of—its exclusive focus on international trade issues.

Postwar institution building to achieve peace, development, and human rights objectives was to include under the United Nations three new institutions: the International Monetary Fund to secure stable exchange rates, the World Bank to provide loans, and a third, eventually emerging as GATT, to ensure stability in trade relations. Instead of a coordinated set of instruments for balanced global development, what emerged were three institutions stripped of many of their development functions. In trade, GATT came equipped solely to eliminate barriers.

At first, GATT had nothing to do with media at all. Developments in the media industry, and especially in the "copyright" industries of publishing, music, film, video, television, and software, were to change this. From early in the middle of the twentieth century, these industries had been concentrating ownership and establishing cross-sectoral linkages, especially in the United States. With growing control over distribution and dissemination of intellectual property, contractual agreements between creators and exploiters of ideas swung slowly but surely in favor of the latter. Media corporations became ever larger, with bulging content portfolios and massive production facilities. As they spread to new markets internationally, they recognized the potential losses accruing from unauthorized copying of their content especially in poorer countries. This accelerated with advances in reproduction technologies of photocopying, audiotapes, video, computers, and printing, raising anew the issue of IPRs. Now, however, industry was less concerned with patent and industrial property rights than with copyright of ideas over which it had effective control. Information was coming to the fore.

The problem facing these industries was that existing IPR regimes, overseen by WIPO and by UNESCO, were, like virtually every international agreement, weak in terms of enforcement. Pursuing cases through national courts, often with only poorly articulated national law and with many countries claiming alternative, sometimes development-oriented, definitions of IPRs, was slow, laborious, and uncertain in outcome. Furthermore, the copyright industries, through the representations of their national delegations, had relatively limited control over these organizations. GATT, over which Western countries had, in practice, much greater control, offered a better prospect. In the mid-1980s, the wealthy countries forced telecommunications and IPRs onto the GATT agenda for the next round. By the completion of the Uruguay Round in the mid-1990s, they had translated this into a comprehensive agreement in IPRs that came into force in WTO member countries in 2000. With the Trade-Related Aspects of Intellectual Property Rights (TRIPS) agreement, the newly formed WTO had the power to police IPRs and to impose major sanctions on countries failing to implement the agreement, including, in many cases, countries that were not members of the WTO.

A few years earlier, international satellite broadcasting of television signals for reception by the public came on the agenda, regarding whether or not prior consent would be required from the receiving nation. Initially enjoying strong affirmative support from many countries—not just developing countries, but also France and the Soviet Union—on grounds of preserving the sovereignty of their airspace and potential social, cultural, and economic damage, the question wound its way through UNESCO and the ITU in the 1970s and 1980s, slowly gaining momentum. The United States, not surprisingly, was the main proponent of the free flow of satellite signals. Others took the middle ground arguing for bilateral agreements. In the end, no agreement was reached, which in practice opened the door to regional and global satellite television broadcasters that have become commonplace today. In effect, this leaves the area free from intergovernmental regulation and primarily though not exclusively in the realm of private broadcasting corporations. Satellite broadcasting companies such as CNN and Sky had a significant ripple effect during the 1990s in turning national media sectors in Europe and elsewhere toward a market model.

Another area in which the winds of change were felt was in the "accounting rate" regime in telecommunications. Since the beginning, the

ITU was the forum in which (mostly national monopoly) telecommunications carriers struck a rate at which each would pay the other for completion of calls over the latter's network. During the 1990s, the system came under increasing pressure as many of its presuppositions—such as monopoly carriers contained within national boundaries—were challenged by the changes introduced with liberalization of the sector. Unilateral action by the United States upped the pace of change, and in practice the old system is being eliminated in favor of market-based mechanisms governed in a general manner through the WTO. The net effect is that the existing (unplanned and fortuitous) financial transfer to many less industrialized countries (as well as some major industrialized ones) is diminishing or has disappeared, with U.S. telecommunications companies being the main beneficiaries. But this was merely a symptom of a liberalization process that transformed the telecommunications sector worldwide from one of national monopolies—many extensions of government departments—interacting through the ITU, to one of competing global carriers interacting on the market. A byproduct of this was the reduction in importance of certain global regulatory activities, especially within the ITU.

In short, this phase saw a significant shift of the regulatory structures toward a market- or industry-dominated model, with robust international agreements in place to enforce economic aspects, and a veering away from an emphasis on the social, cultural, and political roles of media and communications.

The three phases described earlier should not be seen as simply an original industry model of regulation, followed by a brief focus on human rights in the moral afterglow of the Second World War, and then a reassertion of the industry model. Many qualitative changes were wrought by the economic and political dynamics of the different phases, and the specific features of current globalization mold the current phase. The media industry today is different in several vital respects that strongly influence the form of regulation that is required:

- Whereas the media industry up to the middle of the twentieth century was primarily contained within national boundaries, it is now increasingly global, both in terms of the transnationalization of firms and the creation and expansion of global markets
- The means to enforce key aspects of private media industry rights, especially IPRs, are now far more powerful than ever seen before, with the global level now driving national-level regimes
- As compared especially to the second phase, media ownership is increasingly private and driven by market considerations, and its relations with regulatory regimes are more indirect

- At the global level, the industry is highly centralized—controlled by a small number of interlinked corporations
- Distinctions between the different media have declined in the context of convergence and cross ownership, and new media have emerged

While these features point to the dominance of the commercial aspect, it is inaccurate to characterize the social, cultural, and human rights aspects as enjoying merely a temporary flowering, to be relegated to permanent secondary status. The global framework does retain key elements of such regulation, and milestones, such as Article 19 of the Universal Declaration of Human Rights, have not lost their moral force.

Thus, the balance of factors is relatively fluid and dynamic, and in a future phase its guiding rationale could look very different again. The appearance of the Internet, which calls into question so much of received wisdom concerning regulation and governance may indeed be a harbinger of change.

FROM NATIONAL TO INTERNATIONAL: THE SCOPE OF REGULATION

Having looked at the broad temporal phases of regulation, a second perspective emerges from a consideration of which aspects of national regulation have been replicated at the international level and why. At first glance, it might seem plausible that the scope of international regulation would aspire to that previously found at the national level. If so, we could judge the level of maturity of international regulation in terms of the progress made in this process. Yet, there neither could nor should be a simple correspondence between the scope of media regulation nationally and its scope internationally.

Global institutions generally emerge and evolve subject to the principle of subsidiarity, by which decision-making power resides closest to the level at which decisions are implemented. The maxim "If it can be done at national level, then it should be" is backed by both practical and political considerations. Since nations jealously guard their sovereignty, agreement on regulation beyond national level is likely only where a very acute need is felt, and then only in some domains. Thus, the rationale for regulation at the national level will not correspond to an analogous, equally pressing, rationale at the international level.

Nevertheless, an item-by-item comparison of regulation at the two levels does expose any gaps where regulation could have, but has not, been brought to the international level and how in practice they have fared. This in turn will tell us something about the forces and interests that have driven the process.

Two different justifications were set out in chapter 1 for media regulation, with a number of measures under each: industry regulation and societal regulation.

Industry Regulation

Nationally, regulation of the media as an industry sector has given rise to a number of instruments. Internationally, too, the industry aspect has been the major impetus to regulation for most of the last couple of centuries, and it is here we find the most developed instruments.

- The regulation of IPRs, pursued under WIPO by mutual enforcement through the national courts, but now with its own enforcement procedures in the WTO through the TRIPS agreement, has achieved the strongest international dimension of all. Whatever the stated rationale, the force behind the TRIPS agreement was less a mutually recognized need for strong regulatory measures, than the pursuit of self-interest by the most powerful nations and players. For most developing countries, the need for agreement was experienced as a fear of losing out in other areas of vital national interest, for instance directly through the continued exclusion of vital sectors such as agriculture from general negotiations, or indirectly through unilateral retaliatory measures.
- The allocation of radio spectrum also has a global counterpart to national regulation, not only because of the need to regulate transmission across national borders, but laterally because of the invention of satellite and the capacity to broadcast over huge swathes of the world at once. This area, too, has a robust enforcement capacity in the ITU, but the need for agreement is more mutual in that in its absence everyone loses out—radio frequencies are a scarce resource that all can access, but they are valueless if their use is not coordinated.
- Standardization to ensure compatibility, interconnection, and a smoother market is also the subject of international regulation. It is of a voluntary nature, but there are strong incentives to abide by the agreements. Here, the international level has even taken over what had in earlier times been mainly a national concern—the migration of standards from national to international levels is long gone in most technologies. However, the process remains highly contentious since huge commercial interests can be tied up in gaining international acceptance of a standard.

Not all areas of national regulation are raised to the international level.

- Limits on the concentration of ownership in media, to prevent monopoly control and distortion of the market, have no counterpart at the global level. However, an analogous case can be made for them. Global concentration of ownership, major sectoral cross-ownership, and vertical integration of the industry give rise to concerns over the extent of control that is exerted and to how this affects competition, both at the national and global level. On the one hand, global media conglomerates have managed to escape national regulation since they operate from beyond the jurisdiction of most countries; on the other hand, they face virtually nonexistent international regulation.

  Establishing fair conditions of access to infrastructure and to gateways between "layers" of the media industry is another area of national legislation, a step up from regulating for media concentration. Here also there exists no international counterpart, although increasingly the layers of the industry are transnational in scope.

- Regulation for universal service does not exist at the international level, although the same economic argument applies as at the national level—that the extension of a communications network brings about a general improvement in the utility of the network by allowing existing network users to communicate with more people, thereby generating marginal network economies.

  At a macro level, it could be argued that universal service has been achieved without regulation, since satellite technology and market forces have ensured that virtually all of the world's countries have access to international telephone service, with the only ones that are not able to receive satellite broadcast signals or connect to the Internet being those with national policies that prohibit connection. However, universal service does not normally refer to whether a *country* has service, but whether its people do. And on balance, the lack of regulation at the global level has made equitable universal service a more distant goal for many of the world's poor. For example, the collapse of the accounting rate system for international telephony has brought about the end of a system by which international telephone revenues were used by many countries to finance the expansion of basic telephone infrastructure. With the Internet, the situation is even more inequitable since poorer countries must pay the entire cost of their connection to the Internet backbone in Europe or North America, regardless of the direction or origin of traffic. Whether a Peruvian consults an online database in the United States, or a Canadian hunts for a hotel on a Peruvian Web site, Peru pays the full cost of the international connection.

  Efforts to introduce universal service as a global governance issue have consistently provoked a hostile reaction from the rich countries.

The ITU's Maitland Commission proposed that international accounting rates (the mechanism by which telecommunications operators pay each other for completing calls) should be adapted to build up a special fund for telecommunications investment in less industrialized countries. Opposition from the wealthier countries, who pointed to the many anomalies in the accounting rate system, ensured it was never taken up. In the event, as mentioned earlier, the evolution of the accounting rate system was in the opposite direction. A proposal by the UN Development Program (UNDP) to help develop telephone and Internet infrastructure in poor countries with a $0.01 tax for every 100 e-mail messages was quickly dropped when it attracted the hostile attention of U.S. politicians.[1]

Some areas of regulation emerge only at the global level with no direct counterpart nationally, such as the previously mentioned accounting rate system. The need for regulation can also arise in what is already an international context. Regulation of the top-level Internet domain names .com, .org, and .net, for instance, was from the outset international in nature, though it was for a period administered by a single country. However, even here the regulations admitted at the global level have national repercussions and registering an Internet domain name now offers better protection for a corporation than trademark registration.

The development of technical standards has also shifted from the national to the international arena. Whereas telephony, radio, and television were first national and only later international communication media, the Internet began life as an international communication medium everywhere except the United States, where it was born of efforts to provide a national network. The fundamental decisions regarding the technical standards that underpin the Internet were made in the United States to meet the needs of its users and the capabilities of its infrastructures. Standards that might have sacrificed speed for robustness, and thus been better suited to the telecommunications infrastructures of developing countries, were not considered, even though they would have extended the effective life of many countries' infrastructures and saved them vast amounts of money. While the adoption of Internet standards is internationalizing, it is still largely driven by a commercial imperative, with social and developmental standards rarely receiving more than cursory attention.

Thus, a significant number of industry regulatory measures at the national level also receive attention internationally, sometimes even superseding national regulation, though the process of elevation has been somewhat selective.

Societal Regulation

As we saw in chapter 1, regulation at the national level is often justified in order to meet social, political, and cultural ends and to prohibit certain content considered to fall outside accepted normative or ethical boundaries of a given society. Compared to their national counterparts, global media governance bodies rarely engage in this type of intervention and they are much less active in this area than they are in their efforts to regulate global media as an industry.

Controlling concentration of ownership of the media in the interests of diversity and plurality, and to prevent monopoly political and editorial control by private interests, is recognized and commonly practiced at the national level. No such international mechanism exists within global media governance bodies, even in the form of monitoring trends and impacts. Nevertheless, in many countries, especially smaller and poorer ones, unregulated satellite transmission can comprise a large proportion, even the majority, of what is available and can thus distort national efforts at ensuring a diversity of media and sustaining national identity and culture. The inability of countries to regulate beyond their borders combined with the inability or unwillingness of global governance bodies to regulate globally means that as long as their home countries are content, there is little that can be done about the growing concentration of ownership and control of global media.

The other side of regulating for excessive control of media by private interests is ensuring the availability of media geared specifically toward supporting societal aims and sustaining a public sphere through public service media, again widely recognized at the national level. At present, there is no regulation to ensure that alongside private transnational media there could be transnational media for the public interest, although suggestions from reputable sources have called for them and a number of initiatives have been taken, most notably TV5, a French-language public broadcaster owned by national public broadcasters in Belgium, Canada, France, and Switzerland.

While this is clearly an area where UNESCO's mandate would justify it taking a leadership role, it has not done so, although it does work to promote the concept of national public service broadcasting. For its part, the WTO, as we have seen, has refrained from taking action that would define public broadcasting as anticompetitive, largely because of European opposition.[2]

Despite the inactivity, the argument can be sustained that transnational public service is particularly relevant in the context of the construction of a global civil society or public sphere, as a counterbalance to the creation of a globalized market and economy.

Other areas of regulation at the national level could also have global relevance. "Must-carry" obligations on cable carriers for local and nonprofit media, common in North America and Europe, could translate into a percentage of satellite broadcast capacity to be set aside for similar purposes globally. In the United States, the Federal Communications Commission (FCC) requires its direct broadcast satellite operators to reserve 4 percent of their video channel capacity for noncommercial and educational purposes, an interesting national precedent that could be ratcheted up internationally.[3] Universal service in telecommunications for reasons of social equity, as it exists for rural residents and certain social groups in many countries, is promoted by the ITU Development Sector, but there are no regulatory expressions of it and it exists as little more than an aspiration. Attempts by the Group of Eight to bridge the Digital Divide steer well clear of international regulatory actions and are embedded firmly within a highly liberalized unregulated dynamic.

There also exist a range of international conventions on cultural exchange and cooperation, but they have little direct impact on media and communications.

In the area of the release of information into the public domain, the flip side of securing economic IPRs for creators and owners, there is the Berne Convention, the Paris Convention, and subsequent international agreements. However, the TRIPS agreement, whose powerful enforcement measures put it in the driving seat internationally, has no specific support for, or concern for, the expansion of the public domain internationally and nationally, and many fear the gradual erosion of the minimal protection of the long-standing international agreements.

Prohibitive content regulation is a special case of societal regulation, in that its goal is to exclude very specific content, already created, on targeted media. Regulation regarding this exists at the national level everywhere. Social norms, religious tolerance, and political practices (including levels and forms of direct political repression) vary enormously from place to place, and this is reflected in diverse regimes of legal sanctions and censorship mechanisms. Because of this diversity, the prospects for agreement on multilateral regulation of content at the national level are slim—that is, governments are unlikely to cede sovereignty to an international body to regulate content within their jurisdictions. Thus, international regulation will not replace national regulation.

However, in the growing area of what can be termed transnational media—that is, media that originate outside the jurisdiction but whose entry is effectively beyond national control and therefore beyond national regulation—global regulation does become an issue. Shortwave radio, satellite broadcasting, and the Internet are three that have, at different times and in different ways, been subject to national attempts to censor or prevent content reception. Attempts to conclude international agreements to prohibit or exclude unwelcome transnational media, by preventing or influencing transmission in the country of origin, have not succeeded because they are confronted by a range of political and practical obstacles. In the absence of such an enforceable agreement, governments can do little in practice to influence the entry of signals, apart from costly and largely ineffective jamming, and the option of controlling the receiving end is often impractical. Transnational television, subject neither to national nor to global regulation (though sometimes choosing to negotiate with governments for access to larger markets), is now a reality, as has been shortwave radio for decades.

Controlling the content available on the Internet presents quite a different range of problems and possibilities and is still an active area of contention for many countries. For example, in 2001 civil rights groups opposed a Canadian proposal to make downloading child pornography from the Internet an offense punishable by up to five years imprisonment. The groups were concerned with the proposal's precedent-setting principle that merely accessing information was illegal and that policing the law would require technologically sophisticated monitoring of other Internet activities.

With respect to extraterritorial Internet content, the law is generally untested. In one celebrated case, the U.S. Internet company Yahoo! was ordered by a French court to bar French users from visiting Web sites selling Nazi paraphernalia. Yahoo!'s primary legal argument was that its services were U.S.–governed and therefore the sale of the material could not be banned because it would be a violation of the U.S. constitution's free speech guarantees. Yahoo! eventually gave in, removing Nazi material from all of its auctions worldwide, but it continues to appeal the case in the French courts. Meanwhile, urged on by the publicity, other sites have sprung up providing auction services for the banned material. In another case, AOL voluntarily closed down a member's site on its servers that parodied the Koran following protests and threats of legal action. Within days, the site reappeared on a number of servers worldwide, clearly showing the inability of current practices for regulating Internet content deemed offensive.

In 1999, UNESCO called a meeting of 300 specialists to consider ways of combating pedophilia and child pornography on the Internet. The resulting Declaration and Action Plan on Sexual Abuse of Children, Child Pornography, and Pedophilia on the Internet was comprehensive, calling for both indirect action such as research and awareness raising, as well as targeted-regulation by government, self-regulation by industry, and cooperation between government, nongovernmental organizations (NGOs), industry, and civil society. However, it is difficult to imagine this kind of action being taken in many other areas—child abuse is a suitable subject because it is universally rejected, whereas levels of religious and political tolerance or of sexual permissiveness vary widely between countries and are unlikely to build the consensus required for action.

Overall, then, and corresponding to our earlier analysis of the three phases, societal regulation at the international level remains weak and partial and in some areas is retreating with the ascendance of industry regulation. In some aspects, a clear rationale is evident for regulation to remain at the national level, on principles of subsidiarity or sovereignty, and for others to move on to the international and global levels driven by economic or other needs. But the politics of power also play a role. International regulation tends to emerge where:

- There is a compelling and mutually felt economic rationale that obviates subsidiarity (such as in technical standards and the allocation of spectrum)
- There is a rationale that is not universally accepted but is favored by a few players with the power to impose it on others (as in the case of intellectual property)
- There exists, for a period or over time, a strong moral or human rights imperative that potentially affects all parties, based on a mutual normative rationale (such as in the aftermath of the Second World War or the case of child pornography)

Agreement is unlikely to be reached, on the other hand, where there is no mutually compelling rationale for it or where the absence of regulation suits parties in a position to impose their will on others.[4]

INSTRUMENTS OF REGULATION

A third cut on regulation brings us beyond whether specific regulatory measures exist at the international level to the equally important issue of whether such regulation is effective.

In part I, we saw the instruments available at the national level for media regulation, specifically the courts, government departments, regulatory agencies with legislated powers, and various forms of self-regulation. Not surprisingly, these are somewhat different at the global level. The range is broader, extended by a set of possibilities located beyond the binding, and legally enforceable, regulation characteristic of the national level. Among the reasons is that agreements require ceding some degree of power to a collective entity, something that governments and other powerful groups resort to only where no other option better serves their interests (see textbox).

Freedom of Information: Binding but Unenforceable

Freedom of speech is often held up as a fundamental human right, subscribed to by all UN members and a universal standard to which all subscribe. But what does this mean in practice? It offers an interesting case study on instruments and enforceability.[5]

Article 19 of the Universal Declaration of Human Rights states: "Everyone has the right to freedom of opinion and expression; this right includes freedom to hold opinions without interference and to seek, receive and impart information and ideas through any media and regardless of frontiers."

It is a strong statement of rights, but in itself is nonbinding, just like the declaration as a whole. But it is incorporated as a legal standard into another treaty, which is binding, as Article 19 of the International Covenant on Civil and Political Rights (ICCPR), agreed to in 1996, which states that: "Everyone shall have the right to freedom of expression; this right shall include freedom to seek, receive and impart information and ideas of all kinds, regardless of frontiers, either orally, in writing or in print, in the form of art, or through any other media of choice." Various other elaborations on free speech and information rights have been agreed to, such as for children in the Convention of the Rights of the Child (1989 UN General Assembly) and to promote the "free flow of information at international and national levels, press freedom, independent and pluralistic media and a better balanced dissemination of information" in repeated UNESCO resolutions, but only the ICCPR has any instruments for enforcement of such rights.

However, there are limitations.

As a treaty rule, its binding force applies only to those states that have ratified the treaty. (A treaty comes into effect only when it is ratified by legislation in each signatory country, which can be much later or, in some cases, never.) Furthermore, derogation from this article, unlike for some others, is permissible.

The means of enforcement is based on an Optional Protocol to the ICCPR (meaning it is not obligatory to subscribe to it) and on Resolution 1503 adopted by ECOSOC in 1970. The former authorizes the Human Rights Committee of ECOSOC, made up of eighteen experts, to receive and consider communications from citizens of signatories of the Optional Protocol who claim to be a victim of a violation of the rights contained in the covenant. The protocol provides for communications from the complainant, governments, and others, as well as for analysis and reporting. The procedure is slow and confidential, and at the end of it there are no sanctions or compensatory measures available. The most that can be done is the publication of the evidence, along with the commission's views on it. In practice, even these have never been fully exercised by the commission.

It is no surprise that few have ever embarked on this route. Nevertheless, it is better than nothing, and it is important in that it relates to the rights of an individual person as opposed to the rights of the state. Furthermore, the absence of effective enforceability of this binding treaty has not diminished its moral impact over the decades since the signing of the Universal Declaration of Human Rights.

An international agreement can be interrogated with the following questions:

- Is the agreement informal, or is it legally binding?
- Is it specific concerning its intent, or does it sink under the weight of generalities and qualifications?
- Can its terms be readily and easily activated by signatories, or is it tightly controlled by a few?
- Does it contain specific sanctions for noncompliance?
- Does it have instruments to enforce these sanctions?
- Who has access to it? Only member states? Commercial interests? Civil society?

However, the efficacy of instruments does not necessarily rise with each successive affirmative answer.

Many international agreements on media are nonbinding on signatories, such as declarations, resolutions, and some treaties, and are akin to promises about future behavior. Although their force is thus moral, they may have significant influence if, for instance, public opinion mobilizes on the issue. And while they can often be ignored with impunity, in favorable conditions they can encourage relatively deep cooperation. Not just governments but NGOs have developed such accords: The 1992 UN Conference on Environment and Development and many international professional associations utilize common declarations as a means to develop and maintain common agendas.

Thus, it cannot be assumed that a legally binding agreement is necessarily more effective. If a nonbinding agreement yields in practice a greater willingness to cooperate, it may be more effective. Binding agreements can be hollowed out during negotiation by the insertion of numerous qualifying and get-out clauses and through a lack of specifics, or emasculated by voting and decision-making procedures that, legally or in practice, give preference to some groups over others.

Furthermore, in the absence of enforceable sanctions, binding agreements risk a high degree of noncompliance. If the agreement is genuinely to bind its adherents, the consequences of noncompliance must outweigh the consequences of compliance.

Fully enforceable sanctions for failure to meet legally binding agreements offer, in a formal sense, the best guarantee of compliance. They are not an option in most areas since only in the most persuasive of circumstances will governments hand over such power. They tend to emerge in highly contentious circumstances where major interests are at stake and where a very robust agreement is essential to securing the necessary level of cooperation. In other circumstances, attempts to pursue such an agreement could be counterproductive. A voluntary agreement may be adequate, even optimal, where a high degree of implicit consensus has been reached, and it may in its own time and with an accumulation of trust evolve toward a durable binding arrangement.

Within this context, the main instruments, differentiated by these features, can be enumerated as follows:

- Nonbinding instruments include declarations and resolutions of multilateral institutions, agreements to self-regulate, and guidelines for action. The number and prominence of signatories, and how many have been ratified, is a major determinant of their effectiveness.
- Binding instruments include treaties and regulations resulting from multilateral government negotiations, with some administered through the multilateral specialized agencies and others, such as the Universal Declaration of Human Rights, lacking a specific administrating body.
- Enforcement procedures begin at the weakest level with monitoring mechanisms and voluntary cooperation, progress to rules for binding arbitration the results of which are nonlegally enforceable but may risk expulsion, and on to the provision of legal enforcement with robust mechanisms for dispute resolution and the imposition of severe deterrent sanctions. Such sanctions can be delivered by means of agreement concerning prosecution in national courts, as in the Berne Convention on copyright; in the International Court of Justice, such as certain aspects of the Paris Convention on industrial property; or in the most extreme cases by means of instruments specially set up and agreed to for the purpose, such as the WTO procedures, to enforce the outcome of dispute procedures.

Overall, this diversity of instruments and institutions is indicative less of different requirements of regulation than of the extent to which all multilateral agreements and international regulation are subject to the broader political, economic, and institutional context of the time. There are few meaningful recourses to ultimate justice, and the geopolitical configuration of power relations tends to have a major influence in outcomes, irrespective of the actual regulations and instruments available.

A BALANCE SHEET OF REGULATORY ACTIONS

A fourth and concluding cut across media regulation summarizes where each area of regulation stands at the moment and provides a rough balance sheet of benefits. The headings used are familiar from previous sections, rearranged into three groups:

Radio spectrum and orbital allocation:
- The allocation of radio spectrum for telecommunications, television, radio, and other services
- The allocation of orbital slots for satellites, including geostationary positions

Telecommunications infrastructure:
- Standardization
- Universal service/access (between and within countries)
- Trade in telecommunications services

Media content:
- Exclusion of certain content to protect cultural autonomy and economic interests
- Diversity in content, including the effects of concentration of ownership
- Independence and diversity of source, including public service and community media
- Trade in media products
- IPRs
- Freedom of information and media responsibility

Radio Spectrum and Orbital Allocation

Radio spectrum is universally regarded as a natural resource to be utilized for the common good—no private claim can be made to its use or its ownership. The allocation of radio spectrum for telephony, data, television, radio, and other purposes is a key issue internationally, and has been since the earliest days. It involves both a coordination and an allocation element.

The coordination part ensures that the available spectrum is rationally divided up so that interference from broadcasting internationally on the same wavelength and "spillover" effects across borders are avoided. There exists a strong mutual interest between all stakeholders in efficient coordination in this area and there is no disagreement on the need for such coordination.

The allocation aspect is more difficult. This emerges when spectrum becomes a scarce resource through growing demand for its use. Competition for the available spectrum can be between entities within the same media sector or between different media or different sectors altogether, but it is in the interest of all that agreement be reached—either unused spectrum or total anarchy in the spectrum is of no benefit to anyone. Thus, there is little need for an enforceable, multilateral agreement, even though there is ongoing contention in terms of the amount of spectrum to be allocated to each use. In general, the market rules, and demand comes from more developed economies and their media sectors. Only very limited allocation is set aside specifically for development or public service needs.

Satellite orbital slots also require an allocation mechanism when scarcity becomes an issue. In the case of the important, and scarce, geostationary orbit, there is an accepted principle of fair access, but a practice of "first come, first served." Until now, the principle has not been called on to change the practice, but an unenforceable agreement will probably be worth little the day that a small country asks a wealthy one to give up one of its valuable slots.

Telecommunications Infrastructure

Telecommunications infrastructure is becoming the core transmission medium for content, growing in importance as the Internet expands. A number of aspects may be covered by international regulation.

The need for standardization of equipment and of electronic protocols, like spectrum allocation, could not from the earliest time be ignored. As they involve proprietary interests and play a key role in competitive strategies, they were and remain an area of struggle and contention primarily between the largest industry players. Although the ITU and regional standards bodies are widely accepted as fora for agreement of standards, increased competition globally and faster rates of technological innovation exert severe strains on the multilateral system. In practice, it is often merely legitimizing a standoff, a compromise, or a victory of intercorporate struggles. Agreements are thus voluntary, but effective as long as they reflect the de facto situation and balance of commercial forces. The needs of noncorporate interests, such as digital radio standards for small-scale independent stations, can often be jostled aside in these struggles.

Extending universal access to telecommunications has a more complicated history in international regulation. It emerged in the 1980s as an issue between industrialized and less industrialized countries and was recognized as an important factor in economic development. Multilateral resolutions, recommendations, and declarations cover various aspects of access in less industrialized countries, including investment, technology transfer, and tariff policies, but these are mostly unspecific and voluntary and have had little or no impact.

The issue of universal access moved substantially into the international trade area in the 1990s, with the robust and enforceable WTO accord on telecommunications under which domestic sectors are committed to various degrees of opening up and more stringent competition rules will apply. Most countries have signed up, but timescales and levels of commitment vary considerably. The agreement may constrain regulators at the national level in implementing universal service, for instance through the use of cross-subsidization and other measures that might affect competition. The new trade regime will lead to both more external investment in less industrialized countries and more external ownership, with an improvement in services for the business and urban sectors.

At the same time, the settlement procedures for completing calls initiated externally are moving from a voluntary fixed-price basis, which on the whole resulted in some transfers from wealthier to poorer countries, to a cost-based system. This move is happening globally and is being implemented bilaterally (in the case of the United States unilaterally)—no agreement is required since the revenue can simply be withheld for de facto enforcement. The effect will be to reduce or eliminate this source of income, which for some poor countries has represented the bulk of telecommunications income.

Media Content

Increasingly, media content rather than infrastructure or transmission is the driving force of the sector internationally. Issues arising are around sovereignty, impact, and ownership.

With the introduction of satellite television (and, long before, shortwave radio), the sovereignty of nations to exclude content from their jurisdiction by regulating the transmission end became the subject of considerable multilateral activity. The focus was on the question of prior consent. The main fears, especially but not only among less industrialized countries, related to the dominance of the U.S. film and television industry. Concerns were for the preservation and sustenance of cultural identity and for the impact of sophisticated multinational advertising and commercial messages. No agreement was reached and fundamental differences were never resolved, though there are some regional agreements and bilateral accords. This suited the interests of the major powers and media corporations. Since then and as a part of the same trend, this debate has been overtaken by the issue of trade, moving matters further onto a terrain beneficial to the more powerful countries and media corporations.

In relation to diversity of media content, concentration of ownership is regarded as potentially an inhibiting factor. With the growth of media originating outside the jurisdiction, especially satellite television and the

Internet, the issue of ownership extends beyond the national territory. As yet, there are no moves or realistic prospects for the regulation of externally broadcast media to enhance diversity, the introduction of which would not be in the interests of powerful countries and media corporations. Since most of these broadcasters are fully commercial organizations, the effect is likely to be continuing subjection of program content to purely commercial criteria. For the global audiences who are targeted, this may cause restrictions in the diversity and independence of news and other reporting. This is especially true where the national terrestrial options are limited. Indeed, even where terrestrial broadcasting is reasonably well developed foreign content dominates. In Latin America, for example, 62 percent of television programing comes from the United States.

There have been high-level proposals, for instance by the Commission on Global Governance, for an agreement on a cross-subsidy or support mechanism to create a "global commons," including fully independent and educational content channels. But they have yet to have an impact.

Some media products are also included under the terms of the WTO agreement, for instance books and magazines. These prevent governments from introducing measures that would tend to favor national products over imports, on the basis that they distort competition. As in all WTO agreements, they carry strong enforcement procedures, and precedents suggest that cultural protections offer little to no defense. However, audiovisual products are excluded from the WTO agreements because of disagreement between Europe and the United States regarding cultural issues. The issue remains on the agenda and will not go away, even though the interests of the less industrialized countries still do not carry much weight.

In trade, a key factor for international consideration is the ownership of IPRs, especially copyright in film, books, software (including games), and music. Since the beginning, these were the subject of binding multilateral agreements, but their enforcement measures were relatively weak. Various attempts to create an acceptable multilateral solution that would allow for varied regimes of IPRs suited to the less industrialized as well as industrialized countries largely failed. In the end, the major powers moved the matter onto the GATT trade negotiations, where agreement was reached in the mid-1990s, against the protestations of many developing countries who felt pressured into it. This permits only a restrictive definition of IPRs, in line with that of the wealthy countries, but also puts in place very powerful dedicated enforcement machinery. National legislation requires significant modification in many countries to comply with the agreement, posing a serious challenge of interpretation and expertise in many poorer ones. With the continued growth and consolidation of a global market in media products, wealthy countries and transnational media will benefit economically to a significant degree.

Its long-term implications are far reaching for all countries. The trend so far is for the neighboring rights of media owners to be extended in scope (the types of knowledge to which they apply), in duration (the time for which monopoly rights are granted), and in depth (inhibiting partial exceptions for education, development, or other use), against those of creators and of the public. The outcome is a more limited release into the public sphere and the annexation of unprotected knowledge already in the public sphere.

NOTES

1. In an open letter to the U.S. Congress and President Bill Clinton, House Majority Leader Dick Armey questioned U.S. support for the UNDP: "Every time you turn around, it seems there is another agency or bureaucracy looking to get its greedy mitts on the Internet through new taxes. U.S. taxpayer dollars should not be used to support UN reports pushing this kind of redistribution policy."

2. At the regional level, the European Union has included a protocol to the Amsterdam Treaty that exempts government support to public service media from compliance with competition law requirements.

3. The FCC's policy was generally welcomed by public broadcasters, although many, including William Kennard, the FCC chair, felt that it was flawed because it allowed the satellite operators to decide which programing they would carry. Kennard noted that this would reduce the chance that satellites would carry diverse programing "that might not fit neatly into a DBS [direct broadcast satellite] operator's notion of what is commercially viable."

4. For a more complete analysis of international motivations and possible influences, see Cees Hamelink, *The Politics of World Communication* (London: Sage, 1994), chapter 10.

5. Adapted from Cees Hamelink, *The Politics of World Communication* (London: Sage, 1994), 285–289.

10

Actors and Trends
in Global Governance

The previous chapter looked at how regulation happens at the global level and at the instruments used. The governance of these regulations and instruments, if it is to be effective and democratic, requires more than their mere administration as a contractual agreement or a bureaucratic activity of an international agency. This governance is immediately problematic in a way that is not felt at the national level. In intergovernmental agreements and agencies, governments voluntarily cede part of their sovereignty—their right to govern—to a joint entity over which each individually has only limited control. Inevitably, a distinct level emerges at which decisions are taken and power resides, and while coercion and manipulation may sustain the process for a while, inadequate governance will likely lead to the disintegration of consensus as those who are left out refuse to cooperate and reclaim the previously ceded sovereignty over the area. International governance is thus much more problematic than national, in terms both of the loss of sovereignty by national governments, and the reconstitution of such power within new institutional forms that sometimes incorporate actors outside of government. And the emergence of international regulation is always accompanied by the issue of governance and the relative influence and role of each government.

This chapter looks at the forms taken by this reconstitution of power to yield the governance structures in existence today. As we have seen, governance of media and communication is not the exclusive activity of any institution. Rather, it is spread out among a number of them, each of which also has other concerns. A consideration of the governance of media globally must include the governance of the relevant institutions as a whole, as well as, to the extent that they can be differentiated from other functions, of the specific instruments relating to media.

We will begin by examining the main actors involved in governing global institutions and their means of influence. Following this is a discussion of the trends in media governance and their implications inside and—potentially more important—outside these institutions.

THE MAIN ACTORS IN GLOBAL INSTITUTIONS

In the global institutions reviewed in part II, influence is wielded mainly by the following:

- Governments, through their national delegations to international institutions
- Secretariats of intergovernmental organizations
- Private-sector corporations and associations
- Civil society, such as international nongovernmental organizations (NGOs) and professional associations

Governments

In formal terms, only governments exercise the power to vote in intergovernmental institutions on multilateral agreements and treaties—on matters where government sovereignty may be implicated. If decisions implicate or are binding on governments, and only they can follow through with national legislation or other action, then their agreement is essential. Only if governments are party to decisions are they bound by them. On the whole, and in formal terms, governments remain at the center of the international system of governance.

In most UN organizations and specialized agencies of the United Nations, each country has a single inalienable vote in the general member assembly. This is the fundamental touchstone of democracy within the UN system and is not to be underestimated for its moral and practical value. The heads of these institutions, and exceptionally some others, are also usually elected by members for a fixed term.

Beyond these basic common features of democracy, at least at the level of nations, there is considerable variation. The different procedures for voting, the institutional functions and characteristics, the informal methods of conducting work, and the broader interrelationships between countries significantly affect the way power is exerted and the level of influence of different governments.

The formal system may divide membership into layers, a general membership, and then a smaller group, such as a council (ITU), a coordination committee (WIPO), an executive committee (UNESCO), or a general council (WTO), that holds very significant power between plenary meetings of all members. The selection procedures for membership of these groups, and the degree and type of power they hold, are also important features of governance.

Elections to top positions also have their formal and informal sides. The ITU is unique in electing not just the secretary-general but also directors of each of its three sectors. In WIPO, the powerful Coordination Committee nominates the candidate for director-general, and if refused by the General Assembly, continues to nominate others. (The Coordination Committee, which comprises a large proportion of WIPO members, is itself selected in a complex process involving all members.) Similarly, the Executive Board of UNESCO recommends a director-general to the General Conference, which may however refuse the recommendation. The WTO, as we saw in chapter 5, has had difficulty in settling its election procedures for the secretary-general, with the 1999 election of only the second secretary-general resulting in a chaotic situation that satisfied no one.

Elections to high office are often not based wholly on the candidate's merit, if at all. More or less explicit agreements are struck for rotation between or within global regions. Significant pressures and incentives can also be brought to bear by more powerful countries to secure votes for their preferred candidates, as in the case of the failure of Amadou Mahtar M'Bow to get reelected to head UNESCO in the aftermath of the New World Information and Communication Order (NWICO), in other agencies where the multimillion-dollar campaigns of winning candidates were financed by wealthy governments, and, more generally, in the General Agreement on Tariffs and Trade (GATT) and the WTO where only Westerners had ever been elected prior to 1999.

Winning or controlling elected positions is only one way for governments to wield power.

Dues that members pay to fund multilateral agencies can be used to leverage power, through the threat or actual withdrawal from the agency or through stalling payments, a tactic used routinely by the United States as the largest contributor to the UN system. Forcing countries into line by threats of unilateral action, dragging in nonrelevant bilateral or multilateral agendas of crucial interest to reluctant countries, and secret deals among powerful nations revealed only later to the rest are all part and parcel of the realpolitik of multilateral organizations, and indeed they often have their counterparts in national politics. A major instrument of power (not exclusive to governments) can also be knowledge and expertise—negotiations in these institutions are sometimes protracted and extremely complex requiring sustained specialist expertise, which is easier for wealthier countries. Finally, the institutionalization of secrecy in an organization, including in debates covering the justifications for decisions, clearly vitiates its claims to democracy and may discriminate in favor of some members over others, an accusation leveled most notably against the WTO.

As a private-sector organization, the Internet Corporation for Assigned Names and Numbers (ICANN) does not admit governments as members and is, formally, only accountable to the government of California, the state in which it is registered. To date, the most remarkable example of government power in ICANN was at the moment of its creation, a unilateral action by the U.S. Department of Commerce.

Thus, even uniformly applied rules with democratic underpinnings may, in the broader context, yield results that are less than fair and equitable. No institution is free of such influences, nor probably could ever be. However, there is no doubt that a general will, or an irresistible demand, to develop a fairer system would reduce the potential for distortion and render these institutions more democratic.

The Secretariat

The secretariat, comprising the elected leaders and staff, facilitates and administers the actions of the institution, much like any civil service. And like any civil service, it can have significant influence beyond that formally given to it. It exerts its influence through setting the agendas, proposing budgets, executing activities, undertaking external liaison, and by the other means available to bureaucracies.

The key issue is only partly whether, as administrators, secretariats enjoy excessive power. More important is whether that influence is exercised in the interests of one group over others. Policies regarding the hiring of staff vary widely among UN agencies. Some of them hire staff in proportion to the financial contributions of member states, and others put more value in having a staff that more closely reflects the breakdown of the membership at large. As can be expected, the secretariats exercise significant influence in operational areas, but they may also exercise influence in other types of decisions. The way this influence is manifested varies from case to case. In different situations, secretariat staff members can exercise influence through their role as advisors to the agency's executive or in the name of the executive, the latter being particularly apparent in areas where the executive displays little interest. The relative influence of staff, and how it exercises this influence depends on a variety of circumstances, ranging from the structure and constitution of the organization, to the personal characteristics of the executive head and the bureaucratic leaders.

The power of governments and of secretariats by no means excludes others having a major, sometimes decisive, influence on the outcomes of decisions and on the voting choices of governments. Formal power may not, in practice, add up to much for long periods of time. Such exclusive voting power is often concerned only with approving a framework within which decisions are taken by a broader group of actors. This framework itself is anyhow likely to be an expression of external demands from other actors and the general environment.

The ITU's standardization procedures are a case in point. In 1994, the ITU underwent the most far-reaching restructuring since its foundation. For some time before, forces of liberalization were sweeping through the telecommunications industry, hastened by major technological breakthroughs. The ITU's existing procedures could not keep pace, and most important, it feared being overtaken by private-sector and regional bodies. It responded by opening up decision-making procedures and restructuring to bring the private sector into the process in all but internal constitutional matters. It might be said that the private sector, in effect, forced the vote of governments on the matter. But the ITU was merely retaining its relevance in a context in which it had little control over the dynamic of the sector. Furthermore, the change was led by governments with powerful telecommunications interests, who identified their national interests with those of their corporations.

This leads on to ways in which the private sector can have significant, often a determining, influence.

Private-Sector Interests

It is not unusual for governments to invite others onto their national delegations, some permitting participation in all activities short of casting a vote.[1] Canada, for instance, is one of many that includes private-sector organizations and associations, but also NGOs, onto its delegations, selected according to the particular topics under discussion. Canada, like a number of countries, also constitutes national fora within which different interests can put forward and discuss their positions, which are in turn transmitted to the delegations.

Governments may also work intimately, and privately, with specific interests in formulating positions. As mentioned, the interests of the private sector are closely aligned by some governments with the general national interest. A government may even see itself as an "honest broker" between competing factions of national capital.

The multilateral system itself has also been opening up to various ways in which the private sector can become formally involved.

The restructured ITU, as mentioned, allows for direct formal participation in deliberations on most substantive issues. In effect, it has created two membership categories, *sector* and *associate*, distinct from the formal government membership, for each of its three sectors, standardization, radio communication, and development.[2] Any relevant organizations can join, though the membership fee for sector members (which the ITU uses as a source of revenue) is prohibitive for small or noncommercial organizations such as development-oriented NGOs. Associate membership fees are less, but they are also less able to participate fully in ITU activities. For the ITU, this structure makes sense. Private-sector actors and national and regional standards bodies are critical to the development and agreement of standards; and increasingly, radio and telecommunications issues are dominated by private-sector interests. To omit these in any of these areas would likely result in the ITU's displacement as the preeminent body in standards, telecommunications, and even some aspects of radio communication. Most activities of the ITU are agreed to on a consensual basis, as voluntary standards and regulations, without the participation of all those directly involved, the agreements would be meaningless.

The WTO involves the private sector in a less formal but more generalized manner. Industry directors sit on their powerful dispute panels, which can impinge on issues far wider than trade, and there are often close personnel links at various levels—including lucrative private-sector positions for retiring director-generals and senior personnel. UNESCO, too, increasingly reaches out to the private sector. Like the WTO, the participation is not formal, but its Partnerships for the 21st Century Program, launched following the UN Millennium Assembly in 2000, already claims to have established partnerships with 300 firms and business organizations. Among the expected outcomes of the program are increased support from the business sector for UNESCO's mission and projects, reinforcement of internal mechanisms for regular exchange of information and consultation, a stronger and more visible role for UNESCO in the UN system, and a more active presence and enhanced reputation for UNESCO among various partners in civil society.[3]

ICANN, an international but not *intergovernmental* organization, fully and formally incorporates the private sector within its structures.

The ability of the private sector to influence in nonformal ways can have the most impact of all. Most obvious are the well-organized lobby campaigns, targeting governments as well as intergovernmental agencies, and backed by unlimited spending where the issue is considered a strategic one.

However, the future growth of private-sector influence in regulating media and communications on a global scale may not lie within the sphere of the multilateral organizations at all. Of more significance could be the emergence of bodies like ICANN, incorporated under California law as a nonprofit, private-sector corporation, or of quasi-governmental organizations of the private sector intent on regulating key areas of interest as they emerge on the backs of new technologies or are left in a vacuum due to the failure to reach agreement within the intergovernmental system. The section on trends returns to these.

NGOs

The private sector does not have it all its own way. International nongovernmental and noncommercial organizations have enjoyed a special opening to the UN system since its foundation, with the UN Economic and Social Council (ECOSOC) mandated to "make suitable arrangements for the consultation with non-governmental organizations."[4] Specific arrangements were spelled out in 1968,[5] with three categories of involvements for NGOs, depending on their relevance. This only began to translate into significant activity in the 1970s, and then exploded in the 1990s, with the 1992 Earth Summit in Rio de Janeiro, marking a watershed for NGO participation and coinciding with a dramatic increase in both numbers and activities of international NGOs.[6] UN organs and specialized agencies established elaborate mechanisms for the participation of NGOs and began cooperative activities, from exchange of information through to formal rights of consultation. All but a few UN agencies today have developed specific forms of cooperation with international nonprofit NGOs[7] (the most notable exception being the WTO).

UNESCO from its early days saw the value of cooperating with NGOs, especially since so many are active in areas such as education and culture. In 1995, the system was revamped to include two types of relationship. The more formal of the two can be consultative or, for a smaller number of umbrella NGOs in very relevant areas, as associates with more intimate interaction on policy and other matters. NGOs are also involved at the operational level. Every three years an international NGO conference is held to discuss programs and issues, and UNESCO also supports a permanent NGO Committee.

Not so the ITU. Although there is operational involvement in a few of the ITU activities, NGOs are treated in general as if they were an industry interest, and may join any of the three sectors—but for a hefty fee. A few NGOs whose activities are directly dependent on the ITU, such as the International Amateur Radio Union of ham radio operators, do join and actively participate. But for others, the cost is an insurmountable barrier. The recent introduction of associate membership status, with lower fees, will go some way to alleviating this problem. However, for interested NGOs the fees are only a small part of the real cost of participating in extended and often highly technical meetings in Geneva. While ITU decisions, on for instance the allocation of spectrum between different users, could have serious long-term impact on civil society and on development generally, there is no forum for exploring what the impact might be and for interacting with the civil society interests concerned. Rather, it is conceived and designed as a forum for those with a direct immediate interest in these matters and with the resources to maintain a sustained involvement at this level—almost without exception, the private sector and governments.[8] At the same time, however, decisions taken there may have profound, if indirect, impact on many excluded from the process.

Relations between NGOs and GATT, later the WTO, have long been strained, partly because of the culture of secrecy and the lack of transparency that characterizes the organization. The WTO is committed, it claims, to improving public understanding of trade issues and sees relations with NGOs primarily in this light. NGOs have no formal role in WTO activities, nor a right to consultation. At present, the involvement of NGOs is limited to information exchange and briefings. But there has been some attempt at document de-restriction, and the WTO, mainly through its Web site, makes more documentation available than previously.

WIPO admits accredited international NGOs as observers to its meetings. Currently, some eighty NGOs are accredited, primarily industrial and professional associations.

As in so many other areas, ICANN is the exception—it is an NGO itself, but it has no mechanism enabling NGOs to participate in it, other than indirectly through one of its three supporting groups. These supporting groups elect the majority of ICANN board members, with a minority elected by the at-large membership. Like the WTO, ICANN has been criticized for its lack of transparency, but its confused history, ever shifting structures, and ill-defined role make it difficult to determine who exercises power and influence.

Like the private sector, NGOs also have informal avenues for influencing deliberations of these organizations, though they differ somewhat from those of the private sector. This was forcefully illustrated to the WTO during the public demonstrations at various meetings from 1998 onwards—part of a wider campaign on globalization issues in which, however, media-related issues were never brought to the fore. This is considered further in the next section.

INFLUENCES AND TRENDS IN GOVERNANCE

The dynamics of change in the media sector in the context of globalization, outlined in chapter 3, is the backdrop against which media governance structures are evolving.

A new phase of globalization is characterized, on the one hand, by a diminishing role of the nation-state in exercising sovereignty of governance as it (more or less voluntarily) cedes certain powers to multilateral entities, and on the other hand, by the limited and falling capacity of these entities to cope with the expanded global governance tasks and heightened expectations. The process of liberalization across financial, commodity, information and communication technology (ICT), and information sectors, the huge advances in ICTs, and the sheer scale, reach, and pace of transnational corporations threaten to leave many global governance structures struggling in their wake, unable to control or even significantly influence the areas for which formally they held responsibility. Sometimes, with the backing of powerful national governments, who to some extent engineered the vacuum into existence, the globalized private sector and supporting agencies are beginning to fill this expanding global governance gap.

Simplifying somewhat, a core dynamic can be identified in which the UN multilateral organizations, with a sound basis in balanced global development, are struggling against the trade and commercial paradigm based on private property and contractual rights and which is driven largely by non–UN organizations—especially the WTO—more powerful governments, and the interests of private capital. On the side of more balanced development is probably the majority of world governments, though unable to act in concert, as well as most of the UN agencies themselves in terms of their remit and secretariats and civil society.

The media industry is not only one of the lead sectors in the rise of the trade paradigm; it provides many of the tools and instruments that drive it along. The media, and especially the cultural content industries, help prise open new markets internationally through advertising and through the promotion of consumerist lifestyles in which entertainment is usually wrapped. As tools, the pace of globalization would be almost inconceivable without telecommunications and ICTs generally.

Beneath these macro trends and turning the microscope on the media sector, a number of distinct, intertwining strands can be identified that are likely to influence the future governance landscape. The main ones are:

- The declining role of most governments and UN organizations in media and communications governance, and the rise of non–UN agencies such as the WTO and ICANN, coming from narrower trade or technical backgrounds

- The related emergence of quasi-governance organizations controlled by the private sector and the centrality of market mechanisms, and the supporting role of powerful states
- The emergence of civil society as a force to be reckoned with and the rise of independent, alternative, and community media
- The growing sophistication of less industrialized countries in relation to their role in multilateral organizations

These have been sketched out in passing in previous sections, and are summarized and supplemented here.

The Declining Role of Governments and the UN System, and the Ascendance of the Trade Paradigm

Three overlapping global developments need no further rehearsal: The declining sovereignty and relevance of national governments in an era of globalization, the weakness of the UN system and its ability to intervene effectively in major global agendas, and the ascendance of the global trade paradigm and institutions more powerful than governments. In relation to media and communications, these are expressed most forcefully in at least the following six areas:

- The transfer of sovereign government power to the WTO in the area of telecommunications and intellectual property rights (IPRs), and possibly in the future regarding audiovisual products and the capacity to protect cultural diversity and identity
- The loss of IPRs by WIPO and its conventions to the WTO and the consequent strengthening of trade and competition rules over human rights, cultural, and social considerations
- The general decline of the ITU as the global governing body in telecommunications with much of its previous domain moving over to trade and market mechanisms
- The inability of the multilateral organizations to agree on regulating foreign direct satellite broadcasting, and the consequent absence of regulation of the sector
- The careful distancing of UNESCO from political issues and any debates casting doubt on the supremacy of the trade and market paradigm
- The failure of the UN system to gain governance over the Internet, underlined by the creation of ICANN as a nongovernmental and nonrepresentative body that received its power directly from the U.S. government.

It should not be concluded that governments everywhere have lost control of the situation, either at the national or global levels. Most of these have been initiated and actively pursued by wealthy governments and supported by others, and they point to their broader correlation of national interests with those of their transnational corporations and the more general movement toward the market paradigm outlined earlier. Thus, the United States and some EU countries have for decades been advancing the trade paradigm in media and communications sectors, and the loss of state sovereignty is seen by them as a positive move since they believe they will benefit from it. Similarly, the narrowing of UNESCO's media activities primarily into technical assistance and away from more contentious political areas was vigorously pursued by the United Kingdom, the United States, and others, as was the exclusion of Internet governance from the UN agencies.

Nevertheless, the net effect is that governments, who in general have at least some degree of legitimacy and accountability, are losing influence in the international arena, individually and as members of multilateral organizations. This trend shows little sign of abating.

The Emergence of Closed Government and Private-Sector Quasi-Governance Structures

As we have seen, the transnational private sector already has significant and growing influence in multilateral organizations. Yet, this falls short of what they need to achieve for their global ambition, and that of their sponsoring governments, of being free to operate when and how they wish within a relatively unrestricted global market for goods and services. In particular, the exploding ICT infrastructure industries are developing a vision of a world that plants them firmly in the driving seat with others confined to enabling and facilitating roles.

Organizations such as the Organization for Economic Cooperation and Development (OECD) have long been the think tanks and enablers of the wealthy countries pursuing liberalizing agendas. But the first clues of the role to be carved out for the private sector in governing the wave of media growth and expansion appeared in a speech by Al Gore in March 1994 at the ITU's World Telecommunication Development Conference—an ironic occasion since the ITU itself was to be relegated to a spectator in many areas. This Global Information Infrastructure (GII) was further elaborated and agreed to at the (then) Group of Seven meeting in Brussels the following year, in which the major powers outlined the driving forces of globalization of the Information Society, as the European Union preferred to call it, and how they were to be reconciled with the public interest. The engine was to be private investment fueled by competition and liberalization, with promises of universal access and equality of opportunity for citizens. While a few small projects were announced to support the latter aspects, a sweeping regulatory reform process was foreshadowed in relation to liberalization and the privileged role of the private sector.

Particularly striking was the fact that this was the first time the major powers had allowed official status to nonmembers at their secretive meetings—major private-sector corporations were given official status and convened to deliberate among themselves the future of the GII and their part in it. Nonprivate-sector NGOs, refused entry, held their own meeting outside. One commentator described the GII thus:

> Indeed, in every respect, the Global Information Infrastructure is a harbinger of both a certain emerging global regulatory system in communication and a future system of world governance. It is an imperial project with enormous implications for the future of democracy and human rights, insofar as it is based on political decision-making at a level where there is no accountability, the recognized autonomy of private capital, and the formal exclusion of the institutions of civil society. In terms of international relations, it extends the dependency of the so-called less-developed parts of the world. As a social project, it locates human development as a potential benefit of economic investment, rather than as the principal goal.[9]

Emerging from this with a new legitimacy conferred on them, the private sector set up its own parallel initiative called the Global Information Infrastructure Commission, as a coordination, lobby, and research organization bringing together such companies as AT&T, Mitsubishi, Motorola, NEC, Nokia, Olivetti, Oracle, Sprint, Time-Warner, and Viacom. In 1997, Martin Bangemann, the EU commissioner on innovation and telecommunications and a prominent proponent of liberalization, then joined in by calling for an "international charter" to govern the new world order in communication. This was quickly endorsed by the United States, which argued for a new international understanding on policy issues, some based on formal agreement and some on informal understanding and common approaches.

The private sector recognized the opening and soon further entities were formed, aiming more actively to create the global policy environment that would facilitate their continued and accelerated expansion. As the potential of electronic commerce (e-commerce), and the need for a regime that would suit private-sector interests, the Global Business Dialogue on Electronic Commerce (GBDe) was created in 1999 by the world's largest communications companies, chaired by the head of Bertelsmann, then the largest publishing company. The GBDe invited government and multilateral organizations to join with it in designing and planning this global policy framework based primarily on self-regulation—an indication of the growing power and confidence of the sector.

The Group of Eight (G8) continued its approach in relation to the ICTs. At its meeting in July 2000 in Japan, it agreed to a Charter on the Global Information Society, acknowledging the growing Digital Divide between wealthy and poor countries and groups within them. The approach was again twofold: it reaffirmed the leading role of the private sector and it left it up to governments to "create a predictable transparent and non-discriminatory policy and regulatory framework necessary for the information society. It is important to avoid undue regulatory interventions that would hinder productive private-sector initiatives in creating an IT–friendly environment." Meanwhile, a special Digital Opportunity Task Force (DOT Force) was set up to address the Digital Divide and charged with making recommendations on fostering access and use of ICTs and on securing the participation of stakeholders to the subsequent G8 meeting in July 2001. Its membership comprises governments, international organizations, and one each from the three business groups: World Economic Forum (Davos), Global Business Dialogue, and the Global Information Infrastructure Commission. This twin-track approach is the same as before—a global regulatory structure that is fully in line with the demands of industry for open markets and limited regulation, and linked to a limited and nonregulatory action to address the deepening inequalities comprising limited investment in pilot, technical assistance, and human resource development.

As yet, the private sector and its powerful supporters in government are still just experimenting with new approaches and new governance bodies outside the multilateral system. The symbiotic relationship between the G8/industrialized countries and their transnational corporations has yet to yield credible structures that can explicitly take on specific governance roles. The lack of legitimacy is a critical obstacle. Thus, cooperation with not only the multilaterals, but also with civil society may be sought at different levels—which can be interpreted as an attempt at co-optation or an opening toward a broader system.

The trend retains considerable force, although its unwavering adherence to neoliberal trade and regulation policies may provoke the same opposition as has been directed more generally against the WTO, the G8, and others. In any case, these actors, powerful governments, and transnational corporations also continue to pursue their more traditional approach. On the one hand, they undermine or block multilateral agreements where the outcome might go against them and then move in with unaccountable market mechanisms to pick up the pieces—governance by other means; on the other hand, they support strong multilateral approaches where they recognize an advantage, but outside the UN system, in organizations such as the WTO that are largely under their control and that have the power to enforce the more favorable agreements reached.

The Emergence of Civil Society and the Growth of People's Media

Few would doubt that civil society organizations in recent years have grown in their capacity to influence the intergovernmental system and indeed the actions of individual governments and corporations. From the UN Conference on Environment and Development, through to the Multilateral Agreement on Investment and WTO, NGOs have flexed their muscles in a way not seen before.

The growing recognition of the role of civil society organizations is not unrelated to the rise to prominence of transnational corporations and of the market paradigm in general. Within UN organizations, it has given impetus to a renewal of relations with NGOs, or in the case of the ITU that has recently opened extensively to the private sector, perhaps to consider for the first time instigating a formal process for relating to NGOs. Even the WTO is under pressure to open to civil society, though so far it has resisted any significant concessions.

However, civil society organizations are not seen solely as a counterbalance in relation especially to social and cultural concerns, serving to restrain the excesses of market-driven zeal. Emerging governance structures involving a central role for private-sector organizations and groups such as the OECD and the G8 cannot ignore their own tenuous claim to legitimacy in dealing with global affairs. Thus, they may look to civil society to partly fill the legitimacy gap, through incorporation into these new structures in different ways. Civil society is also seen as a link to on-the-ground development activities and as a useful vehicle to determine needs and deliver services.

But there is a limit to the potential role of civil society here. Those promoting the neoliberal paradigm globally have devoted an enormous effort to creating the kind of regime that suits their interests, through the hollowing out of many UN organizations, the strengthening of the WTO, and the creation of new institutional forms. None of these gains are on the bargaining table with civil society. Thus, the invitation of civil society participation will never go so far as to threaten the core tenets of liberalization and the capacity of the global private sector to extend and enforce its interests. Civil society involvement is seen as focused on relatively minor programs to mitigate the negative impact of such liberalization, including targeting needs and delivering services—a role that can have only very limited influence on the larger picture.

Some international civil society organizations recognize the limitations of such incorporation and are working to build broader alliances and deeper roots in communities. A small number of NGOs and looser initiatives have taken up the issue from a global perspective and engage in lobbying the intergovernmental system, such as the People's Communication Charter,[10] the Platform for Communication Rights, and for a decade the MacBride Round-table on Communication (which met for the last time in 1998). However, a lesson learned from NWICO was that a focus on the intergovernmental level alone is unlikely to succeed in bringing about lasting change, and building alliances with other NGOs and community-based and people's organizations is the main focus. Although the international NGO sector as a whole appears to have only a limited grasp of the gravity and urgency of issues arising in media and communications, awareness is growing. At the same time, working up from the ground, membership organizations such as the World Association for Christian Communication[11] (WACC) and the World Association of Community Radio Broadcasters[12] (AMARC) have developed sophisticated policy positions on several global issues.

Indeed, community- and development-oriented media have, through their experience and practice, begun to build a ground-level constituency of people educated in trends in media. Community and independent non-profit radio stations have sprung up all around the world, some in less industrialized countries with explicit development aims, and others primarily giving an alternative voice to communities in a world increasingly dominated by commercial media. Community and open access television stations, as well as alternative video production, exist in significant numbers in South and North America, in Europe, and are emerging in Africa and Asia. Linkages between them are also growing, in terms of exchange of news and feature programing with several organizations devoted solely to such interaction. The Internet is also a further source of alternative media content and international in ambition; though still primarily focused on developing countries, alternative and independent media in the developing world are quickly taking up the new medium and are using it as a source of alternative information and as a low-cost networking tool.[13] Some of these initiatives played a key role in organizing civil society at Seattle and other demonstrations against the WTO.

In relation to governance of media and communications, globally these interconnected strands have not yet attained the critical mass that would see them become a force with which to be reckoned. Nevertheless, their influence is growing and the right catalyst could see them quite rapidly take on a significant role. A conceivable candidate for this role is the United Nations' World Summit of the Information Society, led by the ITU and scheduled for December 2003.

Another trend in mainstream civil society organizations might also be repeated in the area of media and communications: There is evidence that international NGOs are moving to work more closely with governments of less industrialized countries, in building mutual understanding, and in working toward shared agendas and coordination in areas of common concern. Alleviating Third World debt and the structural adjustment policies pursued by the Bretton Woods institutions spring to mind. A sufficient level of common concern regarding media and communications could spark moves in the same direction.

A second mainstream trend is for NGOs to mobilize consumer power to provoke the transnational private sector into setting standards of corporate practice, or "civil regulation" as it has been termed. Forms of pressure include boycotts, direct action, and ethical disinvestments. It is a kind of "induced self-regulation" and can result in significant changes to corporate actions especially where an entire sector is targeted so that all subject themselves to the guidelines. Its limitations are both in the scope of its impact—it is unlikely to seriously impinge on the overall thrust of the regulatory and governance regimes—and in its geographical reach because of difficulties of mobilizing consumers in many societies. Nevertheless, it may open the way for intergovernmental organizations in the future to solidify civil regulation into the global regulatory system.

Finally, a major factor in the form and extent of the growth of influence of civil society organizations, in media and communications and elsewhere, is the question mark over the legitimacy of NGOs themselves. Their claim to represent the general interest of people, or even of their own members in the case of membership organizations, can be vitiated in the absence of acceptable standards of accountability, transparency, and participatory democracy, and the NGO movement as a whole is only beginning to come to grips with this. Certainly, in parallel with their growth in influence they will more and more be taken to task on these grounds.

The Growing Sophistication of Less Industrialized Countries in Global Governance

The relatively low level of influence of less and least developed countries in relation to media and communications governance issues has not been due to a lack of concern on their part regarding some of the matters arising. The liberalization of the telecommunications sector globally demanded sustained effort on the part of wealthy countries, corporations, and their supporters to break the resolve of many countries to retain national control of the sector. For many years, a large number held out against transborder data flows and direct broadcast satellites, and some still continue to do so. The NWICO debate itself, despite its limitations, contained a genuine plea for a more just and equitable regime in media and communications. There is barely a single less industrialized country that has not expressed reservations at the onslaught of mainly U.S. media and the unrelenting promotion of consumerist values through program content and advertising.

Yet, less industrialized countries, and their governments, are highly differentiated, even more so than the wealthier ones, and they cannot be considered in a uniform manner. Many of the poorest lack the capacity to take part in the debate at all, perhaps fully preoccupied with more immediate matters. For others, certain sections of the government, such as the social ministries, may recognize the dangers and propose positions around media, but are then overruled by ministries of trade or finance with quite different agendas. Motivations vary enormously. Repressive governments and dictatorships usually maintain tight control of all cross-border media and communications, though they may adopt the language of national sovereignty when defending their actions. Other countries, such as India, Argentina, and Egypt, which are regional media production hubs with their own not insignificant media industries, may devise more sophisticated strategies and forms of engagement to protect and export them.

Perhaps partly because of the defeat of NWICO, and partly because of the successive crises facing many of them, but also because of acquiescence by many governments to the neoliberal paradigm, there has been virtually no coordinated or sustained criticism, or even awareness among governments or other groups, of global issues in media and communications for some time. The sole exception has been the retention of aspects of the NWICO debate by the Non-Aligned Movement (NAM), a movement that, however, retains a shadow of its former global influence. Despite its many statements on North–South communication imbalances, its efforts to address them, through the News Agencies Pool of Non-Aligned Countries and the Broadcasting Organization of Non-Aligned Countries, have been embarrassing failures. The NAM has also been reticent to enter into alliances with NGOs, to the point of passing a resolution underscoring the intergovernmental character of UN bodies and insisting that NGO contributions to the UN be channelled exclusively through ECOSOC.

Nevertheless, at the broader level, it appears that some less industrialized countries are becoming more organized and sophisticated. The challenges to the WTO over the past few years have derived primarily from the fact that the majority of its members were no longer willing to tolerate the manner in which they are treated by the major powers—and more important, they were able to collaborate effectively if loosely to at least temporarily stall their exclusion and confront the organization with very serious questions about its conduct. Even if the skirmishes regarding media and communications at the WTO were largely between the major powers themselves, less industrialized countries did recognize that the issues were also important for themselves and intervened where they could.

It would be a mistake, therefore, to completely discount the possibility that some combination of less industrialized countries, possibly including both governments and civil society organizations, may become a major force in global media and communications issues in the future, perhaps collaborating with some counterparts in the wealthier countries. Alliances such as those emerging around debt and trade issues, and that include

both developing countries and sophisticated NGOs pursuing more balanced and transparent development, indicate one plausible path.

SUMMING UP

For a long time, governing the regulation of media and communications
was a matter for national governments. When they had to, they negotiated agreements with each other to coordinate the use of shared resources
or to establish the terms for use of each others resources. Now, however,
much of media and communications governance has passed to the global
level. Little by little and in a variety of more or less voluntary circumstances and unplanned ways, countries have ceded upwards the authority to govern.

Overall, the picture that emerges from the various institutions and actors is not a simple one. It is a patchwork of intersecting and competing
interests, clustered around a UN system that has at its core a charter that,
if fully implemented with vision and humanity, would significantly enhance global democracy. Yet, that democratic core is, in practice, in jeop-
ardy of being overpowered or seduced by the interests of the private sector and the neoliberal paradigm. Accountability and transparency do not,
in general, measure up to the better examples of national governments.
As in all institutional contexts, much power is informally exercised, sometimes with no mandate at all. Yet for all that, its main claim to legitimacy
in relation to acting on behalf of people (the UN Charter opens with the
words "We, the peoples of the United Nations") rests on this democratic
core, however tenuously. Extending its relations with civil society will be
key to sustaining the verity of that claim into the future, acting as the main
counterbalance to rising private-sector influence.

Thus, global governance structures in media and communications, as
in so many other areas, are going through a period of instability and
change. Over a long period, they have shifted from the national to the
transnational level, and more recently are drifting horizontally, nationally, and globally, from governments to the private sector and their supporting organizations. Are current trends likely to invigorate or extend
the democratic core, or to cause it to contract and possibly ultimately
disappear? Or could they lead to a transcendence of the current system,
to be gradually displaced by new forms, themselves more or less democratic?

Although there is no doubt that the neoliberal paradigm is currently the
dominant one, supported by the most powerful governments, a consideration of the various trends points in several directions and reveals quite a
fluid dynamic. While the UN system remains on the defensive and losing

ground, the emergence of better informed, more accountable, civil society and of better organized and democratically minded less industrialized countries as potential actors could see a reversal of this and a renewal of the system. Alternatively, or even concurrently, new institutional forms of governance, partly or wholly outside the UN system, might not remain the preserve of the private sector. They may even emerge with extended democratic mandates to incorporate more equitably the voices of those currently excluded.

The final chapter speculates on possible directions for the future.

NOTES

1. The ITU is unique in that, before the recent wave of privatization and liberalization of telecommunications, governments and state-owned telecommunications providers were so closely identified that it was accepted practice for governments to delegate their votes to their telecommunications provider.

2. The associate membership category is not yet available for the ITU Development Sector but will be formally introduced in 2002. The International Labor Organization, another specialized UN agency, goes perhaps farthest of all in this direction by employing a trilateral instrument in formulating its policies. Representatives of employers, of workers, and of governments participate equally in the decision-making labor conferences.

3. See <http://www.unesco.org/ncp/partners/> [last accessed: 26 November 2001].

4. Article 17 UN Charter.

5. UN Economic and Social Council, "ECOSOC Resolution 1296 (XLIV), Arrangements for Consultation with Non-Governmental Organizations," 23 May 1968, <http://www.globalpolicy.org/ngos/ngo-un/info/res-1296.htm> [last accessed: 26 November 2001].

6. A conservative estimate of the growth of international NGOs is provided by the Union of International Associations, which estimates that there are currently more than 38,000 international associations and NGOs, compared to only 6,000 in 1990.

7. A description of the arrangements available for most UN agencies is found in the annually published Non-Governmental Liaison Service and UN Conference on Trade and Development, *The NGLS Handbook* (Geneva: Non-Governmental Liaison Service and UN Conference on Trade and Development, 1997), <http://ngls.tad.ch/english/pubs/hb/hbeng.html> [last accessed: 26 November 2001].

8. A focus group was set up to consider ITU and NGO relations, but little came of it. See <http://comunica.org/itu_ngo/> [last accessed: 26 November 2001].

9. Marc Raboy, "Communication and Globalization," *Trends* 6, no. 2 (2001).

10. See <http://www.pccharter.net> [last accessed: 26 November 2001].

11. See <http://www.wacc.org.uk> [last accessed: 26 November 2001].

12. See <http://www.amarc.org> [last accessed: 26 November 2001].

13. For example, see Undercurrents, <http://www.undercurrents.org/> [last accessed: 26 November 2001]; Media Channel, <http://www.mediachannel.org/> [last accessed: 26 November 2001]; Deep Dish, <http://www.igc.org/deepdish/> [last accessed: 26 November 2001]; Freespeech TV, <http://www.freespeech.org/> [last accessed: 26 November 2001]; Independent Media Center, <http://www.indymedia.org/> [last accessed: 26 November 2001]; and Agencia Informativa Púlsar, <http://www.pulsar.org.ec/> [last accessed: 26 November 2001]. For a discussion on the use of the Internet by rural radio broadcasters in developing countries, see Bruce Girard, "The Challenges of ICTs and Rural Radio," <http://www.comunica.org/tampa/challenge_abstract.htm> [last accessed: 26 November 2001].

11

Scenarios for Media Governance

CALLS FOR CHANGE IN GLOBAL GOVERNANCE

In some respects, governance of media represents a microcosm of global governance as a whole, with the same core issues and contradictions found in both. The broader process also largely determines the parameters within which the evolution of media governance can take place. Overall trends in global governance are likely to greatly influence trends in the governance of media.

We therefore begin with a brief consideration of proposals for reforms of global governance.

There have been many calls for a more equitable global governance, and some too in media and communications. Mostly, these emanate from a human rights and development perspective and tend to focus on two issues, often in tandem: a critique of the Bretton Woods institutions and proposals to reform the UN system.

Tensions in Global Governance

Globalization is not only an economic process involving liberalized markets and open trade. It is also political. The boundaries within which the process of globalization can operate are set politically, through direct negotiations between governments in multilateral fora. Some governments, generally those of the more powerful trading nations, pursue a political agenda of pushing outwards the boundaries of economic globalization. That this same process concurrently reduces their own political sovereignty, ceded to nonaccountable economic forces and to selected intergovernmental agencies, does not unduly concern them since they believe it will rebound to their national economic advantage. Additionally, these governments work closely with transnational capital, regarding them as allies on the global scene, and keep firm control over the intergovernmental agencies involved.

The manner in which this is happening generates a central tension among the intergovernmental organizations themselves. This is not only because more powerful nations are largely dictating the rules to the rest, although this is a source of sharp difference. It is also because the incessant extension of market boundaries pays little heed to the social, cultural, and development aspects of globalization, aspects that are written into the very foundation of the UN system. Thus, the tension is between the UN multilateral system as a whole, set up explicitly if not exclusively on a human rights and development platform, and economic and political forces, including notably the World Trade Organization (WTO), tugging in the direction of economic liberalization and trade expansion. While there is, at least in principle, a great area of mutually reinforcing overlap—opening up trade and exchange potentially benefits all parties—the direction it is taking is perceived by many to be frequently in conflict with the United Nations' social, economic, and development goals. In the longer term, it is also seen as whittling away the public sphere at the national level and blocking its emergence at the global level.

As the contradiction deepens, legally established social, cultural, and economic development principles and agreements, with only limited capacity for enforcement, are being encroached on by the enforceable decisions of trade- and economy-related instruments and institutions. The moral force of international law is little match, in the short term, for the powerful instruments of organizations such as the WTO, backed up by powerful governments—though in the long term the story could be different.

Calls for Reform to Global Governance

Thus, the secretary-general of the United Nations points to the need to reenvision governance, both internationally and nationally, toward a system unequivocally based on human rights, freedom from want, and with a sustainable future.[1] A plethora of reports and initiatives has been launched inquiring into globalization and its impact on human rights, by the UN Economic and Social Committee (ECOSOC), the UN Sub-Commission on the Promotion and Protection of Human Rights, the Committee on Economic, Social, and Cultural Rights, the Commission on Human Rights, the International Labor Organization, and the UN Conference on Trade and Development (UNCTAD), to name but a few.[2]

UNCTAD has been one of the most consistent and forthright critics of current trends, focused as it is on trade and development.

The concluding chapter of the UN Development Program's (UNDP) *Global Development Report, 1999* is entitled "Reinventing Global Governance—for Humanity and Equity" and is representative of the moderate side of UN views. It explicitly recognizes that current structures are too driven by the economic and financial interests of the rich countries "often those of the [then] G-7, sometimes just the G-1," and much vitiated as compared to the original post–Second World War vision. It describes the debate on reform of international institutions as too narrow in scope, often excluding human development as an objective, and dominated by the concerns of industrial countries to the neglect especially of the least industrialized. It calls for a return to the original objectives of the post–Second World War vision, and the UN Charter with human rights and development at the core. "In short, reform driven by concern for people, not for capital." Reforms would include the creation of a global central bank, a fairer WTO with a mandate expanded beyond reducing trade barriers, agreed "principles of performance" for global corporations on human rights standards, and a broader United Nations, including a two-chamber General Assembly to include civil society participation. A reinforced UN system is seen as a means to introduce "international public goods" as exists at national levels, where the market has neither the incentive nor the mechanisms to meet public social and economic needs.

Calls for a fundamental review of governance are not confined to the UN system. Many nongovernment organizations (NGOs) and academics argue for more thoroughgoing reform. Sustained criticism of the Bretton Woods institutions and the WTO emanates from a variety of development and advocacy NGOs,[3] primarily on the perception that they have skewed the global security and economic system slowly but decisively in favor of wealthy countries. Walden Bello, for instance, an outspoken and highly respected development sociologist and economist, argues forcefully for fundamental change to these institutions.[4] The WTO needs not reform, but a radical reduction in power that would "make it simply another institution coexisting with and being checked by other international institutions, organisations, agreements and regional groupings." As a counterbalance, UNCTAD would at the same time be freed from "the cage that rich countries have fashioned for it and carve out a more powerful role in trade and development issues." But UNCTAD would itself also have to open up its decision-making processes to civil society as it has "been too long a club of Southern governments and states that are uncomfortable at the examination of their internal political and economic arrangements." Radical surgery is proposed for the International Monetary Fund, with a global commission to decide whether it should continue to exist at all or be decommissioned, the latter favored by Bello himself.

In a more academic context, David Held propounds the concept of global "cosmopolitan governance." The term points to a global system of democracy that cuts across the territorial boundaries of nation-states, expanding the framework of democratic institutions to encompass different assemblages at local and regional levels. The goals are to bring democratic control to areas that have escaped national control, to rethink global agencies as a coherent and sharper public affairs focal point, and to bring key groups and organizations of civil society and the economy into the democratic process. In practice, this means taking a number of important first steps. He, too, calls for a revival of the spirit of the UN founding principles whereby individuals would have redress for human rights violations at a global level, even at the hands of their own governments. The UN Security Council would be reformed to give an effective voice to developing countries. Global institutions would be supplemented by regional "parliaments" and other bodies to broaden the base of decision making. Crucially, an "assembly of democratic peoples," directly elected by them and accountable to them, would be created. And for global economic coordination, a new agency would be created to ensure equity of development, accountability, and transparency.[5]

Richard Falk has developed a complementary idea of "globalisation-from-above" versus "globalisation-from-below." The former comprises not just the multilateral institutions, but also, and especially, globalization brought about through transnational corporations. He argues that resistance to "economic globalisation is not likely to be effective if it relies on national elections to gain influence and change the role of governments on matters of political economy." The problem is that governments have already bought into, or have been subjected to, the liberalized model of globalization in a manner that leaves them limited room for maneuver—it has become virtually impossible for an individual state to "defect" from the system of globalization in place. Concessions can be wrung from global economic and political elites only through effective opposition from other quarters: "[D]emocratic spaces available to resist globalisation-from-above tend to be mainly situated at either local levels of engagement or transnationally." And globalization at the same time means that "transnational networks of affiliations in relation to gender, race and class have become more tenable." International summits offer one venue to bring the local and global together, as events like the World Summit for Social Development, the World Conference on Women, and the Earth Summit have shown. The other side of the same coin, protests surrounding gatherings of the Group of Eight (G8), WTO, and World Bank, also succeed in broadening public interest and participation in the global agenda. Thus, Falk argues for the centrality of civil society in bringing about the necessary changes.[6]

The Commission on Global Governance, initiated by Willy Brandt, former chancellor of West Germany, and comprising twenty-eight prominent politicians, NGO and foundation leaders, business people, and academics, reported in 1995. It echoes many of the earlier points, regarding enlarging the Security Council, revitalizing the General Assembly, strengthening international law in human rights, involving civil society in UN activities through a Forum for Civil Society, and creating an Economic Security Council to rebalance the coordination of global economic policy, which until now has been exercised by the wealthy nations through the G8 and the Organization for Economic Cooperation and Development (OECD).

All these critiques and proposals come back in their own way to the bifurcation within the governance system between a trade and liberalization paradigm and an economic and social development paradigm, though with different views on the extent and nature of the contradiction between them and on the solutions. All also call for reforms, on the one hand, to make the Bretton Woods institutions and global capital more accountable and responsive to development needs, and on the other hand, for the UN system to become more participatory and inclusive of people and civil society.

There are some who hold views that fall outside these parameters altogether, who welcome the current weakness of the UN system and indeed who would abolish even this thin layer of global democracy. But these views go largely unarticulated in international debates. National political considerations in the United States regularly bring these positions into the public arena, though within constrained and peculiarly colloquial terms. The de facto position of power of the wealthier countries and their capacity to control the system in their interests is not something that merits broadcasting too widely on the international stage. Nor need it be, since there is no evidence yet that the calls for change will yield anything significant in the immediate future.

This could change, even rapidly and from an unexpected quarter, with prospects of imminent change probably leading to far more vocal positions and possibly to greater polarization.

Proposals for Media and Communication Governance

Commentaries and proposals on governance in general have paid scant attention to governance of media and communication, or indeed of any specific sector. But in passing, a number of ideas have been put forward that offer insight into understanding media and communication in the bigger picture.

The 1999, the UNDP *Human Development Report* notes the media's role in encouraging a sense of global responsibility by treating international news and current events from the viewpoints of other countries; calls for regional and private efforts to encourage two-way cultural flows, in film, music, literature, and television programing; and suggests charging rents or royalties for use of the "global commons" such as radio waves to fund new "global goods," by implication including media content.

The idea of royalties for the global commons probably originated with the 1995 World Commission on Culture and Development, which had at least a tangential mandate on media. It suggested a tax on commercial use of radio waves, or even as a small percentage of all commercial media and communications content, explicitly to contribute to the production and distribution of alternative content. It also called for strengthening international cooperation on the media's capacity to support cultural diversity and democratic discourse and raised the issue of concentration of media ownership internationally.

Even the relatively conservative Commission on Global Governance notes widespread apprehension about the media's role in consumerism, cultural homogenization, distortion, and imbalance in world news and concentration of media ownership. These, it says, give rise to suggestions that civil society should try to provide a measure of global public service broadcasting. It also calls for consideration of charging for the use of common global resources, including the electromagnetic spectrum, to provide money for global development purposes. On the telecommunications side, there have been calls from the UNDP, among others, for a global tax on Internet use with revenues to offset the cost of building infrastructure in developing countries.

None of these focus specifically on the issue of governance of media. The Commission on World Communications (the MacBride Commission) of 1980, not surprisingly, had more to say though most is directed at the national level. Global-level proposals tend to vague and qualified, the result undoubtedly of the political polarization surrounding the commission. More than two decades later, many of its proposals are no longer applicable or practical, though the report's comprehensive spirit and egalitarian thrust retain relevance today.

NGOs and academics concerned with governance in general also recognize a role for media. Held, for instance, calls for the introduction of strict limits to private ownership of media and information, as key "public-shaping" institutions.[7] However, only a few focus their research efforts specifically on media and communications governance issues.

Cees Hamelink in 1994 proposes an "as if people matter" system of governance of media.[8] After reviewing the human rights content in each area of media governance and concluding that they are as a whole very weak, he proposes a "right to communicate" that would act as a touchstone for governance agencies and institutions. Such a right was mooted first as early as 1969, and has been fleshed out in several intergovernmental and NGO contexts since. The core idea is that existing rights, such as Article 19 of the Universal Declaration of Human Rights, are inadequate to deal with communication as a two-way interactive process. A right to communicate would go further to ensuring access to the means of communication and the means to engage in dialogues with others.

Hamelink suggests that the way forward is through the adoption of a "robust multilateral convention that provides the basis for people centred political practices in the issue areas of world communication." He argues that such a convention would have to be adopted in a tripartite global conference that would involve governments, civil society, and business, and that would also be ratified at the national level through tripartite negotiations and agreement. The convention would cover a wide range of rights, grouped under information rights, protection rights, collective rights, and participation rights, and robust procedures for enforcement would be essential. He concludes that "a broad social movement in the field of world communication is the essential prerequisite to achieve genuine multilateral negotiations between princes, merchants and ordinary people" and accords the catalytic role to civil society.[9]

More recently, Hamelink has pursued these themes in the context of governance of cyberspace,[10] and the imperative of design, development, and deployment of information and communication technologies. The global Digital Divide further highlights the need for anticipating convergence, and consolidating on this terrain as well, the issue of access to information and communication resources are fundamental to effective political processes and participation. As with other forms of media, Internet governance is systemically demoting users from a status of citizen to that of consumer. Thus, privatization of the Internet has engendered governance activities focusing on facilitation and promotion of commercial activities, rather than promoting and protecting cyberspace as a political space within which citizens engage in political debate and interaction.

Another academic, Marc Raboy, also focuses on the role of civil society in reforming governance of media and communications. Raboy describes four models for regulation of access to communication: the libertarian model (no regulation); the self-regulation model (favored by industry); the top-down institutional model (practiced by the G8, WTO, and OECD); and what he calls the "the long march through the institutions," the slowly developing process, intertwined with initiatives to democratize global governance, by which NGOs are gaining representation in UN agencies and enabling civil society concerns to be given more attention. Raboy argues that the latter model, founded in transparency and public participation, is a robust way of placing a clearer emphasis on the social and cultural role of communication.[11]

However, much work remains to be done before coherent and realistic alternatives are articulated for media and communication governance. The paucity of such effort is a function of how little progress has been made, in civil society and elsewhere, in understanding, highlighting, and organizing around the dangers inherent in current trends and the need for change.

SCENARIOS FOR MEDIA
AND COMMUNICATION GOVERNANCE

Desirable Features and Outcomes of Governance

Exploring the contours of a more equitable model of global media governance is a huge project. As a modest first step, we posit the terrain of governance through delineating two scenarios at opposing ends of a spectrum. Although polar opposites, significant elements of both are well within the bounds of possibility.

Features characterizing a governance system geared toward the general interest of humankind would include the following among its main criteria:

- Its central objectives would focus on the social, economic, and cultural well being of people, with other factors deployed as means to achieve this
- Transparency of operation would be a core value, such that the rationale for decisions and outcomes, and the process by which they are arrived at, are available for scrutiny by all
- It would be participatory and democratic in implementation, encouraging contributions from all stakeholders according to how the outcomes are likely to impact on them
- It would be robust enough to pursue its objectives and enforce democratic agreements in the face of differential access to power of diverse interest groups
- It would respect subsidiarity, such that decisions are taken as much as possible at the level at which their impact will be felt

The outcomes such a system might strive toward:

- Greater diversity of global media content, giving voice especially to marginalized and less powerful communities and cultures
- Better balanced, more diffuse, and decentralized ownership structures, including public, private, and nonprofit media

- Reinforced indigenous content production, across all areas but especially in less industrialized countries
- Better balanced information and media content flows between wealthier and poorer countries
- An enhanced and expanded public domain and the emergence of a global public sphere

In principle, few would deny that these are desirable features of a media governance regime and positive outcomes for people. Yet there is little evidence that they count for much in current constellations and dynamics. Rather, as we have seen, the system is configured and its dynamics driven primarily by commercial imperatives. In the following, scenario 1 is based on the extrapolation of such a commercially driven scenario to its ultimate, but still plausible, conclusion. Scenario 2 builds on the democratic core of the current system.

Scenarios Not Covered

First, however, we briefly review a few scenarios only to set them aside as being outside reasonable bounds of plausibility.

One is a fully libertarian model, in which regulation, and hence governance, is dispensed with altogether. Although arguments are put forward in the case of the Internet, even there history suggests that it would almost certainly soon give way to de facto control by the most powerful players, which already is big business, and eventually become controlled in ways that suits their needs.

A second and related scenario is a future in which self-regulation by industry is at the center of the system as a whole, in which case governance is primarily by industry itself. Although certain subsectors, and parts of all sectors, certainly could be self-regulated, we believe that self-regulation can never be at the core and must always coexist alongside another dominant regulatory system. This is because industry itself realizes that a working marketplace of any kind, whether national or global, requires a structural framework within which to operate and a set of rules to which all players must conform. These rules reconcile the individual tendency of corporations to expand their sphere of control and profits at any cost, with the structural factors that will enable all corporations to continue to exist—put another way, without external structural regulation, competing corporate capital would ultimately undermine its very preconditions of existence. Existing multilateral governance structures are unlikely in the extreme to be rolled back to this extent and replaced by self-regulation. But pressure will remain and perhaps grow for at least partial self-regulation, especially in emerging sectors and where an existing regulatory regime becomes unstable.

Needless to say, a scenario in which civil society holds the key role in governance is also beyond the bounds of plausibility. In addition to lacking the material, power, and legitimacy base, civil society is too enormously complex, diverse, and fluid to adopt such a role.

Finally, a system in which the UN agencies, as currently configured and with the participation solely of governments, gain more or less exclusive control over media governance is also too unlikely to consider. The emergence of other global stakeholders, not least the private sector but also civil society, and the more general dispersion of sovereignty and of power to levels both beneath and beyond national territories would militate against any such outcome.

Thus, if only as a concession to reality, the following two scenarios are hybrids, but retain intergovernmental organizations (somewhat changed) as central players. For conceptual clarity and heuristic reasons, each has a clear dominant strand that impels the scenario toward a particular internally coherent outcome—they are somewhat exaggerated for the sake of the argument.

Scenario 1: A Dominant Trade and Liberalization Paradigm

The first scenario envisages current dominant trends proceeding several steps forward. The main thrust is for the commercial and liberalization logic to permeate virtually the entire media and communication sphere, nationally and internationally, largely at the expense of social, cultural, and political dimensions of the media. Multinational industry reigns, the UN system is in decline and is being displaced by an ever more powerful WTO, closed intergovernmental clubs of powerful governments, and private-sector allies. It leads to a contraction of the public sphere and of human rights imperatives, and an extension of the private sphere and the economic rights of those that can afford to exercise them.

At the macro level, this would require the resolution of current struggles concerning for instance the WTO and Bretton Woods institutions generally in favor of the neoliberal approach, with little structural change and emerging governance needs settled in compliance with the market-driven status quo.

For the media and communication sector, structural conditions and regulation of this scenario would include:

- Unimpeded global trade in media and cultural products, with no protection on the basis of cultural, social, or environmental outcomes—only narrow public health and safety restraints could be invoked as justification for regulating international (or national) trade. This represents the total commodification of media products.

- An intellectual property regime that is fully enforceable, extends the power of investors, and reinforces especially neighboring rights, at the expense of users and the public domain.
- The weakening of universal service instruments in telecommunication, virtually eliminating possibilities for cross-subsidization and any actions deemed to interfere with competition and the operation of the market.
- Much greater commercialization and looser regulation of radio, television, and other mass media, and declining public support for a public service media that is compelled to compete in the market place.
- The commercialization of spectrum terrestrially and in space, which is sold to the highest bidder.
- The gradual extension of industry self-regulation in emerging media subsectors.

Were these trends to gain an inexorable momentum, other global stakeholders would face stark choices. The UN system would be forced to choose between accommodating itself to the new world order and risking redundancy, being cash-strapped, and lacking the internal capacity to devise and enforce an alternative development or human rights–based agenda.

Similarly, less industrialized countries would probably divide between a minority who object, and so are sidelined from the globalization process or perhaps suffer the full rigor of what they have already signed up to, and a majority who believe they have no option but to join in. Although not necessarily supporting the new regime, fear of exclusion and of retribution leave little room for maneuver. They cling to the hope of finding a niche in the global economy in which to claim a comparative advantage. Global media corporations play one country against another, moving media production to the cheapest possible locations, while exploiting global media markets with virtual impunity.

Civil society, realizing the dangers too late to build coalitions and mount an effective opposition, finds itself more or less excluded from this domain altogether, as a spectator while the global media circus rolls on.

The medium-term outcomes of such a scenario might be as follows:

- The number of media channels and sources available grows, especially from international sources by direct satellite broadcast and other means
- Within these, diversity of program content diminishes and quality falls as production investment is spread ever thinner between the channels; emphasis on global market entertainment grows, and content is constrained by advertiser preferences

- Ownership of media globally concentrates and centralizes further, as do media content portfolios and archives of past and present material
- Public service media disappears or dwindles to a niche provider, inadequately funded, in turn reducing the independence and quality of news and current affairs reporting, educational programing, and high-quality entertainment
- Specific support measures for local, community, and people's media disappear, as they are expected to find their own means of support in a commercial climate
- Information available freely in the public domain diminishes, for educational and research purposes and for the enrichment of the public sphere, as the more lucrative parts are gradually hived off by various means to profit-making concerns
- Infrastructure and new telecommunication services grow, but are confined mainly to urban and wealthier markets, leading to greater disparities between different parts of countries and within communities

If brought to an (unlikely) ultimate conclusion, this scenario could lead well beyond anything envisaged in George Orwell's *1984*. Fifty years on, media and communication in the year 2034 might be expunged of all voices of opposition and critical thought and an entire generation may have grown up knowing little else, not just incapable of autonomous political action, but also unaware of the concept and practice. Division between those with access to media and those without would accentuate the already great economic inequalities. All media would be commercial, with production and distribution controlled by a small number of global conglomerates tailoring the same formulas for different regional and national markets. Media content is snatched at birth from its creators—a small number of whom become rich—and vested into corporate hands, who entrench their monopoly intellectual property rights (IPRs) virtually in perpetuity. Media content and information become almost entirely the private property of giant corporations, who control creativity and diversity on the short rein of profit maximization. Most insidiously, the process slowly but surely transforms the very wellspring of ideas and people's creative capacities, in the end yielding a self-perpetuating cycle that stifles genuine diversity and is purged of all dissent and nonconformity.

Public functions of media—of independent news reporting, cultural expression, and social and political interaction—all shrink or are contorted to conform to the imperatives of a commodity. Most national media content sectors, from newspapers, to film, to the Internet, to television are systematically strangled—or die in still-birth—by the inability of the state to provide special support or protection and by integrated industry structures where the international owners of content also control the national distribution and marketing channels. There is now only one imperative, the imperative of profit.

The circle is complete at this point, and the end point feeds back to the beginning. A consistent and coherent pattern of domination impels media in a downward spiral to a new Information Age Dark Era.

Is this the brave new world we are irreversibly careering toward? Probably not. The core weakness of this scenario in practice is the legitimacy deficit it would generate. Current tensions would intensify and the systematic roll out of this agenda through all media would require such an ever growing abuse of power that it could not be sustained for long. The virtually complete subjugation of the public interest to commercial capital, although possible in individual countries and indeed approximated already in the United States, would encounter sustained and deep resentment and opposition globally. Many governments, powerful and less so, would balk at the prospects of such explicitly one-sided development and its long-term implications.

Thus, a more credible basis for retaining this scenario with its driving doctrine of commercialization would require the co-optation of major civil society interest and of the governments of less industrialized countries. This would in turn mean a series of concessions in noncore areas. Such concessions might include, for instance:

- Agreements to limit the encroachment of IPRs on public domain and to protect existing use for education in defined ways
- Exceptions for public service media to market rules
- Agreement that satellite spectrum and other public goods may be allocated to social, cultural, or development activities
- The extension of mechanisms for universal service

Various forms of self-regulation of such concessions are likely to be preferred by the industry and commercial lobbies, since they are difficult to police and enforce and can be (relatively) easily abandoned or cut back. As is the nature of concessions, however, they would never threaten the core paradigm though they could soften the blow somewhat. In this case, the nonnegotiable line would probably be drawn at efforts to significantly regulate market access and conditions for the purposes of social, cultural, or development objectives; any change in the nature of IPRs based, for instance, on the special needs of less industrialized countries; effective controls over concentration of ownership and control, through mergers and other means, of media corporations; and moves toward the displacement of the market as the overriding mechanism, with other requirements being included only as exceptions.

Scenario 2: Multilateral Cooperation Reborn

The second scenario represents a decisive shift in the other direction, reinvigorating the democratic core of the media and communication governance structures. A reformed and rejuvenated UN system, with mechanisms enabling the participation of civil society as well as governments, regains the upper hand in media and communication governance. It instates social, economic, and cultural rights and the satisfaction of human needs as the core objective, and economic and political structures as means to deliver these. Social and cultural needs and equitable economic relations as objectives are elevated above the pursuit of any particular economic model as means.

This scenario would bring some significant regulatory and governance changes:

- A review of the rules of international trade in media products, with higher priority accorded to the preservation and renewal of culture and to potential social risks than to the promotion of competition and uniform market access, and permitting a range of measures by which citizens and governments can influence the impact of external media products, including advertising
- Promotion of a range of measures for providing universal access to telecommunication and media, in rural and remote areas and among marginalized groups, even where these significantly impinge on the operation of market mechanisms
- Support for global public service and development-oriented media, perhaps through a multilateral agency, including ongoing funding from a tax on commercial satellite use, on turnover of the media industries generally, or another similar source
- Enforceable mechanisms to halt, and if needed reverse, the concentration of ownership of media corporations
- An international license system, administered by a multilateral agency, for media transmitted transnationally that includes requirements relating to content quality, diversity, and independence, as well as to freedom from political and other interference
- Reformulation of IPRs to ensure wider and quicker access to the public domain and to support development goals, while preserving the incentives for creativity and innovation in media content
- The allocation of international spectrum, as a global public good, explicitly factoring in social, cultural, and development needs of mar-

ginalized countries and groups, as well as public service and people's media, and dedicated spectrum at no or reduced cost.

Faced with such a panoply of checks and regulations, the transnational corporate sector in this scenario would find itself forced to roll back expectations and operate internationally for the first time within an environment regulated for overall social development. Possibly, existing global corporations would be obliged to split up, where they monopolize one or more sectors or content areas, or to cease transmitting in specific territories where they exert excessive control over content. Profitability would probably suffer a temporary setback, until the sector reorganizes to the new rules of the game, though none of the major players are likely to see their viability threatened.

Civil society, at least some less industrialized countries, and marginalized groups in general, however, would see an expansion of media and communication opportunities and would be offered access they could hitherto only dream of in terms both of participating in media and of promoting their diverse views, cultures, and ideas.

Medium-term outcomes might include the following:

- A significant rise in noncommercial media, with a mission specifically to contribute to a media environment that puts people at the center, from local to global levels
- The emergence of well-funded quality public service media globally and perhaps regionally, alongside the commercial sector
- A reduction of advertising presence and impact, and of the need to maximize advertising revenues, resulting in the alleviation of commercial and consumerist pressures
- The emergence of public communication spaces for informed democratic dialogue on issues of global concern and perhaps of a global civil society
- More equitable access to media services, including telecommunication, thereby reducing the gap between wealthy and poor regions and groups

Conceivably, such a scenario might realistically become a prospect, for instance, were it to be supported by a number of breakaway industrialized country governments, collaborating with a majority of less industrialized countries, and riding on the back of a wave of civil society lobbying and action at the national and international levels.

Realistically, any shift at all in this direction would be (and is currently) opposed forcefully by the United States, and to a lesser extent by the European Union and by some other industrialized countries, and by most of the institutions through which industrialized countries cooperate, such as the G8, OECD, and WTO. A break in these ranks would be an essential prerequisite. The private sector would use all possible means to oppose such trends. Global media owners in the past have not stopped short of explicitly deploying their media to protect and expand their private interests, and the threat in this case is probably strong enough to provoke an extreme reaction.

Such a radical shift would confront other problems. Well-founded concerns exist regarding the capacity of current multilateral governance structures to function democratically and effectively. Should such a scenario appear even on a distant horizon, it would very quickly face its own crisis of legitimacy, given the generally unaccountable, relatively opaque nature of the UN system, and its composition almost entirely of governments. To be plausible and to gain the level of support and legitimacy needed, such a reconstructed UN system would need to develop far greater accountability and transparency and, most important, extend participation beyond governments to embrace other actors, especially civil society and the private sector.

But this underlines also the limited extent to which the media and communication governance structures could realistically be changed in isolation from a broader move for change in global governance. Certainly, circumstances could be imagined in which significant progress could be made perhaps giving rise to new media regulatory instruments, for instance through the emergence of a powerful civil society campaign such as exists for environmental issues, gender, and development. But the full realization of scenario 2 in the absence of a broader move to rethink global governance structures and refocus them on human development stretches credulity somewhat. A full-fledged scenario 2 would require, in the sphere of media and communication, entirely new instruments, even agencies, setting the UN system on a par with, or indeed above, the WTO in terms of its capacity to enforce agreements, and counterbalancing the WTO trade focus with explicit consideration of social and cultural rights and other economic and sustainability objectives. This is likely only against the backdrop of a much wider movement to reinvent global governance.

In the absence of such a movement, scenario 2 may be constructed on a piecemeal basis. A gradual process could begin of establishing throughout the governance system that media and communication are different; that they are not the same as other commodities traded on the market; and that they really do play a key role, and in global terms an increasingly important role, in constituting the social, political, and cultural environment—even the individual psychology and identity formation processes—of the society in which we dwell. Support for global public service media, and for alternative and community media, could be extended from minor grants from UNESCO and others, to regulatory supports through organizations such as the International Telecommunication Union. IPRs could be loosened and adapted to developing country circumstances and to allow for cultural exceptions. The public domain could bit by bit reclaim lost territory and assert its place in the digital world. Genuine international efforts could be made to extend universal service and access to media, even if at the expense of some profits and of pure market principles.

But a very broad, powerful, and robust coalition indeed would be required to wage a sustained campaign to see this agenda through. It would undoubtedly have to incorporate civil society elements globally, especially in the industrialized countries, as well as concerted action from many governments and courageous stances from the UN system.

CONCLUSION

The institutions and system of global governance are in flux. They will never again be the concern simply of governments holed up together behind the closed doors of hallowed institutions, and indeed they never really were. In all areas of global governance including media and communications, other actors, especially the private sector but also civil society, are making their presence felt. New media such as the Internet challenge the structures to adapt, in part harbingers of future generalized change, in part merely expressions of currently dominant trends.

The two scenarios presented represent two polar possibilities. The reality will undoubtedly fall somewhere in between. Just how much the future veers in one direction or the other will be decided by the effort that the various stakeholders put into achieving what they believe to be the best solution and the resources they can mobilize.

Governments will play a pivotal role. They still maintain formal control in most areas of global governance of media and communication. While they individually relinquish formal sovereignty over a growing number of areas, collectively they can change the direction of the institutions and agreements that are the recipients of such sovereignty.

Yet governments are in many ways under the influence of private interests in the form of multinational corporations, in media and communication even more than in most sectors of global importance. Some would argue that this is in the interests of those they formally represent: their citizens. In media and communication, there is no doubt that some countries benefit enormously from the current trend toward liberalization, if measured solely in terms of income and profits generated and repatriated. However, most keep media and communication in that basket of things that can be traded off in the international bartering game against what they regard as more vital national interests, such as agriculture, indigenous manufacturing sectors, financial services, and so forth. Until such time as these governments understand the crucial role that media and communication play in society, in terms of their potential both to wreak enormous damage and to bring about creative and life-affirming change, they are likely to remain in that basket.

If governments play the pivotal role through their formal capacity to reshape global governance, then civil society is the only likely motive force for change. Civil society action directed toward the multilateral agencies themselves will, on its own, be relatively ineffective. Some pressure can also be exerted directly on the private sector, through the mobilization of people as consumers of media products. But this is quite limited, since what is needed is not simply a refinement of media products, but significant changes to the entire production and distribution systems that can shift them away from commercial imperatives.

Thus, civil society must work at several levels, possibly the most important being that of persuading governments of the need for change and of recognizing the central place of media and communication in determining our long-term future.

Action at the national level is not sufficient. If its impact is to reach into the global structures, it must be internationally concerted and coordinated. It must focus on global level obstacles, not simply national ones. An emphasis on the latter alone would allow governments to claim that these matters are largely outside of their hands, since they are already committed through binding international agreements. Progress requires that such agreements are revisited in the global arenas, secured as they were often under duress and in the absence of an understanding of their full implications.

A focus on global issues, and coordinated action, in turn requires a civil society movement organized at the global level, but acting at the national as well as the global level. In the end, only a vibrant civil society at the national level, invigorated and enabled by its counterpart at the global level, can ensure that governments take the lead on behalf of people, in terms of human and development rights, and rebuild the governance system of media and communication with people at the center.

NOTES

1. Kofi A. Annan, *Report to the General Assembly: Millennium Summit*, April 2000.

2. UN Economic and Social Council, Sub-Commission on the Promotion and Protection of Human Rights, *The Realization of Economic, Social and Cultural Rights:*

Globalization and Its Impact on the Full Enjoyment of Human Rights (preliminary report by J. Oloka-Onyango and Deepika Udugama, E/CN.4/Sub.2/2000/13 Section 5), <http://www.globalpolicy.org/socecon/un/wtonite.htm>, June 2001 [last accessed: 26 November 2001].

3. These include: Bretton Woods Project, <http://www.brettonwoodsproject. org> [last accessed: 26 November 2001] and the Third World Network, <http://www.twnside.org.sg> [last accessed: 26 November 2001].

4. For instance, see Walden Bello, "UNCTAD: Time to Lead, Time to Challenge the WTO," *Focus on Trade* no. 44 (January–February 2000), <http://www. focusweb.org/focus/pd/apec/fot/fot44.htm> [last accessed: 26 November 2001].

5. David Held, *Democracy and the Global Order: From the Modern State to Cosmopolitan Governance* (Cambridge: Polity, 1995).

6. Richard Falk, "Resisting 'Globalisation-from-above' through 'Globalisation-from-below,'" *New Political Economy* 2, no. 1 (1997): 11–25.

7. Held, *Democracy and the Global Order*.

8. Cees Hamelink, *The Politics of World Communication* (London: Sage, 1994).

9. Hamelink, *The Politics of World Communication*, 315.

10. Cees Hamelink, *The Ethics of Cyberspace* (London: Sage, 2000).

11. Marc Raboy, *Communication and Globalization—A Challenge for Public Policy* (Ottawa: "Trends Project" Policy Research Secretariat, 1999).

Selected References for Further Reading

BOOKS

Bettig, Ronald V. *Copyrighting Culture: The Political Economy of Intellectual Property.* Boulder, Colo.: Westview, 1996. This is a good and readable account of political, social, and economic issues around intellectual property rights, with a focus on the United States but with an international perspective.

Cammaerts, B., and J. C. Burgelman, eds. *Beyond Competition: Broadening the Scope of Telecommunications Policy.* Brussels: VUB University Press, 2000. This collection is the result of a 1998 seminar entitled "Paving the way for a new public telecommunication policy" that focused on transitions toward an information society. Particularly of interest is part 2 "Social Regulation" and chapter 6 "Media Policy Paradigm Shifts: In Search of a New Communications Policy Paradigm" by Jan van Cuilenburg and Denis McQuail.

Castells, Manuel. *The Information Age: Economy, Society and Culture.* Vol. 2, *The Power of Identity.* Oxford: Blackwell, 1997. This work is the second in Castells's *Information Age* trilogy. This volume in particular unpacks and negotiates emerging issues of individual identities and civil society in terms of globalization, networked society, and convergence of technologies. Castells details particular social movements to illustrate the trends and issues that are being negotiated and played out in new ways and contexts.

Charles Kennedy, and M. Veronica Pastor. *An Introduction to International Telecommunications Law.* London: Artech House, 1996. A useful reference book to the mid-1990s of all aspects of international telecommunications organizations and governance issues.

Commission on Global Governance. *Our Global Neighbourhood: The Report of the Commission on Global Governance.* Oxford: Oxford University Press, 1995. The Commission on Global Governance was initiated by the former chancellor

Willy Brandt of West Germany and comprised primarily of politicians and other prominent names. Relatively conservative in outlook, this book is interesting both for its proposals on governance as a whole and for the small sections on media.

Correa, Carlos M. *Intellectual Property Rights, the WTO and Developing Countries.* London: Zed, 2000. Somewhat legalistic, but nevertheless a good introduction to the TRIPS from the perspective of less industrialized countries.

Goldberg, David, Tony Prosser, and Stefaan Verhulst. *Regulating the Changing Media: A Comparative Study.* Oxford: Clarendon, 1998. The introductory and concluding chapters provide a useful overview of the issues for regulation, and the six chapters in between offer a more detailed account of media trends and regulation in Europe, the United States, and Australia.

Golding, Peter, and Phil Harris, eds. *Beyond Cultural Imperialism: Globalization, Communication and the New International Order.* London: Sage, 1997. Several of the nine chapters in this book review the New World Information and Communication Order from different perspectives, and others offer useful reflections on the culture and media in the context of globalization.

Hamelink, Cees. *The Ethics of Cyberspace.* London: Sage, 2000. Hamelink provides a clear discussion of the issues of governance in the labyrinth of cyberspace. This book is a guide for understanding key human rights entitlements in the context of traditional institutions that are increasingly affected by and migrating to new forms of cyberspacial manifestation, and the implications for morality, democracy, privacy, free speech, and so forth.

——. *ICTs and Social Development: The Global Policy Context.* Geneva: UN Research Institute for Social Development, 1998. <http://www.unrisd.org/infotech/conferen/icts/icts.htm> [last accessed: 26 November 2001].

——. *The Politics of World Communication.* London: Sage, 1994. Though a little dated, this book provides a good account of all the major issues in media and communications globally with historical detail on specific agreements, conventions, and so forth. It analyzes these from a political and institutional perspective and concludes with an argument on the inclusion of a human rights perspective in media governance. Essential reading and reference.

——. *Preserving Media Independence: Regulatory Frameworks.* Paris: UN Educational, Scientific, and Cultural Organization, 1999. A comparative study, this book examines the media regulatory structures of about twenty countries in North America and western and central Europe. It provides a lot of useful data and looks especially at the concept and reality of media independence, defined as free not just from political control, but also from economic and editorial manipulation by owners and the distortions of commercial imperatives.

Held, David. *Democracy and the Global Order: From the Modern State to Cosmopolitan Governance.* Cambridge: Polity, 1995. Held, one of the best writers on governance, presents the basic concepts and justification of "cosmopolitan governance," in quite a readable and succinct form.

Held, D., A. McGrew, D. Goldblatt, and J. Perraton. *Global Transformations: Politics, Economics and Culture.* Cambridge: Polity, 1999. This useful tome is essential for tracing the path of globalization. The authors provide a clear analytical framework in their introduction, which begins by outlining three overarching globalization theses. Chapter 7, "Globalization, Culture and the Fate of Nations," provides a historical account of the globalization of culture and media.

Herman, Edward S., and Robert McChesney. *The Global Media: The New Missionaries of Global Capitalism.* Cassell: London, 1997. An expose and analysis of the corporate takeover of the global media system, covering print media, television, and telecommunications. One of a number of good reviews.

Mansell, Robin, and W. Edward Steinmueller. *Mobilizing the Information Society: Strategies for Growth and Opportunity.* Oxford: Oxford University Press, 2000. A detailed and comprehensive analysis of Information Society developments and trends, in the context of a European Information Society vision. It is particularly well documented and provides much useful detail.

McQuail, Denis, and K. Siune, eds. *Media Policy: Convergence, Concentration and Commerce.* London: Sage, 1998. Although some of the specific media industry information documented in this collection is becoming dated, analysis of the media trends and transitions is strong. Covering a broad range of media sectors, the book spells out underlying definitions and assumptions often taken for granted in media analysis. It is these detailed descriptions and definitions that hold the collection together.

Ó Siochrú, Seán. *Telecommunications and Universal Service: International Experience in the Context of South African Policy Reform.* Ottawa: Information Development Research Centre, 1996. A useful and accessible introduction to the general concepts of universal service in telecommunication and worldwide experience, though a little dated now in the light of rapid evolution in the sector.

South Centre. *The TRIPS Agreement: A Guide for the South.* Geneva: South Centre, 1997. This is a useful summary of the Trade-Related Aspects of Intellectual Property Rights agreement, how it affects poorer countries, and what can be done. However, there is limited emphasis on media and communications per se.

Sussman, Gerald. *Communication, Technology, and Politics in the Information Age.* London: Sage, 1997. Sussman intertwines theoretical underpinnings, historical trends, and specific examples to explore the political content of communications technology. Although some of the media industry information is now dated, this very readable text is a good introduction to the political issues embedded in media and communications.

UN Educational, Scientific, and Cultural Organization. *By Word and Image: Communication, Information and Informatics at UNESCO.* Paris: UN Educational, Scientific, and Cultural Organization Communication, Information, and Informatics Sector, October 1999. This is a succinct and reasonably recent description of UNESCO activities in media and communication.

———. *Many Voices, One World: Report by the International Commission for the Study of Communication Problems.* Paris: UN Educational, Scientific, and Cultural Organization, 1980. This report, otherwise known as the MacBride Commission, represented a milestone in the global political debate on media during the 1970s and early 1980s. Although now quite dated, it still covers a huge territory and raises an enormous number of issues that resonate today. It is out of print and difficult to obtain.

———. *Our Creative Diversity: Report of the World Commission on Culture and Development.* Paris: UN Educational, Scientific, and Cultural Organization, 1991. Although naturally enough concentrating primarily on culture, this text is nevertheless interesting to students of media for its potentially far-reaching proposals relating to media and communications. It includes a chapter on media.

Venturelli, Shalini. *Liberalising the European Media: Politics, Regulation and the Public Sphere.* Oxford: Clarendon, 1998. Although purportedly focusing on Europe, the theoretical chapters in this book offer a wide-ranging review of the philosophical antecedents of media and communications issues and current trends of thought. Although densely written in many parts, even short sections can be rewarding by clearly summarizing complex issues. It is written as a plea to protect and expand the public sphere against current dangers inherent in notions such as the Information Society.

Vincent, Richard C., Kaarle Nordenstreng, and Michael Traber, eds. *Towards Equity in Global Communication: MacBride Update.* Cresskill, N.J.: Hampton, 1999. This takes as its launch pad the MacBride Round Table on Communication that during the 1990s continued debating the issues raised by the MacBride Commission report (officially known as the International Commission for the Study for Communication Problems). A total of fifteen chapters look back at the MacBride legacy and look forward to prospects for media and communications globally.

Wells, Clare. *The UN, UNESCO and the Politics of Knowledge.* London: Macmillan, 1997. This gives a very readable and well-researched account of the politics of the UN Educational, Scientific, and Cultural Organization, hinging especially on the issue of whether UNESCO should be merely a technical assistance agency or take on a greater political role.

World Association for Christian Communications. *Media Ownership and Citizen Access: A Global Overview—Consolidated Report of WACC's Media Ownership Programme.* London: World Association for Christian Communications, 2001.

ARTICLES

Bello, Walden. *Focus on Trade* nos. 41–44 (1999–2000). <http://www.focusweb.org/focus/pd/apec/list.html> [last accessed: 26 November 2001]. In a series of articles from issues no. 41 through 44 on this online journal, Bello outlines the basic critique of the Bretton Woods institutions and proposes how countries of the South should respond. Very clearly written and articulated.

Falk, Richard. "Resisting 'Globalisation-from-above' through 'Globalisation-from-below.'" *New Political Economy* 2, no. 1 (1997): 11–25. This is a prescient summary of the confrontation between neoliberal forces of top-down globalization, and bottom-up civil society–driven opposition. The main dynamics and prospects are borne out by subsequent events, for instance in the confrontations against the World Trade Organization regarding globalization.

Kleinwächter, Wolfgang. "ICANN between Technical Mandate and Political Challenges." *Telecommunications Policy* 24, nos. 6–7 (2000). Kleinwächter's article provides a clear explication and detailing of the disjuncture between the Internet Corporation for Assigned Names and Numbers's self-proclaimed role and definition, and the very real expectations and implications of its reach beyond that role. Many of the political implications of naming and numbering detailed in this account are even more evident now than when the article was published.

Mueller, Milton. "ICANN and Internet Governance: Sorting through the Debris of 'Self-Regulation.'" *info* 1, no. 6 (1999): 497–520. A good article on the early history of the Internet Corporation for Assigned Names and Numbers.

Raboy, Marc. "Global Communication Policy and the Realization of Human Rights." *Journal of International Communication* 5, nos. 1–2 (1998): 83–104.

———. "Public Broadcasting and the Global Framework of Media Democratization." *Gazette* 60, no. 2 (1998): 167–180. The prospects for public broadcasting in current commercializing and globalizing trends is the subject of this article. It argues the need for a reconceptualization of public broadcasting and the pressing need to create global mechanisms to support the emergence of a global public sphere.

———, ed. "Symposium—Global Media Policy: Issue and Strategies." *Javnost/The Public* 5, no. 4 (1998): 64–105. This stimulating set of short articles covers a range of global media issues, from global media regulation and politics to the right to communicate and to the possible roles for civil society.

———, ed. *Global Media Policy for the New Millennium.* Luton, U.K.: University of Luton Press, 2001. This edited volume of fifteen papers shines a much needed spotlight, from different angles, on the emerging global institutional framework in media. After a good overview of the global context and actors by Raboy, subsequent chapters are grouped under the headings of institutions, issues, and practices. This is one of the few books that deals with global media governance issues directly and is essential reading.

Venturelli, Shalini. "Cultural Rights and World Trade agreements in the Information Society." *Gazette* 60, no. 1 (1998): 47–76. This article argues that the emerging global trade-dominated paradigm could transform the idea of content in the information age, privatizing knowledge and transforming human culture into merely another set of products on the market. It provides a succinctly argued overview of this position and of the dangers inherent in these developments.

———. "Information Society and Multilateral Agreements: Obstacles for Developing Countries." *Media Development* (Special Issue: Key Issues in Global Communications) 46, no. 2 (1999).

Selected URLs

Bretton Woods Project. <http://www.brettonwoodsproject.org/>. Monitoring the World Bank and the International Monetary Fund.

Columbia Journalism Review, "Who Owns What." <http://www.cjr.org/owners/>

Comunex. <http://www.comunex.net/>

Comunica. <http://www.comunica.org/>

Fairness and Accuracy in Reporting. <http://www.fair.org/>

FreespeechTV. <http://www.freespeech.org>. Free Speech Internet Television is the first audio/video hub on the Web created and defined by the people who use it.

Global Information Center on Trade and Sustainable Development. <http://www.wtowatch.org/>

Institute for Global Communications. <http://www.igc.org/igc/gateway/>. The mission of IGC is to advance the work of progressive organizations and individuals for peace, justice, economic opportunity, human rights, democracy, and environmental sustainability through strategic use of online technologies.

International Center for Trade and Sustainable Development. <http://www.ictsd.org>

International Telecommunication Union. <http://www.itu.int/>

Internet Corporation for Assigned Names and Numbers. <http://www.icann.org/>

MediaChannel: A Global Vision New Media Production. <http://www.mediachannel.org/>

NGO and Academic ICANN Study (NAIS). <http://www.icannwatch.org/> and <http://www.naisproject.org/>. The NAIS is an international project to review the nature of public representation in the Internet's domain name management organization, ICANN.

The Privacy Forum. <http://www.vortex.com/privacy>

United Nations. <http://www.un.org/>
UN Development Program. <http://www.undp.org/>
UN Educational, Scientific, and Cultural Organization. <http://www.unesco.org/>
World Intellectual Property Organization. <http://www.wipo.int/>
World Summit on the Information Society. <http://wsis.itu.int> Civil Society Division. <http://www.geneva2003.org>
World Trade Organization. <http://www.wto.org/>

Note: All of the URLs listed in this section were last accessed on 26 November 2001.

Index

191

About the Authors

The authors have worked on international communication governance issues for over a decade. Together they recently formed Comunex, to focus on international media and communication issues.

Seán Ó Siochrú is a researcher, writer, and activist in media and communication. As a director of NEXUS Research cooperative, he works for international agencies in media and ICTs and on community issues in Ireland (www.iol.ie/nexus). A founder of the Platform for Communication Rights, he also initiated Community Media Network in his home country, Ireland. He has published several books.

Bruce Girard is a journalist, researcher, and educator. Currently at Delft University of Technology in the Netherlands, he is originally from Canada and has lived for many years in Latin America. He has been highly involved in development communication and communication rights issues, most recently with the Communication Rights in the Information Society campaign and with Comunica, a network supporting use of ICTs by independent media in the South (www.comunica.org). He has lectured and taught on broadcasting, information and communication technologies, and communication rights in more than twenty-five countries.

Amy Mahan is a researcher in the Economics of Infrastructures Programme at Delft University of Technology (TU Delft). She was production editor and coeditor of book reviews for *Telecommunications Policy,* and she coordinates the online journal *TelecomReform.net.* She has lived and worked in Canada (Centre for Policy Research on Science and Technology), Australia (Centre for International Research on Communication and Information Technology), and Ecuador as a private consultant.

Many people helped with this book, offering their suggestions and criticisms and engaging us in discussion. In particular, we are indebted to Cees Hamelink and Marc Raboy for helpful comments. Rohan Samarajiva provided comments and skeptical support. Andrew Calabrese suggested this book at an opportune moment and Brenda Hadenfeldt stuck with us through thick and thin. Bill Melody and Cynthia Hewitt both gave their personal support to the project and the support of their institutions—TU Delft and UNRISD.

Seán Ó Siochrú is more than grateful to Áine for making the writing, and much else, possible. (Bruce Girard and Amy Mahan are grateful to Danielle for making much else impossible.)

For Danielle, Dara, Eavan, Fionn, Sorcha, and generations to come.

About the UNRISD

The **United Nations Research Institute for Social Development (UNRISD)** is an autonomous agency engaging in multidisciplinary research on the social dimensions of contemporary problems affecting development. Its work is guided by the conviction that, for effective development policies to be formulated, an understanding of the social and political context is crucial. The Institute attempts to provide governments, development agencies, grassroots organizations, and scholars with a better understanding of how development policies and processes of economic, social, and environmental change affect different social groups. Working through an extensive network of national research centers, UNRISD aims to promote original research and strengthen research capacity in developing countries.

Current research programs include Civil Society and Social Movements; Democracy, Governance and Human Rights; Identities, Conflict and Cohesion; Social Policy and Development; and Technology and Society. A list of UNRISD's free and priced publications can be obtained by contacting the Reference Centre, UNRISD, Palais des Nations, 1211 Geneva 10, Switzerland; phone: (41 22) 9173020; fax: (41 22) 9170650; email: info@unrisd.org; Web: http://www.unrisd.org.